THE LEGAL ASPECTS OF POLICING

JOSEPH B. SANBORN, JR.
ASSOCIATE PROFESSOR OF CRIMINAL JUSTICE
UNIVERSITY OF CENTRAL FLORIDA

WEST ACADEMIC PUBLISHING

© 2018 LEG, Inc. d/b/a West Academic
  444 Cedar Street, Suite 700
  St. Paul, MN 55101
  1-877-888-1330

West, West Academic Publishing, and West Academic are trademarks of West Publishing Corporation, used under license.

Printed in the United States of America

ISBN: 978-1-63460-481-9

To Andrea

Acknowledgments

I want to extend my gratitude to a colleague at UCF for the last 23 and one-half years, David Slaughter, Esq. Dave went through the entire manuscript and made suggestions that greatly improved the contents of the text. Dave also gave me the confidence to submit the manuscript to West Academic. I also want to thank the reviewer whose observations were very helpful.

About the Author

Joe Sanborn earned his B.A. in 1973 from Villanova University and his PhD in Criminal Justice from SUNY Albany in 1984. Joe spent more than a decade teaching in the Law and Justice Studies Department at Glassboro State College (now Rowan University) in New Jersey. For the last 23 and one-half years, Joe has taught in the Department of Criminal Justice at UCF in Orlando. After 42 years of college teaching, Joe is retiring at the end of the Fall 2017 semester and relocating to Williamsburg, VA.

Table of Contents

Table of Cases

THE LEGAL ASPECTS
OF POLICING

First Principles: Putting Legal Aspects of Policing into Context

THE CONTEST BETWEEN LIBERTY AND SECURITY

The subject matter contained in this text is all about the balance between liberty and security.

Here the contest is our right to be let alone and to be free from physical (arrest; search and seizure; interrogation) and technological (electronic surveillance) interference from the state versus the government's authority to enforce laws and to fulfill its obligation to protect its citizens from criminal conduct. Constitutional rights embody that conflict: at the same time, they represent the basic freedoms and empowerment of the individual, on the one hand, and the limits on the government in exercising its policing power, on the other hand. The relationship is an inverse one: the more rights an individual has the less power or authority the state has. In this text we will examine those constitutional rights, particularly those contained in the U.S. Constitution. U.S. Supreme Court Justices who determine the dynamics of this relationship tend to divide (although not always completely consistently) into two camps: the more "liberal" Justices side with due process, meaning they prefer placing more constitutional controls on criminal justice practitioners; the more "conservative" Justices are more aligned with crime control, meaning they are willing to grant those practitioners more power in dealing with potential criminal elements.

IT'S ABOUT THE U.S. SUPREME COURT

In this text we will examine only U.S. Supreme Court decisions and not those issued by lower Federal Courts or State Courts. What the Supreme Court determines affects the entire country and that Court is the ultimate decision maker. In short, the U.S. Supreme Court owns final say as to exactly what the U.S. Constitution does and does not require. The lower court decisions are important, to be sure, but they cannot be portrayed as Constitutional Law until the country's highest court tells us what that law is. When you see U.S. in the title of a case that tells you it is federal and that may or may not have constitutional implications since only a federal statute or regulation could be at stake. When you see a state's name that not only means the obvious (i.e., a state is involved), but also that it must be of constitutional dimension or the U.S. Supreme Court would not (and could not) be hearing it.

The lower Federal Courts (i.e., district and circuit courts) can disagree with each other, which should make an eventual intervention by the Supreme Court that much more likely and necessary so as to resolve the disagreement. The lower Federal Courts can also disagree with the apparent rulings and suggestions of previous Supreme Court cases, which also should necessitate Supreme Court intervention so as to clarify matters. It should be noted that the Supreme Court is limited in deciding actual cases and controversies, as they are known. That means the Court is not permitted to render advisory opinions. The Supreme Court has the authority to ultimately resolve all questions of federal constitutional law and can modify or reverse any lower federal court ruling considered to be in conflict with its holdings. In short, the U.S. Supreme Court owns final say as to exactly what the U.S. Constitution does and does not require; lower Federal Courts are bound by that final say.

State appellate courts also can disagree with or challenge Supreme Court decisions, but are just as vulnerable as Federal Courts to being reversed by the Supreme Court. There is one critical difference, however. Every state has its own constitution, which can contain rights that supplement or add to the list of rights we enjoy by virtue of the U.S. Constitution. The highest appellate court in each state is the ultimate arbiter of the state constitution. Consequently, these state courts can determine that their constitutions require granting more rights and protections to citizens and more controls on government agents than the Federal Constitution extends. Thus, State appellate courts can be more generous—but never less generous—to its citizens compared to what the Supreme Court has decided. Equally important, however, is that this generosity has to be based upon the state constitution and not the Federal Constitution (whose interpretation belongs to the Supreme Court). The latter principle is captured under what is known as the Supremacy Clause. The Supremacy Clause (Article VI, Clause 2 of the U.S. Constitution) is the official notice to the states that the Federal Constitution is literally the supreme law of the land to which the states are legally bound.

PRINCIPLES NEED INTERPRETATION

Throughout the text we will discuss principles of constitutional law or what comprises our rights. Natural questions will arise, such as, "can the police do this?" or "can I be searched if?" Important to remember is that situations involving these principles must be submitted to and interpreted by a variety of people in order to answer the questions. This interpretation starts with the police who are deciding how they will resolve these questions; the person affected by the police actions must choose whether to complain about them. Defense attorneys are relevant since they decide whether to challenge what the police have done, while prosecutors and judges will also evaluate the police behavior. Finally, appellate courts determine the legality of police conduct.

So, assume the police are routinely and illegally pulling cars over for an examination of their contents (e.g. suspicions arising from having a Florida license plate and travelling north on a New Jersey highway), but do not find anything so there will not be an arrest. Here, the lack of an arrest means there will not be a potential defendant to complain about the police practice; there could be hundreds of these individuals. Those who were stopped but not arrested can complain, but unless they do the practice can continue unabated. If the driver is initially arrested, but later has charges dropped by the police, then, again, there is no one still charged with a crime and it is unlikely that there will be a challenge to the police conduct. Should the driver transition from an arrestee to a defendant, there is a possibility to complain about the seizure of contraband, but only if the prosecutor continues to push the case forward and only if the defense attorney commits to filing a motion to exclude the contraband as evidence. The prosecutor might decide to drop the case and not fight a challenge to the seizure of evidence, while the defense attorney might believe negotiating a plea bargain is preferable to filing that motion. If both opposing sides choose to litigate the matter, a judge would be called upon to make the decision as to the permissibility of the police behavior. Judges vary considerably in their perspectives towards the legality of police actions. Finally, appellate courts could be petitioned to resolve the issue, but only if the losing party elects to appeal an adverse ruling by the judge. There are a lot of people and many ifs involved in this scenario.

A defendant can claim, prior to trial, that constitutional rights were violated by police and/or prosecutors, and that any evidence secured by way of these violations should not be used against the accused at any future criminal proceeding against him/her (invoking the so-called Exclusionary Rule explored in Chapter 3). If unsuccessful, the defendant can appeal that ruling to state appellate courts before the trial begins (called an interlocutory appeal that is allowed in some states) or after conviction (together with any claims concerning mistakes made during trial). If the defendant is acquitted or the case dismissed, the previous lost claims become moot. Should the convicted person not prevail through the state court system, the U.S. Supreme Court can be asked to intervene. Assuming all of these attempts prove futile, the convicted party can proceed to Federal District Court via a writ of *habeas corpus,* complaining that the state actions/proceedings violated a federal constitutional right. An adverse ruling here can be appealed through the Federal Appellate Courts.

FOURTH, FIFTH AND SIXTH AMENDMENT MATTERS

Most of what we will be considering in this text involves a potential violation of the Fourth (searching and seizing an item or person) or the Fifth Amendments (self-incriminating confessions); the Sixth Amendment right to counsel, particularly at interrogation, will also be critical and potentially violated by police or prosecutors. One thing that is important to remember is that should a Fourth Amendment right be found to exist, that right does not present an insurmountable barrier to the police in terms of acquiring that item. All the police would need to secure the item is a search warrant. If a Fifth Amendment right is perceived to exist, however, an effective insurmountable barrier does exist, and the only way for the police or prosecutor to acquire that testimony is to grant the individual immunity from any criminal prosecution. In other words, a right to privacy (4th Amendment) can be overcome, while a right to not self-incriminate (5th Amendment) cannot, unless the defendant makes a voluntary statement or the state surrenders any chance for a conviction on that offense. The Sixth Amendment can serve as an inconvenience to conducting an interrogation and a suspect's request to consult a lawyer should put a halt to the questioning, but the right to counsel does not necessarily constitute an insurmountable obstacle to acquiring incriminating information from the accused.

IT'S THE SUPREME COURT'S CALL

Today, the U.S. Supreme Court wields considerable power in determining lawful procedures in both the federal and state criminal justice systems. While control of the federal system was always the intended design, the Court's domination of the state system did not fully take hold until the mid-1900s, nearly two centuries after the country emerged. In Chapter 1, we will see how this consolidation of power, for better or worse, evolved. What this consolidation means is that it is possible to study one set of constitutional standards that apply to the entire nation instead of their being different standards operating in each state or jurisdiction. This consolidation also means that current constitutional law is always ripe for reversal or modification with either a change in the composition of the Supreme Court (perhaps by only one Justice) or changes in the views of one or more of the Justices over the course of time. Dissenting (or losing) opinions in previous cases can relatively easily become the majority (or determining) opinions of the future. Consequently, this text will give some attention to the views that were originally not the prevailing ones.

One controversy this text cannot address or resolve concerns the context in which the Supreme Court should interpret the Constitution. The conflict involves whether the Court should examine the text of the Constitution in light of the common understanding existing at the time the provision/text was adopted (called originalism) or allow a more current understanding that represents an evolution of the norms/conditions reflected in the Constitution (called living constitution). Supreme Court Justices differ as to which standard should guide their decision making.

The Supreme Court is typically identified by the Chief Justice of the period in question. Thus, during the 1960s, the Warren Court (named after Chief Justice Earl Warren) is credited for engineering a very significant renovation of the state criminal justice systems; we will see the results of these revisions throughout the text. We will also see that the Warren Court established the very significant Exclusionary

Rule and the Miranda Warnings. The Warren Court expanded due process and went far in limiting police powers. Nevertheless, from the 1970s until today, the relatively conservative Burger, Rehnquist and Roberts Courts have had the opportunity to fine tune and modify these two constitutionally driven provisions (among others) by imposing limitations upon and exceptions to them. For four decades the conservatives have "fought back" and have redirected the pendulum in a more crime control direction. Two intriguing questions are: how many of these limits/exceptions would have been devised had the Supreme Court remained more liberal?; and, how vulnerable are these limits/exceptions and other rulings to modification or elimination should a more liberal Court emerge in the future?

Box Introduction-1: Abbreviations Used Frequently in the Text

- REP = Reasonable Expectation of Privacy

- ER = Exclusionary Rule

- TOC = Totality of Circumstances (Test)

- FOPT = Fruit of the Poisonous Tree (Doctrine)

- PC = Probable Cause

- RS = Reasonable Suspicion

- LEO = Law Enforcement Officer

CHAPTER 1

Incorporation and the Nationalization of Constitutional Rights*

THE BILL OF RIGHTS AS A CODE OF CRIMINAL PROCEDURE

The main source of the constitutional rights we have when encountering the police (or later at trial) is the Bill of Rights, which was ratified in 1791. The Bill of Rights is the first 10 Amendments to the U.S. Constitution. Within the Bill is the Fourth Amendment, securing our freedom from unreasonable searches and seizures and setting out the requirements for the police when pursuing a warrant. This Amendment is the major source of control over the police, and the major substance of this text.

There is no debate as to the original target of the Bill of Rights. That would be the newly formulated Federal Government. The Bill of Rights had absolutely no relevance to the operation of criminal justice

---

* Much of the information used to develop this Chapter was derived from three sources:

Raoul Berger, *Government by Judiciary: The Transformation of the Fourteenth Amendment.* 2nd ed. Indianapolis: Liberty Fund, 1997.

Charles Fairman, "Does the Fourteenth Amendment Incorporate the Bill of Rights?: The Original Understanding." 2 *Stanford Law Review* 5 (1949).

Stanley Morrison, "Does the Fourteenth Amendment Incorporate the Bill of Rights?: The Judicial Interpretation." 2 *Stanford Law Review* 140 (1949).

in the states. The spoiler alert is that, today, the Bill of Rights controls the criminal justice systems in all states (plus the federal system). What remains for consideration is what exactly was the original design and how did we get to where we are now.

IN THE BEGINNING: FROM THE ARTICLES TO THE CONSTITUTION

Following the American Revolution, the former British colonies were reluctant to establish a strong, centralized government. The fear was that such a ruling body could reintroduce the tyranny the British monarchy had imposed during the colonial period. The first governing document adopted after the successful revolution was the Articles of Confederation. The Articles reflected the fear of erecting a strong ruling body as they established a rather loosely organized and barely regulated 13 independent states. Today, a comparison would be the European Union; each state was virtually an independent nation. There was no strong central command. Realizing the obstacles this constituted to coordinated action among the states, representatives met in Philadelphia during the summer of 1787 to draft a Constitution that would initiate a new, centralized form of Federal Government over the United States. Despite the general recognition that centralization was a necessity, if not desirable, many prominent figures were concerned that this new entity would be too powerful and would interfere greatly with the internal business of the various states. These individuals were known as the anti-federalists. As the Constitution was being considered for adoption in each state (examining the State Quarters series will tell you the order in which the states adopted the Constitution), the anti-federalists were promised in the state ratifying conventions that there would soon be a Bill of Rights created that would guarantee that very serious limits would be placed on the powers of this new Federal government.

DRAFTING AND RATIFYING THE BILL OF RIGHTS

There were two developments during the drafting and ratifying of the Bill of Rights that arguably would prove to be on immense importance. Both involve James Madison, the composer and "Father" of the Bill of Rights. Madison had been charged with putting the Bill together. He consulted various bills of rights and constitutions from the 13 states. The New York constitution contained a phrase that had been used for the first time in any American document: **due process of law**. Prior to this occasion, and dating back to the days of Magna Charta (1215), the more commonly employed term was: **law of the land**. Until more recent times (late 1800s), both phrases meant the same: access to the courts to claim the existing law. Being denied the law (and rights) of the era encouraged the colonists to rebel against England. Race and gender have historically been linked with denial of the law and (equal) rights in this country. Race was also critical in terms of even gaining access to the courts so as to complain about a denial of rights. Until the 1860s Blacks had not been granted such access. Today we take having access to the courts for granted. Everybody seems to be able to sue everybody else or to force an opposing party into court, including the government. History has shown that this liberal access to the courts was not always the case, however.

Madison's choice to adopt due process (which ultimately became part of the Fifth Amendment) instead of law of the land was critical in this way. Although both terms once meant nothing more than being able to make a claim in court for **the law that *already existed*** (i.e., the law of the land), due process created an opportunity to claim much more, such as, **the law/rights that *should be* or the law/rights that one is *due*** (i.e., the **process** you're **due**). Whereas the first is static and already in place, the latter is dynamic and readily adjustable by the courts. The other major difference is that law of the land suggests that the legislature is the source of law and rights, while due process affords the courts a chance to supplement the decisions of the legislature and to also develop law and rights. The significance of the difference cannot be understated. Madison's choosing due process contributed mightily to the Supreme Court's ability to eventually transport the Bill of Rights to the states. In short, the Court would soon determine and expand upon the process all were due vis-à-vis the police (and the courts) in the federal system and all 50 states.

The second development involved what happened when Madison presented his work to the House of Representatives. Madison had recommended that the Bill of Rights or proposed Amendments should be incorporated into the text of the Constitution. In other words, the Constitution would be edited so as to reflect an updated status, much like a student would edit a term paper on the computer today. Obsolete provisions would be erased; only current standards would remain. What is ironic is that Roger Sherman, an anti-Federalist, opposed Madison's recommendation and argued that the Amendments should be adopted as a separate series of adjustments or revisions at the end of the text of the Constitution. This way all would know not only what the Constitution holds but also what had been revised or removed from the Constitution in the past. A permanent record would exist. Sherman's position prevailed. The irony stems from the fact that the status of the Bill of Rights as a separate document assisted in its eventual incorporation (or transfer) into the operation of the states. Had the Bill of Rights been incorporated directly into the Constitution's text it would have been difficult, if not impossible, to transport the provisions into the states. Never has the Constitution itself been incorporated into state law. As an anti-Federalist, Sherman is likely spinning in his grave. His "victory" has meant an immense increase in the Supreme Court's or federal government's power. The Court has gained control over what occurs in the states by forcing the states to abide by the Bill of Rights. Sherman would likely regard this development as a federal takeover of the states' rights and prerogatives.

One interesting failure on Madison's part was the rejection of his proposed Amendment to control the states, and to prevent them from violating a right to conscience and jury trial, and to ensure freedom of speech and the press. Madison envisioned the states as being as much a potential culprit in infringing someone's rights as would be the federal government. He was relatively alone in this apprehension, however, and his proposal was defeated. It would have been interesting, historically, if Madison had succeeded in having "his" Amendment adopted by Congress. This would-be Amendment might have sufficed (with whatever additions were perceived as necessary through time) in protecting individuals from the states and might have rendered unnecessary the eventual incorporation of most of the Bill of Rights.

PREMATURE ATTEMPTS AT INCORPORATION

It is not surprising that individuals in the states would seek the protections afforded by the Bill of Rights. Why shouldn't state governments be as controlled as the federal government? Wasn't Madison correct about the possible mischief emanating from state authorities? With so many of the provisions aimed at safeguarding those accused of crimes, defense attorneys would certainly have liked to have the same rights for their clients in the state courts (and against state police). However, the first two attempts to steer the Bill of Rights in the direction of the states were non-criminal justice matters. In 1833, in *Barron v. Baltimore* (32 U.S. 243, 1833), the petitioner to the Court requested that the Fifth Amendment's Just Compensation Clause should have equal application to the states or that the states should be similarly bound. The Supreme Court, via Chief Justice Marshall, explained that the provisions of the Bill of Rights applied only to the federal government. Twelve years later, in *Parmoli v. New Orleans* (44 U.S. 589, 1845), the Court similarly rejected an opportunity to apply the First Amendment to the states.

There were two obstacles to holding the states accountable to the Bill of Rights. The first was simply that the document was specifically aimed at the federal system only. That the Supreme Court could just as simply disregard history and its lack of authority to force the states to answer to the Bill of Rights was unfathomable at this time. The second problem was the strength of the concept of federalism. Here, the idea is that there are two separate systems in the United States, the states and the feds. Neither controls the other, and the feds certainly do not dictate to the states. The popularity of a federal government without overwhelming powers was still evident until the mid-Nineteenth Century.

THE CIVIL WAR AND ITS AFTERMATH

A War Between the States and modernization will combine to change the notion that the Bill of Rights should not be relevant to the states. States' rights was dealt a serious blow when the South and its attempt to secede so as to preserve slavery were defeated in the Civil War. The South's reaction to defeat would ultimately contribute to a further diminishing of state autonomy, and to the ultimate extension of the Bill of Rights to the states.

The post-war introduction of the **Black Codes** launched this extension. The Black Codes were an attempt to impose economic slavery upon the newly liberated black person in the South. Although the Thirteenth Amendment had prohibited slavery during the War and the North's victory certainly meant physical slavery could not persist, southern states quickly responded with the Black Codes so as to lessen the extent of true liberty for blacks. There were limits on property ownership, bound apprenticeships and labor restrictions that guaranteed blacks would be beholden financially to whites in the south. Lincoln's party in the North was irate and engineered the passage of the **Civil Rights Act of 1866** in response. This Act granted citizenship to blacks and extended basic business rights as well. The 1866 Act directly negated the Black Codes, but it was nevertheless a mere act of Congress that would be subject to repeal by a subsequent Congress. In order to give the Act more permanence, the Republicans devised the **Fourteenth Amendment** that would guarantee blacks basic business rights (the mission of the Civil Rights Act), and grant citizenship to blacks at the same time. The Dred Scott decision (*Dred Scott v. Sandford,*

60 U.S. 393, 1857) had denied that blacks, even free ones in the North, were citizens. This decision was still "good" law, despite the Thirteenth Amendment and the outcome of the Civil War, and despite the Civil Rights Act, too, since it was merely a legislative act of Congress (which cannot overcome a Supreme Court decision). Thus, the first sentence of the Fourteenth Amendment negates the *Dred Scott* decision since a Constitutional Amendment can overrule a Supreme Court holding. The remaining provisions establish the basic business rights and protection of same; the Amendment was all about race. The Fourteenth Amendment states:

> All persons born or naturalized in the United States and subject to the jurisdiction thereof, are citizens of the United States and of the state wherein they reside. No state shall make or enforce any law which shall abridge the privileges or immunities of citizens of the United States, nor shall any state deprive any person of life, liberty or property without due process of law; nor deny to any person within its jurisdiction equal protection of the laws.

The Amendment has three clauses that are directed at the states, particularly the southern states, and permit federal oversight of state operations. The ***privileges or immunities*** clause refers to the basic business rights (to enter into contracts, to own property, to sue, etc.) to be afforded or at least not to be denied blacks; it does not include political rights, such as the right to vote or to hold public office. The main body of the Constitution (Article IV) has the same privileges and immunities clause within it (and the Articles of Confederation had the same provision), thus limiting the powers of the federal government to invade the basic business rights of U.S. citizens. ***Due process*** would establish for the first time in this country the right of blacks to proceed to court in which they could claim the ***equal protection*** of those basic business rights. Prior to this time blacks were not empowered to take issues and claims to court; they were denied equal protection of all laws. The Amendment constitutionalized the Civil Rights Act of 1866 and gave the federal government a formidable weapon against southern states in the event that they might attempt another method of economic subjugation of blacks. The Amendment also seemed to deal another blow to states' rights since it would appear to allow the U.S. Supreme Court to negate state actions that would violate the Amendment's provisions.

The records of both the debates in Congress during the drafting of the Amendment and the discussions in the states as they were considering ratification of the Amendment do not show any understanding that the Bill of Rights was being incorporated into state operation via the Fourteenth Amendment's adoption. There would have been extensive coverage of the tremendous change in state governance had incorporation been the design of the Fourteenth Amendment. Nearly all the states would have been simultaneously and extensively amending their own constitutions since all would have had at least one provision inconsistent with the many within the Bill of Rights. Moreover, southern states were told that ratifying the Fourteenth Amendment was a prerequisite for readmission to the Union and that their state constitutions had to be compatible with the federal one. If incorporation was a goal of the Amendment, then southern states should have been denied readmission to the Union since their state constitutions were not compatible.

THE SHORT AND LONG HISTORY OF THE FOURTEENTH AMENDMENT

Within five years of its ratification, The Fourteenth Amendment was squarely before the Supreme Court in the *Slaughter-House Cases* (83 U.S. 36, 1873). The state of Louisiana had granted a monopoly to a single company for the slaughter of livestock in the city of New Orleans. The monopoly seemed to directly contradict the privileges and immunities provisions of the Amendment since the right of individuals to conduct business in that city was compromised by a state statute. Nevertheless, the Court determined (in a 5–4 vote) that the principal purpose of the Amendment was to declare freedom for and to extend civil rights to blacks, and to protect the privileges and immunities of citizens of the U.S., not the various states. The decision resulted in effectively excising the Privileges and Immunities Clause from the Amendment; the provision still exists, it just has no meaning. What is remarkable is that the Amendment was stripped of its substance. This opened the door, eventually, for two possible developments: Privileges and Immunities could assume another meaning or another clause, such as Due Process, could be substituted as the substance of the Amendment.

Around the turn of the Nineteenth and Twentieth Centuries, a number of attorneys wanted their state clients to enjoy the same rights that their federal clients enjoyed due to the Bill of Rights; these rights ranged from criminal justice examples (such as indictment by grand jury to the protection against self-incrimination and cruel and unusual punishment to peremptory challenges to jurors) to non-criminal justice elements (such as First Amendment rights). When it was first argued that the Privileges and Immunities Clause was meant to capture all the rights enumerated in the Bill of Rights (*Spies v. Illinois*, 123 U.S. 131, 1887) the Supreme Court ignored the claim. On repeated occasions after that, in pursuit of prohibiting the states from imposing cruel and unusual punishment, the Court specifically rejected the claim that privileges and immunities were intended to have such an interpretation (*In re Kemmler*, 136 U.S. 436, 1890; *McElvaine v. Brush*, 142 U.S. 155, 1891; *O'Neil v. Vermont*, 144 U.S. 323, 1892). If the privileges and immunities clause was supposed to be an equivalent to the Bill of Rights, then the Bill of Rights would not have been needed since its substance was already covered in the Article IV clause. Nevertheless, three Justices in the *O'Neil* decision dissented and stated the privileges and immunities were meant to represent the Bill of Rights provisions; two of these Justices had not held such a position when the issue had been before the Court in previous cases. A final attempt to have privileges and immunities interpreted as the right to a grand jury indictment and a trial jury of 12 members (instead of eight) was unsuccessful in *Maxwell v. Dow* in 1900 (176 U.S. 581).

The more common contention adopted by the lawyers seeking the Bill of Rights enforcement in the states was that the Due Process Clause of the Fourteenth Amendment was substantive in nature and not merely a matter of procedure (i.e., in establishing a guarantee to have access to the courts). Instead, they insisted that Due Process was meant to incorporate the Bill of Rights and to force the observance of these rights in the states. On multiple occasions, the Supreme Court rejected these petitions and offered what seemed to be unassailable logic in defense of that conclusion. The logic is contained in what has been identified as the ***Doctrine of Nonsuperfluousness***. The Doctrine holds that the Due Process Clause of the Fourteenth has to mean the same as the Due Process Clause of the Fifth Amendment within the Bill of Rights. The latter Due Process provision cannot be considered as an abbreviation of or synonym for the numerous other provisions in the Bill of Rights or it would be redundant or superfluous. In other words, if all the other rights were actual versions or manifestations of Due Process, there was no need to mention Due Process itself or again—the other rights already said as much. Madison must have had another right (such as access to the courts) in mind when he put Due Process in the Fifth Amendment, just as the Framers of the Fourteenth Amendment must have had the same procedural notion (and something other than the Bill of Rights) in mind when they drafted the Fourteenth Amendment.

Accordingly, the Court decided that, unlike the federal system, California does not have to provide for grand jury indictment (a Fifth Amendment right) before it can convict someone of murder in *Hurtado v. California* (110 U.S. 516, 1884). While the Doctrine of Nonsuperfluousness was cited with approval in denying the claim that the Fifth Amendment provision was incorporated to the states, the Doctrine was dealt a blow of sorts. Possibly in an attempt to warn the states that it would not look the other way if a state were to act outrageously in dealing with the criminally accused, the *Hurtado* Court reiterated a phrase from a 1926 case (*Herbert v. Louisiana*, 272 U.S. 312) that Due Process would prohibit actions that violate "fundamental principles of liberty and justice." At the same time that the Court was announcing that it was not forcing states to abide by the Bill of Rights provisions *en masse*, it held that Due Process had some (albeit minimal) relevance to prosecuting criminals in the states. Even still, the Court consistently rejected claims that Due Process was meant to include peremptory challenges to jurors (*Brown v. New Jersey*, 175 U.S. 172, 1899) and self-incrimination (*Jack v. Kansas*, 199 U.S. 372, 1905; *Barrington v. Missouri*, 205 U.S. 483, 1907; *Twining v. New Jersey*, 211 U.S. 78, 1908).

The Doctrine of Nonsuperfluousness had been undermined to a considerable extent when, in 1897, the Court declared that the Just Compensation Clause of the Fifth Amendment was incorporated into the states via the Fourteenth Amendment Due Process Clause in *Chicago, Burlington and Quincy Railroad v. Chicago* (166 U.S. 226, 1897). Had the Privileges and Immunities Clause not been negated by the *Slaughter-House Cases*, this illegal seizure of land could have been remedied without resorting to the Due Process Clause and incorporation. Regardless, between the 1920s and 1940s, the Supreme Court incorporated the free speech (*Gitlow v. New York*, 268 U.S. 652, 1925), press (*Near v. Minnesota*, 283 U.S. 697, 1931), assembly (*DeJonge v. Oregon*, 299 U.S. 353, 1937), and religion (*Cantwell v. Connecticut*, 310 U.S. 296, 1937) provisions form the First Amendment via the Due Process Clause of the Fourteenth Amendment. It was only a matter of time before wholesale incorporation would occur.

THE DEVELOPMENT OF MODERN INCORPORATION THEORY

While parts of the Bill of Rights were being incorporated, the Supreme Court held fast against including criminal justice provisions within this list. Nevertheless, there were two occasions in the 1930s in which the Court applied its *fundamental to liberty and justice* standard in reversing state convictions. Both involved black defendants and both prosecutions were in the South. In *Powell v. Alabama* (287 U.S. 45, 1932), the Court ruled that counsel had to be provided to indigent defendants who were facing a capital prosecution. In *Brown v. Mississippi* (297 U.S. 278, 1936), the Court held that coerced confessions (in this case the accused was brutally beaten until he confessed) cannot be the sole basis of a conviction. Interesting is that the Court based these rulings on Due Process itself and not on the right to counsel and the protection against self-incrimination from the Fifth and Sixth Amendments, respectively. During the same decade the Court refused to incorporate the Fifth Amendment's Double Jeopardy provision (*Palko v. Connecticut*, 302 U.S. 319, 325, 1937), but adjusted the standard for potential incorporation so as to include any right that was viewed as "implicit in the concept of ordered liberty." The Court explained that the First Amendment rights that had been incorporated were considered "preferred freedoms," but that criminal justice-oriented rights were not. Similarly, while the right to counsel was guaranteed in capital prosecutions, the right of the indigent to receive counsel in a non-capital case would occur only if the lack of counsel would result in the defendant's being "deprived of a fair trial" (*Betts v. Brady*, 316 U.S. 455, 1942). Later, in *Adamson v. California* (332 U.S. 46, 1947), the Court ruled that the Sixth Amendment right to a jury trial was not binding on the states, since a jury was not essential to securing a fair trial. In this case, however, there were signs of a changing tide on the Supreme Court in favor of adopting incorporation of the criminal justice provisions in the Bill of Rights: four Justices gave notice that they favored a view of the Due Process Clause as incorporating the Bill of Rights. Critical, here, was that Justice Black had changed his opposing incorporation in the *Palko* case to supporting it in *Adamson*. As we will see in Chapter 2, a serious change in the Court's thinking about incorporation was only a few years away (the story about the development of incorporation will continue there).

The incorporation of the criminal justice aspects of the Bill of Rights was achieved mostly during the 1960s under the auspices of the Warren Court. The case that launched this development was the well-known, *Mapp v. Ohio* decision (367 U.S. 643, 1961), which we will examine in greater depth in the next chapter. *Mapp* involved the adoption of the exclusionary rule for the states. For the rest of the decade the Court brought one criminal justice provision after another from the Bill of Rights into state criminal justice, affecting state police, courts and corrections. The provisions/rights that were incorporated were chosen by the Supreme Court due to their being perceived as *fundamental to the American system of justice*. Only two of the criminal justice rights were not and still have not been incorporated: bail and the right to a grand jury indictment. The Court has also proceeded beyond the parameters of the Bill of Rights and has incorporated provisions not included in the Bill of Rights, such as the exclusionary rule and the *Miranda* ruling (see Chapter 9, *infra.*); the requirement to prove guilt beyond a reasonable doubt is also an example. What exists today in terms of the rights that have been enforced against the states is called: ***selective incorporation plus***.

That is, *some but not all* of the Bill of Rights provisions have been incorporated (the selective part), while provisions *not in the Bill of Rights* have been incorporated as well (the plus part). While logic is supposedly essential to the field of law, this approach to incorporation is illogical. If the Fourteenth Amendment Due Process Clause was meant to incorporate the Bill of Rights (contrary to what this text has portrayed), then how is the incorporation not total? How can it be only selective, meaning the Court has simply chosen to incorporate some, while rejecting the incorporation of other rights? This makes incorporation arbitrary or reliant upon Supreme Court approval instead of constitutional requirement. Either the Fourteenth Amendment was meant to incorporate the Bill of Rights or it wasn't; it simply cannot be that it was meant to incorporate only part of the Bill of Rights. That's like being only somewhat pregnant. Moreover, again assuming that the Fourteenth Amendment was meant to incorporate the Bill of Rights how could the Fourteenth Amendment be meant to have incorporated measures not even in the Bill of Rights? That puts no limit to what can be incorporated, except for needing a majority or sufficient votes of the Supreme Court Justices.

FACTORS EXPLAINING THE DEVELOPMENT OF INCORPORATION

Incorporation of the Bill of Rights has likely had some positive results (cleaning up the criminal justice system) and some negative results (consolidation of immense power in the hands of a few Justices; it can reasonably be said that five people—a majority of the Court— run the country). At the same time it is understandable how incorporation happened.

- States' rights had been dealt a significant blow via the outcome of the Civil War.

- The Reconstruction Amendments (13th, 14th, and 15th) reinforced the vulnerability of States' rights while granting meaningful rights to blacks.

- The Fourteenth Amendment had been stripped of its intended substance via the outcome of the *Slaughter-House Cases*.

- There was a huge gap between the rights one had in state versus federal criminal justice systems, which made less and less sense as time went on.

- Both privileges and immunities and due process had a vague and malleable meaning.

- As the notion that everyone is entitled to a "fair trial" caught on (and that neither the federal nor the state system should deprive a defendant of such) it was easy to equate due process with a fair trial.

- States also brought incorporation upon themselves. They engaged in some egregious behavior, such as seizing property without just compensation, repressing speech, press, and religion, and, sometimes handling those accused of crime in horrific ways.

- The U.S. Supreme Court saw a need to intervene so as to clean up state operations, and lacked any other avenue by which to prevent state misbehavior.

- Society had modernized, especially after the mid-Twentieth Century. The idea of federalism was fading, if not completely disappeared; citizenship was not seen as being dual (U.S. vs State).

- The notion that one has rights protecting him/her from federal law enforcement but not from state/local law enforcement seemed irrational.

The composition of the Supreme Court changed dramatically from the 1950s on. An increasing number of Justices not only saw the need for intervention, but also endorsed the idea that incorporation was indeed the original goal of the Fourteenth Amendment.

Box 1-1: Expanding Police Powers During the Last 4 Decades Has Taken a Variety of Forms

Establishing many limits/exceptions to ER (Chapter 2)

Reducing REP (Reasonable Expectation of Privacy) (Chapter 4)

Terry doctrine (Chapter 5)

Establishing many limits/exceptions to *Miranda* (Chapter 9)

The Exclusionary Rule (ER) and the Ways to Circumvent It

NATURE OF THE EXCLUSIONARY RULE

The exclusionary rule (ER) involves the removal of evidence from consideration in a criminal trial when that evidence was secured via a constitutional violation. That violation, in turn, would involve a physical piece of evidence obtained through a search and seizure (typically by police only) or a confession or acknowledgement of guilt obtained through questioning or an interrogation (by police or possibly by prosecutors). Before trial the defense has an opportunity to challenge the admissibility of the evidence that the state proposes to use in the prosecution via what is called a *Motion to Suppress*. The defense might not know the circumstances surrounding the collection of the evidence and thus might not be aware of the appropriateness of filing a motion to suppress. Even if the defense believes there are grounds to argue that the evidence was illegally seized, the defense is not obligated to contest the evidence and, instead, could elect to use not filing as leverage in securing a favorable plea bargain. If a motion to suppress is filed, defense counsel will argue that the evidence was illegally obtained and the prosecutor will defend against such claims. If the judge agrees with the prosecutor, then the case can proceed to trial (or possibly to a plea bargain). If the judge rules for the defense, then the evidence cannot be used to convict the accused. We will soon see, however, that the evidence can be used to impeach the defendant, which may contribute to a conviction. The consequences of a successful motion to suppress range from a partial setback for the state (there could be sufficient legally sound evidence to convict independent of the suppressed evidence) to a fatal blow for the prosecution (there is no independent evidence so the state's case is lost). Thus, the ER can have serious outcomes. As Justice Cardoza famously noted more than 90 years ago:

The criminal is to go free because the constable has blundered.

Justice Cardoza, *People v. Defore*, 150 N.E. 585, 587 (N.Y. 1926).

INITIAL EXPERIENCES WITH THE EXCLUSIONARY RULE

The U.S. Supreme Court's first experience with an exclusionary rule-like scenario occurred in 1886, in *Boyd v. U.S.* (116 U.S. 616). In this case, a federal statute had empowered prosecutors to compel the defendant to produce his private books and papers. Although the Court did not create the ER here, its holding had the same effect in that the statute was declared unconstitutional as violating the Fourth and Fifth Amendments; the federal prosecutor could not use the evidence against the defendant.

The Court rejected a request in 1904 to adopt the ER in *Adams v. N.Y.* (192 U.S. 585). In *Adams*, the Court expressed its concern for competent evidence, not the manner in which it was seized. The idea that evidence relevant or pertinent to the commission of a crime would be disregarded was likely too extreme for the Court at this point. The Court's position would change dramatically within a decade. That change occurred in *Weeks v. U.S.* (232 U.S. 383) in 1914. In this case the Court established the ER. It was important that this was a federal case because the Court has more power over federal courts than over state courts—at least back then. To dictate to a state the Supreme Court must base its opinion on the Constitution. Only then can the Court direct the state to do something or to refrain from doing something—

to be in compliance with the Constitution. In the federal system, however, all the Court needs in order to be the boss is a belief in what it is doing. At this point (1914) the ER was not perceived as emanating from the Constitution. Nevertheless, should the Court believe the ER was an appropriate remedy for wrongdoing in the collection of evidence in federal cases, there was nothing to prevent the Court from adopting the rule in that system. The Court can just as easily determine schedules and procedure for all federal courts.

Weeks involved a search of a house by federal law enforcement officers who did not have a warrant. In some respects it was a wise case for the Court to choose to adopt the ER. The federal offense involved using the mail to send lottery tickets, a nonviolent offense. Excluding the evidence in this case would not result in the release of a dangerous offender. The Court could have eventually chosen a case involving a dangerous federal offender such as one who had kidnapped someone (such as the Lindberg case). Preventing the conviction of this type of defendant (had that been the result of enacting the ER) would have created much more controversy than an offense involving gambling. Also important was that the Court explained the two reasons for adopting the rule. Simply put, the Court believed excluding evidence (a punishment of sorts) was the only way to give the Fourth Amendment any meaning, and that if trial judges were to admit the proceeds of the illegal actions of federal law enforcers, the judges would become the partners of the illegal actors.

It took another 45 years before the Supreme Court was asked whether the ER was binding on the states. In *Wolf v. Colorado* (338 U.S. 25, 1949), there had been a search of a doctor's office without a warrant. Although the case is better known as the one in which the Supreme Court (for the first and last time) ruled that the states are *not bound* by the ER, *Wolf* was the first time a Bill of Rights-situated, criminal justice-related right (here, the Fourth Amendment protection against Unreasonable Searches and Seizures) was considered a part of the Fourteenth Amendment's Due Process Clause. The Court noted that the securing of one's privacy was a core part of the Fourth

Amendment and thus was *implicit in the concept of ordered liberty*. Incorporating a majority of criminal justice rights was just a matter of time.

Moreover, although *Wolf* stood for not incorporating the ER, the Court soon adopted a case-by-case approach to imposing the ER. If the behavior of the state police was sufficiently abhorrent (the Court's phrase was "shocking to the conscience"), the Court promised not to allow the introduction of the evidence in a state criminal court. In *Rochin v. California* (342 U.S. 165, 1952), police forced a suspect to ingest an emetic so as to vomit the two capsules they had witnessed him swallowing after they had forced their way into his bedroom. The Court saw the police behavior as sufficiently shocking and began a selective imposition of the ER in state prosecutions. Even still the Fourth Amendment was not considered the source for the exclusion of evidence in these egregious police search cases. Rather, the Fourteenth Amendment's Due Process Clause was the source.

On two occasions later in the 1950s, the Supreme Court found questionable police behavior as not violating the Fourteenth Amendment. In *Irvine v. California* (347 U.S. 128, 1954), police had a locksmith make a key to gain access to a suspect's residence. They planted a microphone and listened to conversations for a month. In *Breithaupt v. Abram* (352 U.S. 432, 1957), the police directed a physician to draw blood from an unconscious driver suspected of drunk driving (in which there were three fatalities). Neither instance sufficed to constitute the egregious behavior the Court demanded before selectively utilizing an ER to suppress the evidence. Although these cases might have been perceived at the time as a victory for the opponents of the ER, this approach almost had to be unsustainable since it required an analysis of every controversial seizure of evidence and it produced outcomes dependent largely upon the feelings and sensitivities of the Justices.

At the beginning of the 1960s The Court advanced the cause of the ER by outlawing what was called the "silver platter doctrine" in

Elkins v. United States (364 U.S. 206, 1960). This doctrine involved the ability of state law enforcement officers to hand over illegally seized items to federal officers so as to have that evidence admitted in a federal criminal prosecution. *Weeks* had prohibited the direct admission of illegally seized evidence in federal courts, but had not prevented this back-door method where state police handed the material to federal cops on a silver platter. *Elkins* outlawed this practice and explained that the *Wolf* ruling had indeed applied (or incorporated) the Fourth Amendment to the states through the Due Process Clause of the Fourteenth Amendment. By the time of the *Elkins* case, 26 states had adopted the ER on their own accord. So, if the ER was going to be forced upon the states, less than one-half would be impacted.

THE EXCLUSIONARY RULE AND THE LAUNCHING OF INCORPORATION

The case that put the exclusionary rule (and incorporation) on the map was, ironically, *Mapp v. Ohio* in 1961 (367 U.S. 643). From this case forward incorporation became the trend of the 1960s for the Warren Court. Also ironic is that the ER initiated the incorporation movement and yet was not among the provisions included in the Bill of Rights; it simply is not mentioned anywhere in the Constitution (this is the *plus* part *of selective incorporation plus*). *Mapp* was most likely purposely chosen by the Court as the ideal case through which to impose the exclusionary rule on the states. The crime was truly innocuous, which arguably made it most suited for adopting the controversial rule of evidence. That is, no major or serious offender would be set free by virtue of the state's being unable to use illegally seized evidence.

In the *Mapp* case, police were looking for a wanted man and demanded entry into Mapp's home, believing he was hiding inside. The cops lied when they said they had a warrant. They entered without any authority and never found the fugitive. What they found was obscene material, and Mapp was convicted of the possession of that material. She appealed her conviction through the state system and ultimately to the Supreme Court. The basis of the appeal was the First Amendment. Mapp's appellate counsel argued that this constitutional provision protected the private possession of obscenity. At the Supreme Court, Mapp's lawyer was asked if he was asking the Court to reverse *Wolf v. Colorado* and to require states to adopt the ER. The answer was, *No*. Appellate counsel reaffirmed that this was a First Amendment case, and had been argued and treated as such through the appellate court system. Ignoring the Court's rule on having to argue an issue through appeal and before the Court in order for that issue to be resolved, a majority of Justices decided to reformulate the case as one involving the Fourth Amendment and the ER. The case was perfect for this mission inasmuch as throwing out the evidence due to the unconstitutional behavior of the police would not raise too much backlash since the crime involved was merely possession of obscenity; it also didn't hurt that there were multiple cops imposing their will on a single woman, Dollree Mapp. By the way, appellate counsel's argument that the First Amendment protected the private possession of obscenity was ultimately adopted by the Supreme Court in 1969 (*Stanley v. Georgia*, 394 U.S. 557).

Although it may not have seemed significant at the time, one of the most important aspects of the *Mapp* case was that it relied heavily on the need for deterrence. That is, the Court emphasized that it had to require state courts to utilize the ER in order to keep police in line. Without the threat of losing the evidence there would seem to be no other way to force police to obey the demands of the Constitution. The Court's decision to emphasize the deterrence rationale of the ER would prove to be very critical in later years. The more conservative, crime control-oriented Justices used the deterrence rationale as a reason not to employ the ER in numerous situations. As we will see, below, the Court has established many limitations upon and exceptions to the ER based on a lack of improper behavior by the police in several situations and thus no need for the ER to serve as a deterrence to bad police conduct.

The Court also established another important aspect in determining the use of the ER in *Mapp*. In effect, the Court developed a *balancing test*, weighing the need to deter improper police conduct against the costs of losing or excluding probative evidence of guilt (and thus risking an acquittal). This cost-benefit analysis has been employed by the Court after *Mapp* to decide whether the ER will be followed or whether a limit/exception to the ER will be created.

One final observation concerning the ER is necessary. As was pointed out in Chapter 1, the Warren Court was largely responsible for developing the *selective incorporation plus* approach to the Bill of Rights application to the states. Two major parts of the **plus** segment are the *Mapp*-oriented ER and the *Miranda* ruling governing police interrogation, which is addressed in Chapter 9. As the conservative Supreme Court inherited and interpreted these doctrines in the 1970s and thereafter, the constitutional status of both was brought into question. As we will see, the uncertainty surrounding Miranda was resolved by the Court in 2000 (see Chapter 9). The uncertainty surrounding *Mapp* remains, however.

For example, in *U.S. v. Calandra* (414 U.S. 338, 1974), the Court observed that the ER "is a judicially created remedy designed to safeguard Fourth Amendment rights generally through its deterrent effect. . . . (*Id.*, at 348)." Thus, the Court disclosed that it was not convinced the ER enjoyed a constitutional birthright. Two years later, in *Stone v. Powell* (428 U.S. 465, 1976), the Court explained that decisions since *Mapp* "have established that the rule is not a personal constitutional right. . . . (*Id.*, at 486)." While the constitutional status of the ER may be mostly irrelevant at this point, it is likely that the possibility of its being "merely" a judicially created remedy played a role in the Court's establishing multiple limits/exceptions to the application of the ER (see below).

THE FRUIT OF THE POISONOUS TREE DOCTRINE AS A NATURAL COROLLARY TO THE EXCLUSIONARY RULE

The *Fruit of the Poisonous Tree* (FOPT) *Doctrine* holds that initially illegally seized evidence that leads to *secondary or derivative* evidence should cause the latter evidence to be considered tainted or illegally seized as well. Thus, the doctrine is a natural and logical extension of the ER. Although the concept was first suggested by the Supreme Court in 1920 (*Silverthorne v. U.S.*, 251 U.S. 385) and the term FOPT was coined in 1939 (*Nardone v. U.S.*, 308 U.S. 338), *Wong Sun v. United States* (371 U.S. 471) is usually credited with putting the doctrine "on the map" in 1963. Interesting is that while *Wong Sun* formally recognized the doctrine, it also simultaneously created an exception to it.

The question in *Wong Sun* was whether the taint of the original illegal action can ever be sufficiently purged such that the secondary evidence should not be regarded as tainted. *Wong Sun* established the idea that there could be a *break in the connection* between the original and secondary evidence so as to render the latter lawful and admissible. It all depends on what happens in the interim between the two acquisitions of evidence. In *Wong Sun*, there were days between the illegal arrest and his confession, he had been released from custody, had consulted a lawyer, and he had returned to the police station on his own accord. The Court believed those intervening factors sufficed to purge the original illegal arrest of its taint on the confession. The confession was not regarded as illegally seized. The purged taint element does not serve as a limit or an exception to the ER, then, but rather as an *exception to the fruit of the poisonous tree extension of the exclusionary rule*. The evidence is not FOPT.

What will suffice to remove taint from the secondary evidence will depend on the intervening factors. In *Brown v. Illinois* (422 U.S. 590, 1975), the Court first explained that a simple reading of *Miranda* to a suspect will not be sufficient to purge an illegal arrest, and then identified three factors that will be examined to make this determination: (1) the "temporal" proximity of the illegal police conduct and the confession (or whatever evidence is derived from the illegal action); (2) any intervening events or circumstances; and, (3) the purpose and flagrancy of the police misconduct (*Id.*, at 603–604). Accordingly, the Court has held that Mirandizing a suspect was not enough to purge even a voluntary confession because there had been an illegal arrest without probable cause that was followed by involuntary transportation to the police station (*Dunaway v. New York*, 442 U.S. 200, 1979; *Taylor v. Alabama*, 457 U.S. 687, 1982).

A more recent case, *New York v. Harris* (495 U.S. 14, 1990) demonstrated how taint can both continue and dissipate in a single encounter with the police. In *Harris*, the police arrested the defendant at his home without a warrant, which was a constitutional violation (see Chapter 3). After he was warned of his rights, the suspect gave an oral confession. Harris was then transported to the police station, again was warned of his rights and signed a written confession this time; the latter interview was videotaped to which he objected. The Supreme Court ruled both the original oral statement and the videotape were inadmissible as tainted by the illegal arrest. However, the written statement was admissible because the illegal arrest did not render the continued custody unlawful once Harris was removed from the house. The police securing of the statement at the station was not an exploitation of the illegal entry into the defendant's house. The Court explained that challenged evidence has to be the product of illegal government activity, which was not applicable to the transactions in the police station.

By far, the most controversial ruling that "de-contaminates" illegal police behavior is the very recent 2016 case, *Utah v. Strieff* (579 U.S. ____, 136 S.Ct. 2056, 2016). *Strieff* involved an investigatory stop (see Chapter 5) that, for the purpose of argument, was labelled by the Court as illegal. During the stop, the officer contacted a dispatcher who revealed that Strieff had an outstanding arrest warrant. The officer then arrested and searched him incident to arrest (see Chapter 6), and found drugs. Applying the *Brown* criteria, the Court found that "temporal proximity" favored suppressing the evidence since it was found only minutes after the stop. Nevertheless, there was a significant "intervening circumstance" in the discovery of the outstanding warrant. That circumstance authorized the subsequent arrest, which permitted the search for and discovery of the drugs. Finally, the initial behavior of the officer was not seen as purposeful or flagrant misconduct, but rather as negligent behavior at most. The majority (5–3 decision) allowed the admission of the drugs because they had been sufficiently purged from any illegal police activity; attenuation had been satisfied.

As we will see, below (Exceptions to the Exclusionary Rule), there are also two ways in which FOPT-linked evidence that has been unconstitutionally seized may yet be admissible in court due to critical exceptions to the ER.

VARIOUS WAYS TO REVERSE THE TREND OF EXCLUSION AND TO EXPAND THE ADMISSIBILITY OF EVIDENCE

As we have seen, the liberal Warren Court established an obligation for states to abide by the restrictions resulting from the exclusionary rule in 1961. Most of the other provisions of the Bill of Rights were incorporated throughout the remainder of the 1960s. Together, the liberal Supreme Court erected numerous constitutionally-oriented blockades to the police and their ability to secure evidence of guilt against offenders. However, from roughly 1971 the more conservative Supreme Court has campaigned to expand the admissibility of probative evidence of guilt in several capacities. These measures include:

Box 2-1: Avoiding/Limiting the Exclusionary Rule

- Establishing rules that limit the applicability of the ER (see below)

- Adopting exceptions to the ER (see below)

- Easing the restrictions on securing a warrant (see Chapter 3)

- Reducing the areas protected by a reasonable expectation of privacy (see Chapter 4)

- Extending the situations qualifying for investigatory stops/ stop and frisk (see Chapter 5)

- Expanding the areas that qualify for warrantless searches (see Chapter 6)

- Reducing the Chances of a *Miranda* Violation (see Chapter 9)

- Limiting the Negative Consequences of a *Miranda* Violation (see Chapter 9)

Various Ways to Curtail the Exclusionary Rule

For 40 plus years the Supreme Court has waged something of a war against the ER (and in Chapter 9 we will see a very similar war waged against *Miranda)*, trying to reduce the negative results of its exclusionary nature. The war has been operationalized in two capacities: ***rules to using the ER (perhaps better phrased as limits)*; and, *exceptions to the enforcement of the ER.***

Limits to the Application of the Exclusionary Rule

One sentence can fairly well capture the complex and multifaceted nature of the limits the Court has imposed on the applicability of the ER:

The ER applies to only ***certain proceedings*** (and even then there might be only a *harmless error* if a mistake is made) in which only ***certain people*** can complain about only ***certain violations*** (and only once about some violations).

This one sentence above, then, captures the ***three questions*** surrounding the limits of the ER:

The Question of *When*

Taking these in order, the Supreme Court has made it clear that the ER prohibits the introduction of illegally seized evidence only in *certain proceedings*, namely a ***criminal trial*** (i.e., in order to convict the accused). Both of these highlighted words are critical limitations. With regard to *criminal*, illegally seized evidence can be admitted at *civil trials or prosecutions*. Thus, illegally seized tax records can be used by the IRS in a civil action for tax delinquency (*U.S. v. Janis*, 428 U.S. 433, 1976). Similarly, a number of *criminal-related proceedings other than trial* can witness the use of illegally seized evidence. There is no prohibition against considering this evidence at a *grand jury proceeding* (*U.S. v. Calandra*, 414 U.S. 338, 1974) or a *probation/parole revocation hearing*. The ER also does not apply to the *sentencing stage* of a criminal prosecution. A defendant convicted of crime A can receive the maximum sentence for that offense due, in part, to the possession of a weapon during crime A that was inadmissible (and did not result in a conviction) at the trial on crime A.

In all of these situations the Court has employed a ***balancing test*** to determine whether the value of and purposes served by the ER outweighs the loss of evidence suffered by its imposition. In conducting the test the Court has relied heavily upon the deterrence rationale of the ER as justification for establishing its rules or limits. According to the Court, police are focused solely on the prospect of having offenders convicted and are not motivated by other collateral possibilities (such as parole revocation). Simply put, then, if the police would not be deterred by allowing the use of illegally seized evidence in these other proceedings, there is no utility in or necessity of enforcing the ER in these contexts. Moreover, even if illegally seized evidence is mistakenly admitted at a criminal trial, it will be nevertheless be considered a *harmless error*, if the evidence is insignificant and would not have contributed to the guilty verdict; in other words, the error is harmless if there was overwhelming legal evidence to support the verdict (*Chapman v. California*, 386 U.S. 18, 1967).

The Question of *Who*

The *certain people* aspect of the limitation involves who may complain about the illegal behavior of police or prosecutors. In order to file a motion to suppress the person claiming a constitutional violation must have standing. To have standing a person must have what is called a *reasonable expectation of privacy* (REP), a concept we explore at greater length in the next chapter. Simply stated, a person must have possession (actual or joint) of *the premise or location searched* in order to have a REP. Once upon a time an individual legitimately on the premises (such as a passenger in a car) would have been thought to automatically have standing to object to an illegal search (*Jones v. U.S.,* 362 U.S. 257, 1960). This ruling was reinforced years later when the Court emphasized that one does not need to have a possessory interest in or title to the premises searched in order to have standing (*Mancusi v. DeForte*, 392 U.S. 364, 1968). The Court put an end to that thinking in a 5–4 decision in 1978 (*Rakas v. Illinois*, 439 U.S. 128). In the car context, a passenger would have standing if the search involved his/her clothing or belongings, but typically would lack standing if the search was of the trunk of the car (then only the owner of the car would have standing). The dissent in *Rakas* observed this restriction on standing could encourage the police to illegally search a vehicle, thinking that only the owner would be authorized to challenge the search.

Similarly, ownership of an item would have usually granted standing to the person affected by the illegal search. In 1980, however, the Court held that owning an item is irrelevant to standing if the item is searched and found on someone else's property (*Rawlings v. Kentucky,* 448 U.S. 98, 1980). Obviously, by narrowing the individuals who can contest the state's illegal collection of evidence, the Court has taken a lot of the "sting" out of the exclusionary rule. It needs to be noted, as well, that while having standing is a prerequisite to filing a motion to suppress, that does not mean that this person has to file such a motion. Defendants are allowed to *waive* this constitutional right and to not object to the admission or use of illegally seized evidence. There are myriad reasons (such as ignorance or incompetence of the defense attorney, fear of a judge not likely to grant the motion, or forgoing the right as part of a plea bargain) that could explain why the accused would not pursue the exclusionary rule option.

The Question of *What*

The Supreme Court has determined that only *violations of the U.S. Constitution* suffice to trigger the ER. In *U.S. v. Caceres* (440 U.S. 741, 1979), the Court ruled that the violation of a federal regulation or statute does not require the exclusion of illegally seized evidence (unless the statute itself calls for exclusion). Similarly, violating a state constitution only does not require an exclusionary result, unless the state has a provision for its own ER in this context (*California v. Greenwood*, 486 U.S. 35, 1988). In order to better ensure compliance with this rule, the Court has specifically restricted the *supervisory power* of the lower federal courts (i.e., district courts and courts of appeal or circuit courts) such that they may insist upon the exclusion of evidence in a federal court only when there is a federal Constitutional violation (*U.S. v. Payner*, 447 U.S. 727, 1980). Historically, the lower federal courts were authorized to exercise their supervisory power in situations that did not amount to a constitutional violation, such as when a federal agent had acted unethically or immorally. *Payner* put an end to this practice.

In addition, the Court has placed a limit on how many times a Fourth Amendment claim is entitled to a review. In *Stone v. Powell* (428 U.S. 465, 1976), the Court held that when a state has provided a defendant a "full and fair litigation of a Fourth Amendment claim," there is no right to federal habeas corpus relief on the basis that illegally seized evidence was used to secure a conviction in a state court; this limitation has not been extended to Fifth Amendment claims, however. Finally, in this type of limitation, the Supreme Court has simply held that there are *two constitutional violations* that do not result in an application of the ER. First, an *Illegal arrest* does not prevent the government from taking the defendant to trial (*Ker v. Illinois*, 119 U.S. 436, 1886). Even in an extreme case in which a murder defendant was kidnapped in Chicago and brought back to Michigan to stand trial the Court said this "forcible abduction" does not prevent a subsequent trial; a person will not escape justice simply because he was brought to trial against his will (*Frisbie v. Collins*, 342 U.S. 519, 1952; see also, *U.S. v. Alvarez-Machain*, 504 U.S. 655, 1992). Similarly, a violation of the knock and announce (K&A) rule in executing a warrant (see Chapter 3) does not result in an application of the ER. In *Hudson v. Michigan* (547 U.S. 586, 2006), a 5–4 decision, the Court ruled that since a K&A violation has nothing to do with the seizure of evidence the ER does not apply. The Court noted that fear of losing evidence via the ER could cause police to delay, which could both endanger them and lead to the destruction of evidence. Moreover, other remedies were said to exist, such as increased professionalism, internal discipline, and, citizen review. The dissent, however, believed that imposing the ER in this situation would promote deterrence of illegal police behavior.

Exceptions to the Exclusionary Rule

Whereas limits to the ER restrict when, how, and by whom it can be invoked, exceptions to the ER actually permit illegally seized evidence to be used at trial to convict the defendant. As in the case with establishing limits to the ER, the deterrence rationale emphasized in *Mapp* has led to the development of several important exceptions to the exclusionary rule. There are four major categories of exceptions: *impeaching the defendant; independent source; inevitable discovery; and, good faith.*

The ability to *impeach a defendant* by using illegally seized evidence was the first exception to the ER; the Court established it in 1971. Important to note is that this exception to the ER does not permit the introduction of the illegally seized evidence by the prosecution so as to convict the accused. Instead, it permits the use of the evidence to challenge the defendant's testimony; the exception was created so as to prevent the defendant from being able to commit perjury on the stand. In *Harris v. New York* (401 U.S. 222, 1971), the Court determined that an illegally secured confession may be used to impeach the defendant's credibility during the defendant's direct testimony; here, there had been defective *Miranda* warnings (see Chapter 9). A few years later, the Court similarly allowed an illegal confession (where the request by the accused to consult a lawyer was ignored) to serve as impeachment material (*Oregon v. Hass*, 420 U.S. 714, 1975). The Court subsequently held that an *involuntary* confession *cannot be used* for impeachment purposes (*Mincey v. Arizona*, 437 U.S. 385, 1978).

Finally, in 1980, the Court ruled that an illegally seized item (a T-shirt that had been fitted to transport cocaine had been suppressed) can be used in an impeachment capacity during cross-examination of a defendant (*U.S. v. Havens*, 446 U.S. 620, 1980).

Independent source is relevant to both the ER and Fruit of Poisonous Tree. The 1920 *Silverthorne* case had alluded to the possibility that any information that has been gained from an "independent source" would be admissible, even when that same evidence was acquired illegally as well. In 1980, in *U.S. v. Crews* (445 U.S. 463), there had been an illegal arrest and identification of a suspect. Nevertheless, the Supreme Court allowed an in-court identification of the defendant because the police were already aware of the existence of the witness at the time of the illegal arrest; also, the accuracy of the identification had not been affected by the illegal police action. More recently, the Court reaffirmed the exception in *Murray v. U.S.* (487 U.S. 533, 1988). In *Murray*, federal police conducted a warrantless search of a warehouse for drugs; suspected traffickers had been arrested outside the locked warehouse, but that action did not authorize the warrantless search. Inside the agents observed wrapped bales of suspected marijuana. They left the warehouse and filed a warrant application, which relied upon information the agents possessed when they made the first illegal entry (the Court did stress that the legal source must be genuinely independent). The agents re-entered the warehouse with a warrant and found 270 bales of marijuana. Emphasizing the deterrence rationale of the ER, the Court held that to exclude the evidence that had a legal independent source would be to place the police in a "worse" position had the illegal search not occurred. They would lose evidence that they had obtained independently of the improper search. The ER was designed to force police to lose the product of their illegal actions, not to end up worse off than if there had been no illegal activity. In dissent, Justice Marshall commented that this exception to the ER/FOPT will encourage police to illegally search in order to discover whether the findings justify the inconvenience of pursuing a warrant. There might be some merit to this observation inasmuch as a nearly identical fact situation had led to the same conclusions by the Court four years earlier (see *Segura v. U.S.*, 468 U.S. 796, 1984). While the *Crews* case was truly a FOPT situation, *Murray* was not about derivative evidence but rather the "rediscovery" of initial evidence.

The lead Supreme Court case for ***inevitable discovery*** is *Nix v. Williams* (467 U.S. 431, 1984). In this case an illegal interrogation of a murder suspect produced a statement that led to finding a young girl's dead body. This interrogation has gained fame as the "Christian burial speech," which we will discuss in Chapter 9. The Court held that, despite the connection between the illegal interrogation and the location of the body, the latter could be admitted as evidence because 200 people had been looking for the girl so she would have been found or discovered eventually inevitably. Important to this case was that, in addition to the illegal acquisition of the evidence, there was an independent, legal avenue (the search party) that would have discovered the evidence inevitably. The state will have to prove by a preponderance of evidence that the discovery would have been accomplished inevitably and lawfully.

The Good Faith Exception

Good faith is big enough and important enough to warrant its own section. Before good faith was actually called or known as this, there was an early example of its allowance. In *Michigan v. DeFillippo* (443 U.S. 31, 1979), Detroit police arrested the defendant for violating a Stop & Identify ordinance; they found drugs. An appellate court in Michigan granted the defendant's motion to suppress the drugs because the ordinance was unconstitutionally vague, rendering the arrest and search invalid. The Supreme Court reversed this decision, noting that the police had probable cause to believe the accused had violated the statute and that there was no way for the police to have known that the ordinance would ultimately be found to be unconstitutional. The Court held that the statute was presumptively valid, and thus the evidence was admissible. As with so many exceptions, the Court highlighted the lack of need for deterrence for police misbehavior in this context. Instead, police were operating in (what would eventually be known as) good faith. They were legally authorized to do what they did here, so this "illegal" search would constitute an exception to the ER.

When good faith officially entered the vocabulary a few years later it was originally associated with a technical violation or error committed by the police that would not have been considered to be on a constitutional level. A good example is using a search warrant form that is not relevant to the item being sought by the police, such as using a drug warrant in the pursuit of weapons. This is an error on the part of the police, but the mistake is technical at most since it is a violation of a rule or regulation and not the Constitution. If all other rules were satisfied, there would have been probable cause for the search and the judge would have signed off on granting the warrant, which is really all that is constitutionally required for the search to be valid (see Chapter 3). This scenario was indeed the fact situation in *Massachusetts v. Sheppard* (468 U.S. 981) in 1984, but *Sheppard* was merely the companion case to the one in which good faith was given a more significant and controversial interpretation.

U.S. v. Leon (468 U.S. 897, 1984) identified good faith as when the police had acted in "the objectively reasonable belief" that they were acting constitutionally. Rather than a technical flaw, *Leon* involved the granting of a search warrant for drugs without a demonstration of probable cause; the information upon which the police had relied was six months old. Nevertheless, the Court observed that the ER was designed to deter police misconduct and not to punish judges for their errors (it was the judge who made the ultimate mistake in *Leon*). According to the Court, judges have no stake in the securing of evidence and there was no indication that judges, in general, are ignoring Fourth Amendment requirements or would be deterred by the ER. Thus, the Court characterized this situation as a "good faith" mistake, and not as a fundamental flaw in the warrant application process, and concluded it was sufficient to serve as an exception to the ER. The Court did note that probable cause cannot be completely lacking and that the warrant cannot be completely defective; judges also cannot be perceived as partners of shoddy police work (i.e., there cannot be collusion between the two parties). One potential negative outcome to this context of the good faith exception is that it removes negative consequences for judges' being sloppy or too law enforcement inclined, and it allows, if not encourages, police to be equally sloppy in seeking to obtain a warrant. Two wrongs (police seeking a warrant without having probable cause and judges granting the warrant in the same condition) effectively equal a right (to execute a warrant). Basically, if the police "get by" the judge, the case is not subject to second guessing. Prior to *Leon*, both police and judges had to worry that an appellate court would eventually determine that a search warrant was unconstitutional and that all evidence secured via that warrant would be suppressed. If the police lie to the judge in seeking the warrant or don't execute the warrant properly (such as going beyond the parameters of the warrant), the search should be declared unlawful.

The Good Faith Exception Extended

Besides the *Leon* defective warrant situation there are numerous (at least six) examples of good faith that the Court has sanctioned in recent years; all are based on the notion that no deterrence is to be gained by applying the ER in these contexts since police were obeying the law in each. In *Illinois v. Krull* (480 U.S. 340, 1987), Chicago police had engaged in a warrantless inspection of a junkyard. This activity appeared to be authorized by an Illinois statute, but it was later found to be unconstitutional. Since the police had relied upon the then-current legality of the statute, the Court allowed the illegally seized evidence to be admitted at trial. Whereas *DeFillippo* had involved unconstitutionally criminalizing behavior, *Krull* dealt with the authorization of unconstitutional searches; the Court had previously held that any statute that allowed for unconstitutional searches required imposition of the ER (*Berger v. New York,* 388 U.S. 41, 1967). Nevertheless, the Supreme Court in *Krull* declared there was no meaningful difference between the two situations (*DeFillippo vs Krull*) and that both should be included within the good faith category. The Court also saw no difference between *Krull* and *Leon.* Whereas in *Leon* the police relied upon the decision of a judge, the police in *Krull* (and *DeFillippo*) relied upon the decision(s) of a legislature. The Court believed that the threat of the ER would not deter legislatures, mirroring the feeling it had that the ER would not deter judges in *Leon.*

In the same year as *Krull,* the Court extended the good faith exception to a serious mistake the police made in what is called the *particularity requirement* (see Chapter 3). In short, a search warrant must specify the proposed location of the search. The initial investigation conducted by the police in *Maryland v. Garrison* (480 U.S. 79, 1987) indicated there was only one apartment on the third floor of the building the police were targeting for a drug search when there were actually two. The warrant simply stated it authorized a search of *the* third floor apartment. The police ended up searching Garrison's residence, not knowing they were in the wrong apartment. The Court determined that the factual mistake did not invalidate the warrant, and that the conduct of the police must be judged in light of the information available to them at the time they applied for the warrant. The dissent believed that the failure to discover that the third floor had two apartments was not a reasonable mistake, and, moreover, that the reasonableness of the error should not affect the admissibility of the evidence obtained.

A different type of mistake was accepted by the Court in a *third-party consent* situation in 1990 (*Illinois v. Rodriguez*, 497 U.S. 177); we will address this topic in Chapter 6. A former girlfriend and former co-tenant of Rodriguez complained that he had assaulted her; she led police to his apartment. Along the way she referred to the residence as "our" apartment and she had a key, which the police used to gain entrance. Inside the apartment they found both the defendant and drugs. The police thought she still lived there and would thus have the common authority to give the consent necessary for them to access the apartment without a warrant. Her being a *former* resident stripped her of that authority, however. Nevertheless, the Court held that since the police reasonably believed she still lived with the defendant that *apparent authority* was sufficient to let this illegal search constitute an exception to the ER under the good faith umbrella.

The mistakes made in *Garrison/Rodriguez* were serious such that they could be considered sufficient to render the searches unconstitutional. The Court rejected that conclusion and explained in *Rodriquez* that police do not always have to be correct, but, rather, they always have to be reasonable. It could be reasonably argued that the *Garrison/Rodriguez* cases are not really examples of good faith because the Court held that since the behaviors of the police were not unreasonable, there were no Fourth Amendment violations. But, they have been included under this category in this text because in both cases the police lacked actual, proper authority to enter the premises. Thus, constitutional level mistakes, if not violations, occurred, and the only reason the Court did not impose the ER was because the errors in both situations were both reasonable and the result of good faith on the part of the police.

The next two examples of good faith are very similar. In fact, both involved erroneous information being supplied to police who then acted on that misinformation. In *Arizona v. Evans* (514 U.S. 1, 1995), a court clerk reported that there was an outstanding misdemeanor arrest warrant for Evans, but it had been quashed 17 days earlier. The latter information had not been entered on the computer, however, due to a clerical error of a court employee. Evans had been stopped for a motor vehicle infraction, but the misinformation on the outstanding warrant led to his arrest, which led to the discovery of drugs. Since the police did nothing wrong themselves and were simply relying upon inaccurate information, the Court saw no deterrence potential in applying the ER to this situation and decided to adopt another good faith exception to the ER, referring here to *the clerical errors of court employees*. Interesting, the dissent wanted the ER to be enforced against all government officials, and not just against police.

Negligent bookkeeping by a police employee led to another mistaken report that there was an outstanding arrest warrant for the defendant in *Herring v. U.S.* (555 U.S. 135, 2009). Although the warrant had been withdrawn five months earlier, the database had not been updated. Herring was arrested as he left a police impound lot, and drugs and a gun were found on him incident to the arrest. As in *Evans*, the police acting in a law enforcement capacity in *Herring* were not culpable, according to the Court, which is a prerequisite for the ER to apply. Good faith was extended in *Herring* so as to include *the clerical errors of police employees*. The dissent in *Herring* attempted to launch a new direction for the ER. These Justices believe deterrence is not the only rationale for the ER, but rather should include allowing the judiciary to avoid the taint associated with becoming a partner in the lawlessness of police (an original purpose of the ER announced in the 1914 *Weeks* decision), as well as preventing the government from profiting from its own lawlessness.

The final extension of good faith, to date, resembles the concept furthered in *DeFillippo* and *Krull*. In *Davis v. U.S.* (564 U.S. 229, 2011), the Supreme Court held that when police rely upon an established constitutional precedent (here, *New York v. Belton*, 453 U.S. 454, 1981; see Chapter 6) and that precedent is latter overruled (here, *Arizona v. Gant*, 556 U.S. 332, 2009; see Chapter 6), searches conducted in the interim will not be subjected to the ER because they were made in good faith (here, upon *constitutional precedent*).

Another way to look at the good faith exception to the ER is that a majority of the Justices likely do not view these searches and seizures as unreasonable, which is the major requirement of the Fourth Amendment. To be sure, some of the cases dealt with police actions that were extremely reasonable in light of the law of the time: *DeFillippo, Krull, and, Davis*. Some of the cases, however, involved what is unavoidably illegal behavior on the part of the police regardless of whether deterrence would be served: *Leon, Garrison, Evans, Herring, and, Rodriguez*. In the latter cases the police were acting without constitutional authority or legitimacy, mistakes aside. The bottom line for the good faith exception is that there are two competing realities: on the one hand, the police did not knowingly do anything wrong, but, on the other hand, the defendant was convicted using unconstitutionally seized evidence.

Between the *limits and exceptions* to the ER the Supreme Court has established a broad area in which illegally seized evidence can have significant impact in a variety of ways upon the lives of those against whom the illegal activities have been directed; that impact even includes potentially convicting the person so affected. To be sure, the conservative-oriented Justices have constructed a weighty and varied precedent that can curtail the effect of the ER, and forgives the mistakes and illegal behavior of the police. Important to remember, however, is that most, if not all, of this precedent can be eliminated by a change in composition of the Supreme Court Justices.

Box 2-2: Various Dimensions of Good Faith

Relying on a statute later declared unconstitutional

Relying on a previous U.S. Supreme Court decision later reversed

Wrong information on existence of an outstanding warrant

    Via police

    Via court worker

Particularity requirement—mistake in the address

Third-party consent in searching—lacking authority

Deficient warrant—relying on a defective warrant

Box 2-3: Balancing Tests Are Employed

Entire ER area—benefits of deterrence must outweigh the costs (Chapter 2)

Summers Rule (Chapter 3)

Use of force—amount of intrusion vs need for apprehension (Chapter 3)

Whether to grant a warrant to conduct surgery (Chapter 4)

Dog sniffs—at airports or traffic stops (Chapter 4)

Telling motorists and passengers to get out of cars—invasion of privacy vs officer safety (Chapter 5)

Terry stops—government interests/crime prevention vs intrusion on 4th amendment (Chapter 5)

Checkpoints: sobriety/illegal aliens—slight intrusion vs substantial interest (Chapter 5)

Breath tests without a warrant incident to arrest of DUI suspects (Chapter 6)

Special needs searches (Chapter 6)

Cell phone searches incident to arrest and finding crime/criminals vs. privacy (Chapter 6)

Taking blood samples (Chapter 10)

CHAPTER 3

The Fourth Amendment: Design Flaws, Limitations, and Requirements

The Fourth Amendment reads:

Amendment IV

The right of the people to be secure in their persons, houses, papers, and effects, against unreasonable searches and seizures, shall not be violated, and no Warrants shall issue, but upon probable cause, supported by Oath or affirmation, and particularly describing the place to be searched, and the persons or things to be seized.

It is interesting that the Founders were quite upset with Colonial policy, which put the houses and effects of colonists at the compete mercy of the British military, and yet they did not establish anything like an insurmountable barrier between the newly created U.S. government and the property of its citizens. Searches and seizures need to be merely reasonable, while warrants validate the intrusion into anyone's home and need only probable cause to be legitimate.

At first glance, the Amendment may seem pretty straight forward. Greater scrutiny of the wording, however, will reveal what has become the material over which many Supreme Court Justices have differed in very significant ways. Some of the disagreement deals with what were the original intentions of the Framers of the Amendment; some of it concerns simply what was the Amendment meaning to say in common parlance, and how was that meaning meant to evolve over time.

So, before covering what the Fourth Amendment demands of the police, it is important to discuss the Amendment's ambiguities (i.e., problems in interpretation), and to consider what the Amendment does not control.

Box 3-1: Fourth Amendment Interpretation Problems

Vague Words

Two Independent Clauses

No Remedy Provided

Focus on the Physical

All Items Created Equal

Applying for a Warrant

Executing a Warrant

PROBLEMS WITH THE FOURTH AMENDMENT AS DRAFTED BY THE FOUNDERS

The Amendment employs **vague words**, such as *unreasonable* and *probable* cause. Much like beauty, the definitions of unreasonable and probable cause will vary by the perception of the individual. Both terms are judgments so their purported existence, especially in close calls, will yield different opinions.

It is not only the adjectives that present definitional hurdles, however. Precisely what constitutes an arrest (e.g., is it every situation in which a person's liberty is constrained, however briefly?) or a search (e.g., is it every situation in which a police officer is looking at an item or place?) can be a serious judgment call.

The Amendment contains **two independent clauses**: one prohibits unreasonable searches and seizures, while the second describes the requirements for securing a warrant. So which is it? Do searches and seizures just have to be reasonable or should we infer that the only way for a search to be reasonable is to mandate that police have a warrant before they search. Are reasonable and probable cause inextricably tied, such that the only way a search can be reasonable is if it is backed by probable cause? One might infer that since the first clause demands reasonableness only, that was the primary concern of the Founders. But then a legitimate question would be, if reasonableness only was the focus, why did the Founders add the second clause addressing the warrant procedure? During the first one hundred and fifty years of the Amendment's existence the first clause seemed to dominate the Supreme Court's approach and interpretation. From the mid-Twentieth Century on, however, the warrant requirement has taken center stage. The more conservative, pro-law enforcement type of Justice is likely to want only reasonableness, while the more liberal, pro-accused type of Justice is likely to want a warrant to justify most, if not all, searches.

Perhaps the most significant deficiency is that there is **no remedy** provided. The Amendment simply states there shall not be any unreasonable (or warrantless) searches and seizures. This is much like what the Ten Commandments do. Well, what if. . . . ? With violating the Commandments there is a possibility that eternal damnation follows from a violation. There is no clear cut reaction identified, however, for a violation of the Fourth Amendment.

The Amendment was focused on **physical interference** (trespassing someone's property—houses) and the **seizure of physical items** (persons, papers and effects). That was the procedure with which the Founders would have been familiar. The Founders could not have anticipated modern technology, such as wiretapping and even more sophisticated devices, in which there is neither a trespass nor a physical seizure (e.g., only a conversation overheard).

Assuming a warrant was desirable or necessary, did the Framers want or expect arrests to be justified with a warrant in the same manner searches would be? The Amendment **appears to treat persons equally with houses, papers and effects**, but it is unlikely the Founders considered them to be on an equal footing, and history has not seen people (for whom a warrant to arrest is rarely required) given as much constitutional protection as the physical items (for which a warrant to search is preferable, and mostly a norm). Similarly, were **all seizures meant to be treated equally**? Would a brief detention or stop of someone require any or the same level of evidence as an arrest? The history of Supreme Court decision making shows less evidence is required when the intrusion is less significant, as in a stop versus an arrest. Moreover, **not all places are treated equally**. As we will see, for example, houses are given substantial (and the most) protection against governmental interference, automobiles significantly less, and the fields and the property surrounding one's home virtually none, provided the area is outside the curtilage of the house.

There were no police operating at the time of the ratification of the Amendment (1791). So **does it matter who is applying for the warrant** (and exactly who can and cannot apply), and is it important who is supplying the information that will constitute the probable cause—a cop, a well-respected citizen—a criminal or "unsavory" type who has turned informant? It is seemingly obvious that the Fourth Amendment was aimed at government searchers, but precisely who is restricted by it? Is the answer only the person we consider having a state law enforcement identity, such as a police officer or a prosecutor or does that include private law enforcement, such as private security officers or private investigators who are privately employed, but are licensed by the state? Would other non-law enforcement state employees be eligible (or controlled by) to apply for a search or arrest warrant, such as those who work for state colleges or government bureaucratic types? Related to this uncertainty is the question as to **who may issue a warrant**? Is it only a judicial figure or may someone else, such as an attorney general, be qualified to grant a warrant request?

One completely unaddressed aspect of the Amendment was the **legitimacy in using force in order to effect an arrest or even a search**, for that matter. The same applies to **executing a warrant**, assuming one is necessary. Arrest was an understood concept at the time and could have reasonably been thought to have produced a discussion as to what should be allowed if the individual resisted arrest or attempted to flee the area. There is no guide as to what force may be reasonably applied in this context. Searches might as easily have been anticipated to require force in order to be carried out, since a person could resist this maneuver as well, such as not allowing police entry into a house. Regardless, there is no guide for this activity either. Can the police utilize force to gain entry into a house; does that depend upon resistance experienced? Are the police obligated to announce their identity and purpose before executing the warrant? Even if the individual cooperates with a search of the house, are there limits on how long a warrant stays in effect or the time of day during which it can be executed?

In light of the many questions and uncertainties inherent in the contents of the Fourth Amendment, it should come as no surprise that an immense amount of litigation and controversy have surrounded its history.

LIMITS ON THE APPLICATION OF THE FOURTH AMENDMENT

Two elements must exist for someone to be able to complain that a Fourth Amendment violation has occurred. The first is that a *government agent* must be involved. This position has been clear for nearly a century (see *Burdeau v. McDowell*, 256 U.S. 465, 1921). In addition, this government agent must be working in a law enforcement capacity, such as a police officer or a prosecutor. Others who work for the government, such as professors who teach at a state college, but are not in the field of law enforcement, are in the same status as all other private citizens. For all of them, a constitutional violation in not possible. The one exception to this rule is that elementary and secondary school teachers have had a water downed version of the Fourth Amendment applied to them in the search of students. As we will see in Chapter 6, these teachers must *act reasonably*, but do not need a warrant to search (*N. J. v. T.L.O.*, 469 U.S. 325, 1985). Also beyond the control of the Constitution are private police and investigators who are engaged in law enforcement-like activity, but are not employed by the state. Like all the rights listed in the Bill of Rights, the government is the target of the intended control or limitations. The second necessary element is that the individual claiming the violation must have had *a reasonable expectation of privacy (REP)*. This element is relevant usually only for searches (arrests have not been the subject of much in the way of Fourth Amendment coverage, and a person's body in terms of arrest is not protected in the same way as a person's personal belongings are) and was derived from a 1967 Supreme Court case, *Katz v. U.S.* (389 U.S. 347) (we will return to this case in Chapter 7).

REASONABLE EXPECTATION OF PRIVACY AND POLICE INVESTIGATORY POWERS

The *Katz* decision established serious protection against a state-sponsored invasion of privacy by requiring a warrant before police can wiretap a person's phone conversation. Prior to that time (see Chapter 7) wiretapping had not been considered to involve either a physical intrusion (the interception typically would occur outside the house or establishment in which the landline phone had been used) or a physical seizure (only a conversation was caught). In *Katz*, the Court emphasized that the Fourth Amendment protects people, not places. The landmark decision held that one's having an expectation (the adjective *subjective* was implicit, but was not used by the Court) of privacy was sufficient to trigger Fourth Amendment protection. Justice Harlan concurred in the opinion, but was insistent that the expectation of privacy had to be *reasonable*, one that society would accept as such. Remarkable is that Justice Harlan's concurrence has actually become the holding. Today the standard is that one must have a *reasonable expectation of privacy* in order for the authority of the police to be constrained by the Fourth Amendment. The most likely explanation for this is that the *Katz* opinion was handed down by liberal Justices who favored a more expansive Amendment that better controlled police power, but the decision was handed down near the end of the Warren Court era. The succeeding four decades have been dominated by more conservative Justices, likely more comfortable with the notion that not just anyone's subjective expectation should be the standard for triggering Fourth Amendment relevance. Theoretically, a subjective expectation of privacy could be argued to exist in a public street. The conservative Justices prevented such a development by seizing upon Justice Harlan's modifying adjective, reasonable, which now controls the Fourth Amendment's application to searches.

These ideas, although controversial at times, have been settled law for many years. One caveat to these principles must be noted, however. Recently, the Supreme Court has indicated that when the government physically intrudes on someone's property, a search has taken place, whether or not the target of the activity had a reasonable expectation of privacy (*U.S. v. Jones*, 565 U.S. 400, 2012). This new holding has the potential of revising some of what constitutional law currently provides and some of what this text will report as established practice.

FOURTH AMENDMENT REQUIREMENTS

Assuming there is a government agent and a reasonable expectation of privacy on the part of the individual against whom the government is taking action, the Fourth Amendment has relevance. As we've already mentioned there has been disagreement as to whether a warrant was intended to be required for all arrests and searches conducted by the government. Those favoring the reasonableness-only position will cite the desirability of quick and efficient law enforcement that is not hampered by interjecting a judge into the process. Criminals can escape and evidence can be lost in the time it takes to secure a warrant. Those favoring a warrant will point to the judge's providing confirmation of reasonable government action and interference into peoples' lives. Here, the judge is an objective outsider who can be better relied upon to prevent government abuse of power. The warrant also guarantees that the police had a legitimate reason to invade someone's privacy *before* the interference.

SECURING A WARRANT

Neutral Magistrate

Assuming a warrant is necessary, the procedure is pretty straightforward. Perhaps the easiest aspect of a warrant is the person authorized to issue one: a neutral and detached magistrate. Even here, however, there have been some hiccups in the past. We know today from Supreme Court case law that a warrant cannot be authorized by:

- a state attorney general (*Coolidge v. New Hampshire*, 403 U.S. 443, 1971);

- an unsalaried justice of the peace whose financial compensation depended upon every signed warrant (*Connally v. Georgia*, 429 U.S. 245, 1977); and,

- a town justice actively involved in a search for pornography (*Lo-Ji Sales, Inc. v. New York*, 442 U.S. 319, 1979).

DEFINING PROBABLE CAUSE, ARREST, SEARCH AND SEIZURE

The next questions are more complicated and involve *what exactly is an arrest, what is a search*, and *what is a seizure*. Answering these questions can be difficult, but is critical since the government needs a certain amount of evidence to justify all three activities, and lacking that evidence puts arrests, searches, and seizures, and any acquired evidence in jeopardy. An arrest, which rarely needs a warrant to be valid, requires **probable cause to believe** both that **a crime has occurred** and that **the person being arrested committed that crime**. A search, which much more likely needs a warrant to be valid, requires **probable cause to believe** both that **an item is connected with a crime** and that **the item is located in the place to be searched**. A search involves a governmental violation of a person's reasonable expectation of privacy (*U.S. v. Jacobsen*, 466 U.S. 109, 1984). One interesting feature of the government's searching powers is that a warrant may be secured against a non-suspect (i.e., someone with no personal connection to a crime) provided that the criminally connected item is located on that person's property. The Court made this ruling in *Zurcher v. Stanford Daily* (436 U.S. 547, 1978). A seizure entails some meaningful interference with a person's possessory interest in property (*U.S. v. Jacobsen*). A seizure is the government's gaining control **over a person** (perhaps culminating in an arrest) due to the commission of a violation or crime, or **over an item** due to a connection with some illegal event. Examples of the latter include contraband or items one is not entitled to possess legally (such as drugs), the proceeds of a crime (such as stolen merchandise), instruments used to facilitate the commission of a crime (such as a gun), and materials that serve as evidence that corroborates a person's having dome a crime (such as clothing worn during the crime). Although probable cause to believe that a criminal connection exists must be present, a warrant may or may not be required.

Probable Cause Defined

Probable cause is perhaps best explained as a quantum of evidence that is relatively situated along a continuum of possible levels or amounts of information. It represents more knowledge than a mere and/or reasonable suspicion, and less than clear and convincing evidence. Probable cause is certainly much less evidence than that that would constitute beyond a reasonable doubt. To quantify it, there would have to be slightly more evidence suggesting guilt than there is suggesting lack of guilt, perhaps a 51% or so level. The Supreme Court rarely defines terms, and possibly the best definition it gave of probable cause dates back to 1949, when, in *Brinegar v. United States*:

> Probable cause exists where the facts and circumstances within the officers' knowledge, and of which that have reasonably trustworthy information, are sufficient in themselves to warrant a belief by a man of reasonable caution that a crime is being committed (338 U.S. 160, 161, 1949).

An interesting recent twist to the probable cause requirement is that the Supreme Court has upheld both **pretext arrests** (*Arkansas v. Sullivan*, 532 U.S. 769, 2001; *Devenpeck v. Alford*, 543 U.S. 146, 2004) and **pretext searches** (*Whren v. U.S.*, 517 U.S. 806, 1996). Alford was arrested for unlawfully taping a conversation. The original offense that drew him to the attention of the police, however, was impersonating an officer. A unanimous Court ruled that there must be *probable cause for some offense*, even if it is not the one or is not even similar to the one that initiated the police attention. The Court explained that there is no such thing as a "closely related rule" concerning the connection between the initial suspicion and the ultimate reason for the arrest. The Court rejected the rule because it would make the validity of the arrest dependent upon the motivation of the police officer. Instead, the Court indicated that the motivation is irrelevant provided there is probable cause to arrest. The Court also held that there is no requirement that the suspect be told the reason for the arrest at the time of arrest. While it may be good practice or policy, informing the suspect of the charges at the time of arrest is not constitutionally required, according to the Supreme Court.

Finally, The Supreme Court determined that, if one police officer (X) requests another officer (Y) arrest a suspect, police officer X must have probable cause, not police officer Y (*U.S. v. Hensley*, 469 U.S. 221, 1985).

Arrest Defined

An arrest is probably best defined as interfering with a person's liberty extensively, such that they are physically restricted and detained. At its extreme an arrest is easy to discern. So, if an individual has been taken into custody, transported to the police station, booked by the police and placed in jail, it's pretty safe to conclude that an arrest has occurred. None of these actions is necessary for an arrest to occur, however. An arrest can be consummated on the street, at an airport or in someone's home. The important and necessary ingredient is depriving someone of his/her liberty beyond a temporary stop or detention.

It is interesting that more time and energy have been spent on *what is not an arrest*. Substantial interference with liberty can occur without an arrest, as can be seen in motor vehicle stops and field detentions of persons on the street. We will see in Chapters 5 (Investigatory Stops/Stop and Frisk) and 6 (Warrantless Searches) that brief and temporary seizures or detentions (as opposed to arrests) can be justified on less than probable cause. An arrest without probable cause, however, is unconstitutional, as is any evidence secured from the individual who has been subjected to an illegal detention. Moreover, police are prohibited from moving a suspect from a private residence to the police station without probable cause (*Dunaway v. New York*, 442 U.S. 200, 1979).

The level of the detention is important also as to whether *Miranda* warnings are required when police are questioning someone. If the person is in custody, *Miranda* warnings are necessary prior to any interrogation; if the person is in a temporary detention status, however, warnings are not likely to be required (see Chapter 9).

Historically, police never needed a warrant to arrest, and they still do not need one if the person is in the public sector, even if there is ample time to secure a warrant (*U.S. v. Watson*, 423 U.S. 411, 1976). There is also no warrant needed for an arrest that begins in a public place, but then the suspect escapes into a private place and is arrested there (*U.S. v. Santana*, 427 U.S. 38, 1975). In this case, Santana tried to retreat into her house, but officers chased her and caught her inside.

Recently, the Court upheld a warrantless arrest for a minor criminal offense, namely a misdemeanor punishable by fine only (this case involved a failure to use a seat belt). The Court saw this behavior as neither unreasonable nor as a violation of the Fourth Amendment (*Atwater v. City of Lago Vista*, 532 U.S. 318, 2001). Although all 50 states allow this type of arrest, this was a 5–4 decision; the dissent saw this as an unreasonable search and seizure, and that an arrest here was a pointless indignity, serving no discernable state interest. Seven years later, the Court also authorized warrantless misdemeanor arrests (*Virginia v. Moore*, 553 U.S. 164, 2008). In *Moore*, a driver was stopped for driving with a suspended license. While Virginia law called for a summons in lieu of arrest in this context, the officer arrested the driver. Seeing no Fourth Amendment violation, the legality of that choice was upheld by the Supreme Court.

One final important note is that most defendants are arrested without a judicial determination of probable cause. There is neither a warrant nor an indictment preceding arrest so the police officer is the only one, so far, who has alleged that probable cause exists. If this is the case, the Fourth Amendment requires a judicial finding of probable cause as a prerequisite to extending custody following arrest (*Gerstein v. Pugh*, 420 U.S. 103, 1975); this finding must take place (in an initial/first appearance) within 48 hours of arrest (*County of Riverside v. McLaughlin*, 500 U.S. 44, 1991).

DEVELOPING A CONSTITUTIONAL REQUIREMENT FOR AN ARREST WARRANT

As we have seen, historically, a warrant was not needed to arrest anyone in any location. The Supreme Court put an end to that situation in 1980 in *Payton v. New York* (445 U.S. 573). Absent exigent circumstances or the valid consent of the homeowner, police are now required to obtain a warrant to effect an arrest *in the person's home*. The Court held that the Fourth Amendment applies equally to persons and property and, since the police cannot enter a home to remove property without a warrant, the same should apply to people (so as to preserve the privacy of the home). At this time 24 states allowed warrantless entry, 15 clearly prohibited it, and 11 had no clear position. The Court explained that this longstanding practice was not immune from constitutional scrutiny or change. *Payton* was interesting in that it broke new ground. It was a 6–3 decision that had three liberal Justices (Brennan, Marshall, and Stevens) joining three more conservative Justices (Stewart, Powell, and Blackmun) in the majority. Justice White wrote the dissent and argued that Common Law and the Fourth Amendment permitted warrantless arrests in the home, that most of the states allowed (or at least did not prohibit) such an entry, and that even Congress had not required a warrant for federal arrests in the home. This is a situation in which Originalists will complain that the Supreme Court is amending the Constitution by a simple majority vote instead of by following the procedures spelled out for adopting amendments.

Four years later the Court explained that the police desire to apprehend a suspect in a DUI case, which has an exigency element since alcohol will dissipate and evidence will thus destroyed, is not sufficient to justify a warrantless nighttime entry of suspect's house to effect an arrest (*Welsh v. Wisconsin*, 466 U.S. 740, 1984). It was critical to the decision that the incident involved only a non-jailable traffic offense, and that the entry was made at night. A change in either of these characteristics could very well change the outcome of the Court's ruling. And we already noted that if the entry to the house involves a hot pursuit of the suspect from a public place, no warrant is necessary (*U.S. v. Santana*, 427 U.S. 38, 1976).

An arrest warrant is needed also to arrest an overnight guest because that person has a reasonable expectation of privacy (*Minnesota v. Olson*, 495 U.S. 91, 1990), but visitors packing drugs for a short period of time are not equally protected (*Minnesota v. Carter*, 525 U.S. 83, 1998).

Visitors do not seem to enjoy the same level of privacy entitlement, but it should be noted that *Carter* was a 5–4 decision. Interesting is that an additional search warrant is required to arrest a suspect who is located in someone else's home, unless that person gives consent to enter his/ her home or there are exigent circumstances (*Steagald v. U.S.*, 451 U.S. 204, 1981).

Search Defined

A search is probably best defined as an intrusion into an area in which a person has a reasonable expectation of privacy. In Chapter 4, the *Public Domain* concept will address the situations in which that expectation is absent so that a search has not occurred, thus dispensing with both the probable cause and warrant requirements. We will soon see where a "limited search" can take place during a "limited detention" without a warrant or probable cause in Chapter 5 (Investigatory Stops/ Stop and Frisk), and where full blown searches can occur without a warrant and perhaps without probable cause as well in Chapter 6 (Warrantless Searches). Apart from these three major and important categories, both probable cause and a warrant are required for police to legally search.

ESTABLISHING PROBABLE CAUSE

As we've seen, to achieve probable cause the police must have reliable evidence that makes it appear more likely than not—or probable—that an arrest or search is called for. Essentially any information qualifies for consideration here, regardless of whether the evidence would be admissible at trial. In determining whether the required threshold has been reached, a judge will use a *totality of circumstances* test or analysis. This test is used in a number of contexts, as we will see throughout the text, and simply examines the factors upon which police relied to make a conclusion probable cause existed, such as the behavior of the accused, statements by the suspect, physical evidence, location of the alleged offense, prior record of the suspect, information provided by others, etc.

The evidence amounting to probable cause must be *particularized*, meaning it must directly implicate a person. So, when the police had a warrant to search a bar and the bartender for drugs, they were not authorized to frisk or search other patrons of the bar as well (*Ybarra v. Illinois*, 444 U.S. 85, 1979). The Supreme Court has indicated it might allow some leeway, however, depending upon the context. There was a case in which the police stopped a vehicle for speeding and the driver opened the glove compartment to retrieve his license and registration. Visible was a roll of money. The driver gave police consent to search the car, which uncovered nearly $800 in cash and five small bags of cocaine. All three occupants of the car denied owning the money or the drugs; all three were arrested, however. At the police station, one the occupants confessed to owning both items. At trial, he tried to suppress the confession, arguing his arrest was illegal due to a lack of probable cause. The Court upheld the arrest, holding that it was reasonable for the police to infer that "any or all three" of the occupants knew about and "exercised dominion and control over, the cocaine. Thus a reasonable officer could conclude that there was probable cause to believe Pringle committed the crime of possession of cocaine, either solely or jointly." (*Maryland v. Pringle*, 540 U.S. 366, 372, 2003).

Obviously, if the arrest or search requires a warrant, the police will have to convince a judge that the circumstances that constitute probable cause already exist *prior to the actual arrest or search*. The advantage of the warrant requirement is that police cannot claim the presence of probable cause via information they learn while conducting the arrest or search.

If a police officer or a non-criminal citizen is the source of information regarding alleged criminal activity, credibility will be mostly assumed by the judge. If an informant with a criminal history or reputation is the source of the information, however, the judge is likely to have some skepticism regarding the integrity of the individual providing that information. In 1964, the Warren Court created a *two-prong test* to determine the acceptability of an informant as the source of probable cause (*Aguilar v. Texas*, 378 U.S. 108, 1964). What was needed was a *reliable informant* and *valid information*. Reliability was gauged by variables such as whether the informant had provided valid information in past or perhaps by whether he/she was exposing him/herself to prosecution by revealing what they had. Validity was estimated by the scope and depth of the information provided by the informant, how this information was acquired and in what context and over what length of time had the informant had access to the criminal enterprise. In short, did the informant possess facts that would lead the judge to conclude that the information was correct? One problem was that *Aguilar* basically guaranteed that anonymous tips could never be used. There would be no way for the police to demonstrate the reliability of an informant that was unknown to them. *Aguilar* remained law for nearly four decades.

In 1983, the more conservative Supreme Court developed a new formula for evaluating the information provided by informants. The Court established a *totality of circumstances test* that allows for anonymous informants (*Illinois v. Gates*, 462 U.S. 213, 1983). In *Gates*, a letter had supplied an abundance of information as to what the defendants (a married couple) would be doing in the near future, especially in terms of travelling around the country. The police corroborated those predicted activities, then obtained a warrant to search the couple's house when they returned home. The police did find drugs inside the home. Interesting is that there was good detail in the anonymous letter, but that none of the activity described was criminal, per se. All of the predicted and described behaviors were ostensibly legal. The Supreme Court said that, nevertheless, the depth of the information (corroborated by the police) established probable cause. *Gates* ended up abandoning the two-prong test of *Aguilar*; it simply allows the deficiency in one prong (which means the reliability prong) to be compensated by the strength of the other prong (the validity or extent of the information). One disturbing prospect to come out of *Gates* is that it opens the door for police to be the anonymous source as well.

APPLYING FOR A WARRANT

The police can use any relevant evidence, including hearsay and other sources of information that would not be admissible at trial. The police include this information in a sworn affidavit that is submitted to the judge. Police cannot commit perjury or a "reckless disregard for the truth." If either of these occurs and the remainder of the affidavit fails to establish probable cause, the warrant should be invalidated, and all evidence secured therefrom should be declared inadmissible (*Franks v. Delaware*, 438 U.S. 154, 1978). In *Franks* the defendant made a showing that police had knowingly and intentionally used a false statement (or had acted with a reckless disregard for the truth) in the warrant affidavit. When the defendant can show by a preponderance that there is not adequate probable cause independent of this "bad" information, the warrant will be invalidated. If the police had relied on an informant, the defendant might be able to learn the identity of informant, especially if the judge cannot resolve the probable cause question without further information.

PARTICULARITY REQUIREMENT

As discussed earlier, the warrant must describe the items to be seized and the place to be searched. This is known as the *particularity requirement*. Where problems or mistakes seem most likely to occur, here, are in describing the place to be searched, such as a wrong address or misplaced numbers amounting to a mistake in the exact location (e.g., a 335 West Avenue instead of 353 West Avenue). The Supreme Court was asked whether a mistake in this context was fatal for the warrant and the evidence seized in *Maryland v. Garrison* (480 U.S. 79, 1987). The Court answered no. Garrison was the case in which the police thought mistakenly that there was only one apartment on the third floor of a building when there were actually two. The police didn't know there were 2 apartments until after they had entered the wrong one and had found drugs and cash. The Court held this to be a Good Faith exception to the particularity requirement since the warrant was valid when issued. The dissent did not see the mistake as being reasonable.

Particularity errors can also involve the items being searched. In *Groh v. Ramirez* (540 U.S. 551, 2004), the Court held that a search warrant containing no description of the items to be seized (weapons and explosives) was completely ineffective, and was not saved by the fact that the affidavit had mentioned the items. The Court explained that the motivation for the warrant provision in the Fourth Amendment, especially the particularity requirement, was to prevent general searches. Consequently, a search warrant must contain a particularized description of the items to be seized. Otherwise, the warrant is unconstitutional, even if application for the warrant has the descriptions. The Court observed that the only way to save the warrant would have been to have the affidavit (with the description) accompany the warrant. It is interesting that the Court did not perceive this mistake or oversight to constitute a good faith exception situation.

The police can also secure what is called **anticipatory warrants** with probable cause (*U.S. v. Grubbs*, 547 U.S. 90, 2006). The Court said this type of warrant is permitted as long as there is current probable cause to believe a person or an item will be on the premise when the warrant is executed. A unanimous Court held that this future aspect doesn't violate the particularity requirement since the item is not currently at the location when the police secure the warrant. All that is required, according to the Court, is that the item/person has to be at the location when the warrant is executed. In order to acquire this type of warrant there must be probable cause to believe that there is a triggering event or condition that will account for the ultimate location of the item/person, but this information does not have to be disclosed to the suspect.

EXECUTING A WARRANT

There is usually a time limit during which the police must execute a warrant (such as a matter of days or months), and the search might have to occur during the daytime. Nighttime execution of warrants is possible, however, especially if the target is drugs. Operating outside the limits imposed by the warrant authorization could lead to the warrant's invalidation.

There is a requirement to **knock and announce** prior to entry into a house to execute a search warrant. The Warren Court first identified this responsibility in *Ker v. California* (374 U.S. 23, 1963). Even the liberal Court was willing to identify *exceptions* to this overall rule, however:

- Victim or someone in danger;

- Risk of injury to police;

- Possibility of flight;

- Destruction of evidence.

A constitutional duty to knock and announce was established more recently by a more conservative Court in *Wilson v. Arkansas* (514 U.S. 927, 1995). In *Wilson,* the Court explained that common law had required the police to knock and announce unless there had been an emergency or exigent circumstances and that most states had adopted the rule. The Court saw this rule as constituting a part of the Fourth Amendment's requirement for reasonableness, although the exceptions noted above were also recognized as potentially reasonable by the Court.

The Court has acknowledged that knock and announce should be the assumed ordinary procedure so people have a chance to comply and to avoid destruction of property (that attends a no-knock entry). The Court determined that it would not grant a category-based exception to knock and announce, meaning that simply because the target is drugs does not give the police an assumption of being able to enter without knocking and announcing. Instead, the validity of a no-knock entry is gauged on a case-by-case decision (*Richards v. Wisconsin,* 520 U.S. 385, 1997). The police must have reasonable suspicion that a knock and announce entry would be dangerous or futile.

A no-knock entry is valid even if the entry causes destruction of property (*U.S. v. Ramirez*, 523 U.S. 65, 1998). In *Ramirez*, the police had probable cause that there was an escaped felon in the residence they searched (belonging to Ramirez); they dispensed with the knocking and announcing rule. The Court noted that the Fourth Amendment does not require a higher standard of proof when the no-knock will involve destruction of property.

Unless there is an emergency or exigency of some sort, police are expected to wait for a refusal or a slight time lapse (15 to 20 seconds can suffice) after a knock and announce has occurred before entering. The validity of the police action in this context will be subjected to a **Totality of Circumstances test**; drugs can be considered as one of the circumstances justifying a quick entry by the police (*U.S. v. Banks*, 540 U.S. 31, 2003).

As noted in Chapter 2 one interesting facet about the knock and announce rule is that is a violation of it does not result in the loss of evidence by police; there is no ER in this situation (*Hudson v. Michigan*, 547 U.S. 586, 2006). *Hudson* was a 5–4 decision so its longevity is questionable. Nevertheless, the Court held that a knock and announce violation has nothing to do with seizure of evidence so the ER does not apply. The Court believed that the ER in this situation could cause the police to delay, which could endanger cops and lead to the destruction of evidence. The dissent saw the ER as promoting deterrence here.

The Fourth Amendment does not require the police to provide a copy of warrant before searching (*Groh v. Ramirez*, 540 U.S. 551, 2004), but it does mean that the police cannot bring the media inside the home while searching (*Wilson v. Layne*, 526 U.S. 603, 1999). The scope of search is defined by the object of the search or the items mentioned in the warrant. If an arrest is involved the police are authorized to look for a person, while if a search is the target, the police may look for the item described in the warrant anywhere that there is probable cause to believe the item can be found, provided there is authorization via the warrant to look in that location. A warrant that permits the police to search for a stolen car in a garage would not authorize the police to search in a basement of a house for the same car, even though, theoretically, the car could be located there. As with an arrest, a search extends to the entire area covered by the warrant's description (e.g., a garage, a basement, etc.).

The *Summers* Rule

The police are authorized to detain someone found on the premises while executing a search warrant (*Michigan v. Summers*, 452 U.S. 692, 1981; the origin of the so-called *Summers Rule*). This authority applies also to detaining someone else who was not a target of the search, but was found inside the house (*Muehler v. Mena*, 544 U.S. 93, 2005); the individual's immigration status can also be ascertained. Mena had been handcuffed and detained for 2–3 hours in a garage, even though she was not suspected of criminal activity. Utilizing *a balancing test* (between the amount of intrusion versus the special law enforcement interests), the Court saw this limited intrusion and restraint as reasonable. However, the Court prohibited detaining a suspect after chasing him for a mile after that person had left the target house. This activity was not sustainable under the *Summers* Rule, according to the Court (*Bailey v. U.S.*, 568 U.S. 186, 2013).

The police can also detain someone while they are pursuing a warrant (*Illinois v. McArthur*, 531 U.S. 326, 2001). The police held McArthur outside his trailer for two hours while pursuing a warrant so as to prevent the destruction of evidence. The police had probable cause to believe that there were drugs inside the trailer (they just didn't have the warrant they needed), and there was good reason to believe the suspect would destroy the drugs if the police had simply left the scene. McArthur also had access to the trailer, although he was never out of the sight of the police. And the restraint was for a limited amount of time.

The Court noted that these detentions in order to:

- minimize the risk of harm to the police;

- facilitate the completion of the search;

- prevent flight; and,

- preserve the integrity of the search.

FORCE USED TO EFFECT AN ARREST

The police use of force is much more likely to arise as an issue in dealing with an arrest rather than a search, and the use of deadly force is particularly controversial. The lead case in this area is *Tennessee v. Garner* (471 U.S. 1, 1985), which overruled the *fleeing felon rule*. The fleeing felon rule, from the common law era, allowed police to use lethal force against all those suspected of committing a felony if they attempted to escape from police apprehension. The Court put an end to this in the *Garner* case, which involved an unarmed juvenile who ran away from the police after he had committed a residential burglary. The Court ruled that the police use of deadly force against a nondangerous suspect is excessive and unreasonable, and thus is a violation of the Fourth Amendment. The Court ruled that to use deadly force the suspect must be attempting to escape apprehension, and the police must have probable cause to believe that the suspect poses a threat of death or serious physical harm to the officer or others. That belief would require that the suspect either presented a current deadly threat or has committed a crime that resulted in serious physical harm. It is interesting that more than one-half of the states still had observed the fleeing felon rule at this time. Nevertheless, the Supreme Court observed that the rule originated at a time when all major felonies were capital crimes, while most felonies in 1985 were punishable by prison sentences at most. It is also interesting that Justice White, who dissented in the *Payton v. New York* decision (because the Court was effectively amending the Constitution) wrote the *Garner* opinion and explained that the Fourth Amendment was not frozen in its Eighteenth Century context.

In *Scott v. Harris* (550 U.S. 372, 2007), the Court allowed an officer to ram Harris's fleeing car so as to terminate a 10-mile high speed chase. The Court saw the suspect's flight as a continuing serious threat to innocent bystanders, authorizing the police to use the necessary force to terminate the chase, even though that force placed the suspect at risk of death or serious injury. The suspect sustained serious injury; he became a quadriplegic as a result of being rammed by the police. The Court did not believe this use of force constituted a violation of the Fourth Amendment.

Plumhoff v. Rickard (572 U.S. ___, 134 S.Ct. 2012, 2014) involved another motor vehicle incident. Here, the suspect (Rickard) fled a traffic stop and a car chase ensued. Rickard crashed his vehicle into a patrol car. As officers approached the suspect's car he continued to try to get away in his car. One officer (Plumhoff) fired three shots into Rickard's car. Rickard drove away and almost hit another cop. Then, multiple officers fired a total of 12 shots into the car. Richard lost control and the car ran into a building. Rickard and a passenger died from the crash and gunshots; his daughter sued. The Court declared that there was no Fourth Amendment violation in this case and that the officers were allowed to use deadly force. The Justices explained that 15 shots by the police were not excessive since Rickard continued to constitute a threat until he rammed the building with his car. The exchange between the police and the suspect was rapid and the threat never ended until the final crash.

It should be noted that the police are subject to liability for using excessive force under Federal Statutes 42 U.S.C., popularly known as **Section 1983**. The standard for the use of force is "objective reasonableness." In *Graham v. Connor* (490 U.S. 396, 1989), the Supreme Court noted that it uses a TOC test to determine the validity of the use of force:

> Our Fourth Amendment jurisprudence has long recognized that the right to make an arrest or investigatory stop necessarily carries with it the right to use some degree of

physical coercion or threat to effect it. . . . Because '(t)he test of reasonableness under the Fourth Amendment is not capable of precise definition or mechanical application . . . however, its proper application requires careful attention to the facts and circumstances of each particular case, including the severity of the crime at issue, whether the suspect poses an immediate threat to the safety of the officers or others, and whether he is actively resisting arrest or attempting to evade arrest by flight (*Id.*, at 396).

The Supreme Court posed the critical question as what would a reasonable officer due at the time, rather than adopting a retrospective, Monday quarterbacking approach. The Court observed:

The calculus of reasonableness must embody allowance for the fact that police officers are often forced to make split-second judgments—in circumstances that are tense, uncertain, and rapidly evolving—about the amount of force that is necessary in a particular situation (*Id.*, at 396–97).

The standard for liability applies to the use of both deadly and nondeadly, but excessive force. In *Plumhoff v. Rickard*, the Court found that the officers were entitled to qualified immunity.

FORCE USED TO EFFECT A SEARCH

The one case dealing with force used to search is *Winston v. Lee* (470 U.S. 753, 1985). This case involved the surgical removal of evidence (a bullet) from a suspect's body. The Court established the principle for searches such as this, as follows: "The reasonableness of surgical intrusions beneath the skin depends on a case-by-case approach, in which the individual's interests in privacy and security are weighed against society's interests in conducting the procedure (*Id.*, at 754)."

In *Winston*, the first thought was that the proposed operation was superficial, but then it turned out to be more complicated and threatening. The Court believed that no surgery could be permitted when the life of the suspect was threatened by the operation. Here surgery was somewhat intense and intrusive, and the state did not really need the evidence. The bullet merely would have corroborated the victim's account of being robbed by the defendant (the victim's bullet was the target of the search). Since the victim could identify the accused the state did not really need the bullet and thus it failed to demonstrate a compelling need for the evidence.

The question of the relationship, if any, between the exclusionary rule and the use of excessive force for either arrests or searches has not been addressed or resolved by the Supreme Court.

Now that we have covered the elements and requirements of the Fourth Amendment it is useful to detail when and how the Amendment is either dispensed with altogether or modified due to the context in which the police activity takes place. The next three chapters explore when the requirements of the Fourth Amendment are:

- mostly inapplicable (due to the *Public Domain* nature of the investigation; Chapter 4);

- somewhat watered down (due to "only" a *stop and frisk* occurring rather than an *arrest and search*; Chapter 5); or,

- mostly put aside (due to an area in which a *warrant* has simply been determined to be *unnecessary*; Chapter 6).

Box 3-2: Totality of Circumstances (TOC) Test Is Applied:

Establishing PC or RS (Chapter 3)

- Cop's determination of PC—for arrest or warrant or investigatory stop
- Using an informant
- Drug courier profile and all *Terry* stops (Chapter 5)

Executing a warrant and how long must police wait before forcible entry (Chapter 3)

Use of deadly force by police (Chapter 3)

Length of detention/stop (Chapter 5)

Exigent Circumstances (Chapter 6)

Voluntariness

- Consent search (Chapter 6)
- Confession (Chapter 9)
- Understanding and waiver of *Miranda* (Chapter 9)

Suggestibility of identification procedures (Chapter 10)

CHAPTER 4

Public Domain and the Lack of a Reasonable Expectation of Privacy (REP)

As long as there is no reasonable expectation of privacy—wherever that may be—the police activity of observation is not considered a search. Without a search, there is no Fourth Amendment relevance and thus no constitutional controls (such as probable cause or a warrant). This "area" will be referred to as **Public Domain**, although as we will see, some of it is not within the public sector as we know it. The Supreme Court has increased the dimensions of this category in recent years, usually in order to assist law enforcement in the "War on Drugs." Some of the adjustment has been natural and obvious, perhaps, while some of the Supreme Court's conclusions as to where people reasonably lack a right to privacy have been quite controversial. As the situations within this area grow, the right to privacy shrinks and the police power to investigate expands. An important caveat is that using the word, search, in this subject area is technically (and legally) incorrect. Thus, it is not a plain view search. Rather, using words such as inspection, observation and investigation is more legally correct.

PLAIN VIEW

Before launching into the actual areas covered within the Public Domain, it is helpful to consider what is called *Plain View* and some related areas that deal with other human senses. This topic is often classified as a search that dispenses with the warrant requirement (see Chapter 6). That is not correct, however. Whatever is in the officer's plain view is *not a search* at all; it might be better characterized as an observation. *As long as the police are in a location in which they are entitled to be and do not engage in a physical search*, whatever is in the officers' vision is in plain view. This activity, alone, does not constitute a search, period. This principle was established by the Court a long time ago (*Harris v. U.S.*, 390 U.S. 234, 1968). Of course, plain view can occur within the Public Domain as when the police observe something from a public location, such as a sidewalk or a street. In this context, the police will obviously not need any special authorization to be where they are located. Plain view can also occur within a very private location, however, such as inside someone's house. In this context, the police will need special authorization to be where they are located, such as having a warrant to conduct a search.

So, it is critical that the police officer is legally situated and does not conduct an actual search, such as opening doors or drawers or moving objects so as to see an item better. The object must be plainly visible *as is*. This limitation became critical in *Arizona v. Hicks* (480 U.S. 321, 1987). The police in *Hicks* responded to a complaint that the defendant had fired a bullet through the floor of his apartment and injured a person in the apartment below. While searching the apartment for weapons, the police discovered stereo equipment thought to have been stolen. At this point there was only reasonable suspicion to believe the stereo was stolen, and not probable cause. One officer moved the item to see the serial number, which disclosed it had been stolen. This activity was found by the Court not to be a plain view situation and amounted to a warrantless and illegal search of the stereo equipment. It should be noted that the object that is in plain view cannot be *seized*, moreover, unless the police have probable cause to believe that it is contraband or evidence of a crime in some way. Earlier the Court had ruled that "certain knowledge" of an item's incriminating nature was not required in order for it to be seized, only probable cause was (*Texas v. Brown*, 460 U.S. 730, 1983). The *Hicks* decision stated that the stereo could have been seized legally without a warrant if the police had probable cause (before the search) to believe it was stolen. If the police could have seen the serial number without moving (i.e., searching) the stereo, they would have had probable cause and could have seized it. So, plain view can justify a *warrantless seizure*, but should still not be regarded as a *warrantless search*.

In early plain view cases, another requirement for the plain view discovery to be valid was that it be inadvertent (*Texas v. Brown*). In other words, the plain view discovery had to be exactly that, a discovery and not a confirmation of what was already known by the police. The Court subsequently held, however, that the plain view discovery of an item (and its seizure, assuming probable cause exists) does not have to be inadvertent. In *Horton v. California* (496 U.S. 128, 1990), the Court explained that although inadvertence would exist in most "legitimate 'plain view' seizures," it is not a prerequisite. In *Horton*, the police had a warrant to search for stolen property and had hoped to find other evidence of a robbery, which happened when they found weapons as well. This activity was upheld by the Court, despite the lack of an unexpected discovery. Important was the fact that the warrant allowed the police to look where they did and found the weapons in plain view. As the Court noted, it would usually be in the best interests of the police to identify all the items they expect to find since that would almost have to expand the scope of the search automatically.

The plain view concept has also been applied to the sky when the police use aircraft in order to inspect an area. Where this activity becomes complicated is when private property is the target of the surveillance so discussion of this topic is reserved for the Open Fields section of this chapter (see below).

Plain view is best considered as an *extension or enhancement* of the cops' investigatory powers, and it overlaps most areas of searches with or without warrants. So, if the police are executing a warrant and see something not itemized in the warrant, this sighting is legitimate and is not a search as long as the police are looking in a location in which the warrant would authorize their searching in the first place. Thus, if police have a warrant to search for drugs and during that search they come across illegal weapons in plain view, the weapons have been found without a search having occurred. Similarly, if a person gives the police consent to look into the trunk of their car, any item in the officer's plain view in that trunk has been found without a search. Probably the only three categories in which plain view is irrelevant are *searches incident to arrest*, *inventory searches of automobiles*, and *border searches*. Why plain view should be irrelevant here is that the officer has complete dominion over the person/area being searched and no enhancement of investigatory powers should be necessary. The police are already authorized to "look" everywhere in these situations, and should not have to rely upon simply "coming across" an item.

Plain but Enhanced View

Probably the least controversial location for plain view is the public domain, meaning if the police are situated in the public sector, they cannot be accused of conducting searches of areas that fall within their common vision. Police are also permitted to utilize devices that merely enhance what they can see by their own eyes. Thus, employing flashlights does not convert an inspection by the police into a search that would be controlled by the Fourth Amendment (*Texas v. Brown*, 460 U.S. 730, 1983).

At the same time, plain view has been applied to a method of detection that could not be definitively ascertained without the assistance of an enhancement device: field tests to determine whether a substance is cocaine. In *U.S. v. Jacobsen* (466 U.S. 109, 1984), the Court ruled that ascertaining the physical characteristics of such a substance was not a search. Congress had criminalized the possession of cocaine so there was no legitimate expectation of privacy violated when the government accomplished no more than establishing the physical elements of cocaine.

The use of tracking devices that would monitor the progress of a vehicle is also permitted, provided that the monitoring occurs in the public domain (*U.S. v. Knotts*, 460 U.S. 276, 1983). In *Knotts*, the police had placed a beeper in a container with the owner's consent, and that container was eventually placed by Knotts in his vehicle. Once the vehicle that is tracked enters private property (*U.S. v. Karo*, 468 U.S. 705, 1984), however, Fourth Amendment protections become relevant. How the vehicle and the beeper become associated is also critical.

Permissible Enhancement Depends upon Context

A recent decision by the Supreme Court, *U.S. v. Jones* (565 U.S. 400, 2012), has disclosed the importance of the way in which some tracking devices are used. In *Jones*, police had a warrant to install a GPS (Global Positioning System) tracking device underneath the defendant's jeep (but the warrant had expired). The jeep had been parked in a public lot, which would raise the question as to whether Jones had a REP. Police monitored the movements of the jeep for 28 days, and tracked the operation over public roads. The GPS disclosed that the jeep had been driven to a drug house where large amounts of drugs had been found. A unanimous Court held this was an unconstitutional search. Interesting is that the Court unanimously found that a search had occurred due to there being a physical intrusion by the police and that it *didn't matter whether there was a reasonable expectation of privacy*. What was critical to the Court's decision was that the police had physically intruded on the defendant's private property (i.e., the car that constitutes an effect entitled to Fourth Amendment protection), and that they did this to obtain information.

Justice Scalia wrote the opinion and emphasized that this physical intrusion would have been considered a search when the Fourth Amendment was adopted (an originalist position). But, with Justice Scalia's death the *Jones* rationale could be vulnerable as well. Four Justices agreed with the decision to identify the police behavior as a search and to invalidate it, but did so only because of the length of the monitoring via GPS. These Justices made a cogent point: "If the police attach a GPS device to a car and use the device to follow the car for even a brief time, under the Court's theory, the Fourth Amendment applies. But if the police follow the same car for a much longer period using unmarked cars and aerial assistance, this tracking is not subject to any Fourth Amendment constraints (181 L.Ed. 2d at 931)." Thus, Justice Scalia's replacement could alter the balance of decision making found in *Jones*.

The government had argued in *Jones* that the lack of a reasonable expectation of privacy meant there had been no search, especially for the monitoring that occurred on public roads. The *Jones* majority, however, ruled that the reasonable expectation of privacy standard announced in *Katz* provided an additional protection (rather than a substitute for) common law notions of physical trespass. Thus, Jones' constitutional rights were violated even without his having a REP.

Impermissible Enhancement Devices

Perhaps the most interesting case dealing with the use of enhancement devices in the plain view context is *Kyllo v. U.S.* (533 U.S. 27, 2001). In *Kyllo*, the police aimed a thermal imaging device at a house in order to detect excessive amounts of heat within the house. Such intense heat is typically associated with the high intensity lamps needed to grow and cultivate marijuana. The device detects infrared radiation not visible to the naked eye. The police spent a few minutes scanning the house from the streets in front and behind the house and found hot spots over the garage and side wall of the house, indicating this was a "grow house." The Court saw this activity as a physical intrusion into a constitutionally protected area that amounted to a search, even though the device captured only heat emanating from a house and did not detect any private activity occurring inside the house. Particularly important to the majority of Justices was that the device or technology in question was not in general public use. So, although there had been no significant compromise of a person's privacy, because the government had employed a device that was not used by the public so as "to explore details of the home that would presumably have been unknowable without physical intrusion, the surveillance is a 'search' and is presumptively unreasonable without a warrant (*Id.*)." *Kyllo* is the first time the Court has identified the *general public use element* as a criterion for Fourth Amendment relevance. Also interesting is that Justice Scalia wrote the decision (and with whom Justice Thomas agreed) even though he (and Justice Thomas) had typically supported outcomes that did not further the cause of privacy the way *Kyllo* did; equally interesting is that Justice Stevens dissented, even though he typically championed privacy at the expense of effective law enforcement.

PLAIN SMELL/ODOR

Complementing plain view is what is popularly known as plain smell. As with plain view, plain smell is not a search. The easiest (and lease controversial) example of this is a police stop of a vehicle and the unavoidable odor of alcohol on the driver's breath or burning marijuana emanating from the car (perhaps envisioning a Cheech and Chong or Harold and Kumar movie will assist the picturing of the event and this assumes the possession and use of marijuana is still illegal). In this example, the police have "found" the presence of marijuana without having conducted a search. Probable cause to believe possession of drugs exists and a search of the car without a warrant would be permitted (this action is examined in Chapter 6 on Warrantless Searches).

The plain smell concept received its biggest boost from the ability of dogs to sniff out drugs, even when the drugs are packaged and not emitting an obvious odor (i.e., detectible by humans). The Supreme Court endorsed the non-search aspect of a sniff test by a narcotics trained dog in *U.S. v. Place* (462 U.S. 696, 1983). It would be reasonable to consider drug detecting dogs as an *enhancement device* the police use to locate drugs. In *Place*, the police became suspicious of a traveler in Miami's airport. The departure of the plane prevented a search of Place's luggage in Miami, although he had consented to a search. The police notified DEA authorities in New York (Place's destination) that they suspected Place was transporting drugs. DEA agents met Place at LaGuardia airport and seized his luggage. There was no canine patrol at LaGuardia so the agents took Place's luggage to Kennedy airport. There a dog reacted to one of the bags, suggesting the presence of drugs. The agent used that information to secure a warrant; the search discovered cocaine. Ultimately, the Court invalidated the seizure of the bags, but that was due to the unreasonably long duration of the seizure (90 minutes) rather than because of any intrusion into Place's privacy, which the Court identified as minimal and as disclosing only the possible presence of drugs (and not any other item within the luggage). Critical for the investigative powers of the police, the Court held in *Place* that reasonable suspicion was sufficient to seize the luggage and to begin a dog sniffing test, that the dog sniff was not a search, and that the dog's alert constituted probable cause.

More recently, the Court determined that the police do not have to provide extensive proof a dog's training and performance in order for an alert to establish probable cause (*Florida v. Harris*, 568 U.S. 237, 2013). Instead, the Court explained that the presence of probable cause will be evaluated by "whether all of the facts surrounding a dog's alert, viewed through the lens of common sense, would make a reasonable prudent person think that a search would reveal contraband or evidence of a crime. A sniff is up to snuff when it meets that test (*Id.*, at 70)."

Place Extended

The Supreme Court has also extended *Place* in terms of whether reasonable suspicion is required to initiate a dog sniffing test as suggested in *Place*. In *Illinois v. Caballes* (543 U.S. 405, 2005), a K-9 officer overheard a radio report that another officer had stopped a vehicle for speeding. The K-9 officer drove to the stopped car and walked his drug-detecting dog around it; this entire transaction took about ten minutes. The dog alerted at the trunk. Drugs were found and the driver was convicted. The Supreme Court stated that reasonable suspicion was not required to launch a dog sniffing test of a lawfully stopped vehicle. The Court perceived the incident as not changing the character of a traffic stop and as being executed in a reasonable manner. The Court rejected the defendant's contentions that the dog sniffing test both extended the routine traffic stop and amounted to a drug investigation.

The Limits of Plain Smell/Odor

Finally, location is as important to plain smell as it is to plain view. A dog sniff does become a search when it occurs within the curtilage of one's home. In *Florida v. Jardines* (569 U.S. 1, 2013), the police brought a dog and its handler to Jardines' home. The dog alerted as it approached the front porch and also alerted (by sitting) at the base of the front door. The police secured a warrant and found marijuana plants. The Court ruled that this action by the dog amounted to a search that was invalid since probable cause would have been needed before the search by the dog. The Court noted that while people generally invite others, including strangers, to their home, "introducing a trained police dog to explore the area around the home in hopes of discovering incriminating evidence is something else. There is no customary invitation to do that (*Id.*, at 502)."

PLAIN TOUCH/FEEL

Assuming the police have the right to be touching an area (such as a frisk), what is discovered via a plain touch or feel is not a search. In *Minnesota v. Dickerson* (508 U.S. 366, 1993), a police officer's sense of touch during a protective pat-down search was not considered a search. In this case a cop felt a "small lump" in the suspect's nylon jacket that seemed similar to "a lump of crack cocaine in cellophane." The Court said police may seize any object for which there is probable cause to believe is contraband, weapons or some other form of evidence. However, the Court also ruled in this case that the officer did not have probable cause to believe what he felt was contraband and excluded the evidence. In the end, police may utilize any sensory perception without committing a search.

At the same time, police cannot feel and manipulate luggage and have that action included under the plain touch category. In *Bond v. U.S.* (529 U.S. 334, 2000), an officer squeezed a canvas bag that belonged to a bus passenger. The Supreme Court described this action as a physically invasive inspection that was much more intrusive than a visual inspection. The Court explained that when a bus passenger puts a bag in the overhead bin there is an expectation that the bag will be handled, but not felt in an exploratory manner or physically manipulated. Consequently, when the officer first squeezed the bag and felt drugs he violated the defendant's reasonable expectation of privacy. Moreover, the belief that there was a brick-like object in the bag did not establish probable cause to open the bag.

PUBLIC DOMAIN

Whatever someone exposes to the public (i.e., whatever is located in the Public Domain) is not entitled to a REP. Thus, a good deal of investigation can occur without a search having taken place in the eyes of the Supreme Court. In the next section we will discuss the ways in which one's "private" property is considered to be in the public domain. Within the "true" public domain there is virtually nothing preventing the police from exploring areas without Fourth Amendment restrictions.

A vehicle located in a public area will likely lack any REP. There is no doubt that the police can place the car under surveillance and observe its progress through public streets. That doesn't mean the police have carte blanche to perform any type of investigation they want as we just saw with the *U.S. v. Jones* decision. Nevertheless, the Supreme Court has suggested in previous case law that the exterior of a car is exposed to the public and is not entitled to a REP. Consequently, law enforcement can likely collect paint scrapings and tire impressions from a car parked on a public thoroughfare without needing to comply with Fourth Amendment requirements (*Cardwell v. Lewis*, 417 U.S. 583, 1974). In this case, the vehicle was associated with a suspected homicide. The Court held that the exterior of the car was knowingly exposed to the public, there was no invasion of privacy and thus the driver was not entitled to any Fourth Amendment protections.

Motorists stopped on the highway for a traffic violation can likely be ordered to move any item that obstructs an officer's view of the car's VIN number on the front dash (*New York v. Class*, 475 U.S. 106, 1986). Ascertaining the VIN number can inform the police as to whether the vehicle has been reported stolen. We will see in Chapter 6 that probable cause dispenses the need for a warrant in the automobile context.

When a person puts trash on the curb to be picked up, the Supreme Court has determined that, regardless of whatever subjective expectation exists, there is no REP; the owner cannot reasonably expect that trash to be private (*California v. Greenwood*, 486 U.S. 35, 1988). In *Greenwood*, the police asked the trash collector to pick up the plastic garbage bags from the curb and then turn them over to them. Cops found evidence of narcotics use. These agents then secured a warrant and found drugs inside Greenwood's house. The Court acknowledged that Greenwood likely did not expect that the contents of his trash would become known to the police (or to any other members of the public), but nevertheless stated that society was not prepared to accept that expectation as reasonable. Thus, this is another example of the importance of the Court's adoption of REP in lieu of a subjective expectation of privacy originally adopted in the *Katz* decision. Most interesting, Justices Brennan and Marshall not only believed a person has a privacy interest in his/her trash, but also that this expectation is objectively reasonable. Bolstering Greenwood's claim of privacy was that state constitutional law prohibited the police from examining his trash. In addition, state courts had ruled the examination of the trash as an unreasonable search. The Supreme Court rejected these claims and held that the reasonableness of a search does not depend upon the law of a state in which the search occurs. As in the case with trash, any other abandoned property (such as a house, vehicle, and items left in a hotel room) would similarly lack a REP and could be examined without a search taking place.

Transfer to a third party presents another way in which public domain has been recognized by the Supreme Court. Material (such as bank copies of individuals' checks, deposits, and financial statements) can be subpoenaed by the government without a warrant. The Court ruled there was no REP in these materials. Instead, the depositor takes a risk in revealing these items to another (i.e., the bank employees) and risks that this information, in turn, will be conveyed by that party to the government (*U.S. v. Miller*, 425 U.S. 435, 1976).

Similarly, there is no REP as to the numbers one uses to call someone via a phone. While the contents of the conversation are entitled to a REP, the numbers do not enjoy the same status. Cops can thus install a pen register to record numbers one dials (*Smith v. Maryland*, 442 U.S. 735, 1979). Once again, the Supreme Court admitted that the defendant in this case had a subjective expectation, but held that society was not prepared to recognize that expectation as reasonable.

For mail sent out via private carrier (such as FedEx) when workers of the carrier searched the contents of a package and then turned over that material to DEA agents, there was no Fourth Amendment implications because the government's inspection did not exceed the original private search. The mailer had no REP against the government search that was initiated after private one (*U.S. v. Jacobsen*, 466 U.S. 109, 1984). This is the same case in which we saw previously that agents can field test for drugs without Fourth Amendment restrictions.

Finally, if a merchant knowingly exposes obscene magazines for sale, the purchase of these items by undercover sheriffs in an adult bookstore does not constitute an unreasonable search or seizure. Here, the dealer had no expectation of privacy, subjective or reasonable (*Maryland v. Macon*, 472 U.S. 463, 1985). Entering the place of business did not amount to a search, and the purchase of the magazines did not amount to a seizure, according to the Court so no Fourth Amendment-related activity took place.

Open Fields

The first consideration of the open fields category did not raise much controversy. That is because the first case, *Hester v. U.S.* (265 U.S. 57, 1924), dealt with law enforcement being permitted to effect an open field observation from a highway. No search had occurred here according to the Court. In more recent times, considerable controversy has characterized this topic. The controversy stems from the Court's holding in *Oliver v. U.S.* (466 U.S. 170), delivered in 1984. *Oliver* is a prime example of the importance of *reasonable* ultimately being identified as the qualifier of the expectation of privacy (via Justice Harlan's concurrence), instead of the term, *subjective* (which was the suggestion of the majority in *Katz v. U.S.*).

In *Oliver*, the Supreme Court verified that a person's reasonable expectation of privacy on one's property is restricted to the curtilage or area immediately surrounding the domicile or home (*Hester* had said as much). A person's subjective expectation of privacy is irrelevant here. So, even if someone fences off the property, erects "no trespassing" signs, prevents any possible observation of the property from a public location or from an aerial observation, or conducts business within a structure that is neither part of nor serving as a domicile, whatever expectation of privacy there is, it is not reasonable, according to the Court. The Court opined that people cannot demand privacy for activities that are conducted outdoor in open fields, unless that activity occurs within the curtilage of the home (in other words, within a few feet of the house). The rationale here is that the Fourth Amendment was intended to protect intimate activities from government surveillance, but not when those activities take place within an open field. The Court explained that there is no societal interest in protecting activities in open fields, and that, generally, fences and no trespassing signs do not effectively prevent the public from viewing what occurs or exists in open fields. In the Court's view:

> The test of legitimacy is not whether the individual chooses
> to conceal assertedly 'private' activity. Rather the correct

inquiry is whether the government's intrusion infringes upon the personal and societal values protected by the Fourth Amendment (*Id.*, at 182–83).

The common law did distinguish open field from curtilage, and, in a concurring opinion. Justice White stressed that a reasonable expectation of privacy is actually irrelevant because open field is neither a house nor effect mentioned in and protected by the Fourth Amendment. Very interesting, the *Oliver* opinion pointed out that James Madison, the author of the Amendment, had written originally that houses, papers and *other property* were to be protected from government interference, but the *other property* provision was eliminated as Congress considered the Fourth Amendment for ratification. Also interesting is that the dissent (Justices Marshall, Brennan, and Stevens) noted that neither phone booths nor conversations occurring within a phone booth can be described as persons, houses, papers or effects, but the Fourth Amendment nevertheless prohibits the police from eavesdropping on such a conversation without a warrant (see *Katz v. U.S.*). These Justices also believed there was a reasonable expectation of privacy in the context of open fields.

Oliver Extended

The Court fortified the notion of the inviolability of the premise when, in the same year as *Oliver*, it ruled that while beepers are allowed when police track activity in the public sector, there are prohibited in tracking activity in the interior of a house (*U.S. v. Karo*, 468 U.S. 705, 1984). Three years later, however, the Court authorized even more intrusive police investigations in the open field area by extending or applying *Oliver* to structures located on private property. In *U.S. v. Dunn* (480 U.S. 294, 1987), federal agents inspected Dunn's ranch, which consisted of 198 acres that were completely surrounded by a perimeter fence, and a number of internal fences as well. There were a ranch house, a greenhouse and two barns, one of which had a locked gate surrounding it. The agents climbed numerous fences to get to the barn. They shined a flashlight through netting that had covered the barn and saw a drug laboratory. Rather than enter the barn the agents secured a search warrant. Although the lower federal court had ruled the activity an unconstitutional search, the Supreme Court reversed. In *Dunn*, the Court established criteria to be used in determining whether a structure is within the curtilage of a house:

- Proximity of the area claimed to be curtilage to the home;

- Whether the area is included within an enclosure surrounding the home;

- The nature of the uses to which the area is put;

- The steps taken by the resident to protect the area from observation by people passing by (*U.S. v. Dunn*, at 301).

The Court held that the police had not engaged in a search because the barn was not within the protected curtilage (there were 50 yards between barn and house). In addition, there was a fence around the house, but the barn was not within it. The federal agents had substantial information about illegal activity on the ranch and could smell an odor that suggested the barn had been used to make drugs and was not associated with domestic life. Finally, Dunn had done little to protect the barn area from observation by those standing in his open fields; the fences were designed to corral livestock and did not tend to bar observation. The Court rejected Dunn's claim that he had a privacy interest in the barn. Justices Brennan and Marshall noted in dissent that lower courts had consistently held that barns are within the curtilage, and that, even if the barn is not within the curtilage, the barn and the surrounding area are entitled to Fourth Amendment protection.

Oliver Going Airborne

As noted earlier under plain view, the Supreme Court has classified aerial observation by the police within the plain view category. Where aerial observation becomes most controversial is when that observation occurs in proximity to one's house. In *California v. Ciraolo*

(476 U.S. 207, 1986), the Court determined that as long as the aircraft is in public, navigable space, the observation is not a search. The police activity here involved the use of a fixed-wing aircraft at 1,000 feet. The subject's yard was within the curtilage of the house, and a fence shielded the yard from observation from the street. Regardless, the yard could be seen with the naked eye from the air so there was no reasonable expectation of privacy. The Court explained that since private and commercial flight in the public airways is routine no warrant is needed to see what can be seen with the naked eye. Moreover,

> the area within the curtilage does not itself bar all police observation. The Fourth Amendment protection of the home has never been extended to require law enforcement officers to shield their eyes when passing by a home on public thoroughfares. Nor does the mere fact that an individual has taken measures to restrict some views of his activities preclude an officer's observations from a public vantage point where he has a right to be and which renders the activities clearly visible (*Id.*, at 213).

Similarly, in *Dow Chemical Company v. U.S.* (476 U.S. 227, 1986), the Court upheld the police use of a precision aerial mapping camera over a Dow plant in Michigan sequentially from 12,000, 3,000, and 1,200 feet (the company hadn't prevented aerial sight of their equipment), and in *Florida v. Riley* (488 U.S. 445, 1989), the Court allowed police to utilize a helicopter from 400 feet so as to investigate a partially covered greenhouse. The sophisticated aerial photography employed in the *Dow Chemical* case could be considered an enhancement device.

*Oliver (*and *Place)* Restricted Somewhat

A violation of the privacy established via curtilage did result in the invalidation of a search in a recent case, the *Florida v. Jardines* case we covered under the plain smell/odor area above. To recap, police brought a trained drug-sniffing dog onto the defendant's front porch to investigate for the presence of drugs. The Court ruled 5–4 that this was a search. So, even though the reaction by the dog indicated drugs, which in so many previous cases has been held to not be a search, and then the police secured a warrant, the eventual discovery of drugs inside the house via that warrant was unlawful. The Court held that the police learned what they did only by physically intruding on the defendant's property (i.e., the porch) to gather evidence, and that this amounted to a search. What is interesting and confusing is that the majority stated that the police would have been allowed to enter the porch and to approach the front door without having committed a search, and then would have been permitted to pursue a warrant on that information. Assumedly, the police could have used their plain view and plain smell capacities without engaging in a search. It would seem, then, that the enhanced ability of the dogs to detect odors that are potentially oblivious to humans is what rendered the activity a search. In fact, the four dissenters in the case noted that the police were on the porch for only a minute or two and that an "implied license" extends to everyone, including the police, to be at that location. The dissenters also stated that they did not consider the police activity to be a search. They stressed that there was no violation of a REP since there is no REP as to odors that can be detected by humans who are standing where they are allowed to be, and that there is no reason to distinguish humans and dogs.

The majority did explain that the house owner's consent to the dog sniffing exercise would have led the Court to redefine the activity as a non-search. As we will see in Chapter 6, consent negates Fourth Amendment restrictions such as probable cause and/or a warrant.

As of now, then, the location of a dog sniff determines whether there is a search. The holding is somewhat confusing. Police are permitted to stand on the porch without a dog without any Fourth Amendment implications, but bringing along a dog to detect drugs (which has consistently been held not to constitute a search) transforms the activity into a search (without any necessary connection to a REP). But, if the dog sniffing exercise receives the owner's consent (which has never been connected to plain smell), then no search has occurred.

Once again, Justice Scalia was instrumental in this ruling; he wrote the decision. Thus, his death and replacement on the Court could result in a reversal of the reasoning and ruling in *Jardines*.

Undercover Agents

The War on Drugs often requires that police pose as undercover agents who set up buying opportunities from dealers. A question that has been resolved for half a century is whether the location of the buy matters. Specifically, does the fact that a transaction took place inside the dealer's home implicate any Fourth Amendment concerns or restrictions? The Supreme Court answered in the negative in *Lewis v. U.S.* (385 U.S. 206) in 1966. Simply put, the dealer who sells drugs from his/her house has effectively converted the home into a place of business, according to the Court. That place of business lacks a REP, and thus the Fourth Amendment provides no protection to the dealer.

Another version of undercover agent is the informant. In *Hoffa v. U.S.* (385 U.S. 293, 1966), the Court ruled that an informant working with police to obtain information disclosed by the target of the operation (here, the infamous Jimmy Hoffa) does not violate any Fourth Amendment rights of the target by posing as a member of the target's group and by obtaining that information inside the target's hotel room (or any other private location).

Physical Characteristics

There are a variety of ways in which the police will seek to identify individuals as perpetrators of crimes. It is what CSI is all about. We will consider this topic at greater length in Chapter 10. The Fourth Amendment aspects of this category will be addressed here. At least three methods of identifying offenders have a potential connection to the Fourth Amendment via a right to privacy: one's handwriting and voice, which can be examined through exemplars, and one's face, which can be recognized in a lineup.

The Supreme Court has refused to extend Fourth Amendment protections to these elements. Both voice (*U.S. v. Dionisio*, 410 U.S. 1) and handwriting (*U.S. v. Mara*, 410 U.S. 19) exemplars were the subject of grand jury subpoenas in cases that reached the Supreme Court in 1973. The defendants had claimed a Fourth Amendment right not to supply the samples, but the Court rejected the claims and held there is no right to privacy in these contexts because they are routinely exposed to the public. (The Court also ruled that the Fourth Amendment generally does not apply to grand jury proceedings that are comprised of private citizens, and a subpoena is not equal to a seizure). The lack of a REP would mean police should not face any Fourth Amendment obstacles in obtaining these products from suspects. Similarly, suspects cannot claim a Fourth Amendment right to privacy so as to prevent inclusion in a lineup (*U.S. v. Wade*, 388 U.S. 218, 1967).

"Private" Areas Stripped of a REP

It is also possible to be stripped of any REP and to be subject to what are truly searches, but will not be categorized as such due to the status of the target of the search. There is some overlap here with warrantless (or administrative) searches that are allowed for regulated businesses (and some other contexts) as we will see in Chapter 6.

A prisoner has no legitimate REP in a prison cell, according to the Supreme Court (*Hudson v. Palmer*, 468 U.S. 517, 1984). Thus, a guard can "search" the inmate's private possessions, without having that activity classified as a search (there were four dissenters in this case). "Searches" of probationers have been handled the same way by the Court (*Griffin v. Wisconsin*, 483 U.S. 868, 1987).

More recent cases have signaled that states (and the feds) are allowed to raise the stakes for those seeking probation and parole by forcing them to surrender any REP in order to secure conditional release to the community. In *U.S. v. Knights* (534 U.S. 112, 2001) the Court upheld a term of probation in California in which the probation agreement demanded the offender to submit his person, property, residence and vehicle to search by any probation officer or law enforcement officer at any time. Knights signed off and subsequently a cop searched Knights' apartment and found evidence of vandalism as suspected. Interesting, the lower federal court granted Knights' motion to suppress, which was upheld on appeal, because the court believed only the probation officer could search, and that the investigatory search conducted by the police here was unreasonable. Nevertheless, a unanimous Supreme Court reversed and held the search to be reasonable. The Court emphasized that probationers do not enjoy the absolute liberty every law abiding citizen enjoys. Moreover, the Court explained that reasonable conditions may be imposed on probationers that will severely diminish an expectation of privacy. Nevertheless, the Court did rule that, while no warrant was necessary, reasonable suspicion was required for this type of search. The reasonable suspicion requirement was short lived, however. In *Samson v. California* (547 U.S. 843, 2006) the Court upheld the elimination of reasonable suspicion if the parole condition agreement specified such. Suspicionless searches of parolees is justified, according to the Court, because parolees have a lesser EOP than probationers since parole is more akin to prison than is probation. In *Samson*, the parolee knew and agreed to the terms, including searches any time for any reason by any probation officer or law enforcement officer. Consequently, the Court declared that "petitioner did not have an expectation of privacy that society would recognize as legitimate (*Id.*, at 852)."

Box 4-1: Bright Line Rule Areas

Open fields reducing privacy to the curtilage (Chapter 4)

Robinson and all criminal offenses equal search incident to arrest (Chapter 6)

Ross and PC for auto search w/o warrant (Chapter 6)

Belton and search of passenger compartment incident to arrest (but narrowed) (Chapter 6)

Berkemer and *Miranda* applies to all crimes (Chapter 9)

Edwards rule shutting down interrogation (Chapter 9)

CHAPTER 5

Investigatory Stops: Stop and Frisk and Traffic Stops

In the previous chapter we dealt with activities that were not considered searches and thus the Fourth Amendment did not supply any protection to the target of police scrutiny. In this chapter we address police behaviors that are not regarded as full-fledged searches, and, consequently, the Fourth Amendment does not provide full-fledged protection to a suspect. The moral here is going to be: less search/seizure equals less protection.

In the midst of the Warren Court era, the otherwise liberal Court issued a rather conservative-oriented holding that has done much to advance the cause of policing. The case was *Terry v. Ohio* (392 U.S. 1) in 1968, which involved investigatory stops. Investigatory stops are what they imply, namely an interference with someone's liberty for the purpose of investigating a possible criminal activity. These stops occur in two overlapping contexts. The first is a so-called field detention that deals with a pedestrian (at stake in the *Terry* case), while the second is a traffic stop involving a motorist. The principles behind and policing powers associated with *Terry* apply equally to both contexts; this chapter will review the two areas jointly as well as separately.

TERRY AND THE AUTHORIZATION OF *STOP AND FRISK*

In *Terry v. Ohio*, the Supreme Court examined what was probably very reasonable police behavior and responded with what was probably a very reasonable ruling. A seasoned police officer observed what he believed was multiple suspects "casing" a store in order to rob the owner. He intervened and found weapons on two of the suspects. There were *many* characteristics that made the intervention very reasonable. It is very unlikely that the Court would have both sustained what the officer did here and allowed the admission of the weapons at trial that convicted the suspects had *all* of the following circumstances not existed:

- Veteran cop—39 years as cop—35 years as detective—30 years patrolling area;

- Prolonged direct observation—10–12 minutes;

- Witnessed probable violent crime about to happen—2 suspects kept looking into store;

- Suspects went back and forth to the corner a dozen times and kept talking to each other—3rd man joined them—armed robbery inside store appeared to be about to happen;

- Brief detention—took less than a minute before frisk yielded gun;

- Limited intrusion/frisk—patted the outside of clothing—felt a pistol—removed it and found another weapon on 2nd man—found nothing on the third; and,

- Frisk aimed solely at weapons to protect officer and the public.

In this scenario the officer had reasonable suspicion (RS), but lacked probable cause (PC) to believe a crime was about to happen. Arguably, it could be said that the officer lacked the authority to infringe on the liberty of these individuals. Nevertheless, this scenario also disclosed capable and reasonable law enforcement, according to the *Terry* Court. The officer interrupted a violent crime and possibly saved lives, including his own. Moreover, the officer conducted a limited intrusion into the privacy of the suspects via the *frisk* (which had been aimed solely at *weapons*) for only a limited amount of time, which rendered the encounter a mere *stop*. Finding all of these circumstances to be reasonable, the Court permitted lesser evidence (i.e., reasonable suspicion instead of probable cause) to serve as justification for a stop and frisk, which amounted to a lesser search and seizure. In other words, since a frisk was considered less than a full-fledged search, and the brief detention was regarded as less than a full-fledged seizure or arrest this police activity required less than full-fledged Fourth Amendment application.

What was involved in *Terry v. Ohio* is a **balancing test**: balancing the amount of intrusion with the level of evidence required for the intrusion or making the two elements proportionate to one another. The more significant the intrusion is, the more substantial is the required amount of evidence:

	Very Brief Encounter	Stop and Frisk	Arrest and Search
Level of Intrusion:			
Level of Required Evidence:	**None**	**RS**	**PC**

The *Terry* doctrine announced by the Court held that *searches and seizures of limited intrusion* and *aimed at weapons* may sometimes be justified on *less than probable cause*. As proof that the frisk had to be aimed at weapons, the Court announced in a companion case (*Sibron v. New York*, 392 U.S. 40, 1968) that a frisk for drugs was not permitted under *Terry*.

While the Warren Court seemed to have gone out of its way to be reasonable in sanctioning this investigatory tool or weapon of the police, Justice Douglas was alone in dissenting in the case. His objection to the formula constructed by the Court was that the police officer in the street ended up having more authority and ability to act against an individual than would a judge. As Justice Douglas saw it, a judge could not authorize interference into someone's life without a warrant for which there would have to be probable cause. A cop, however, could interfere in very meaningful ways with just reasonable suspicion due to the *Terry* decision. It may all be reasonable, but to Justice Douglas it was not constitutional.

Also at stake in *Terry v. Ohio* was another balancing test, namely the weighing of the intrusiveness or violation of privacy at hand versus the protection of society realized through stop and frisk activity. Simply stated, the Court favored more effective law enforcement.

DETERMINING WHAT IS A STOP/ DETENTION

The norm for field investigations and traffic stops is that the encounter will be brief (i.e., will remain a mere stop) and will require limited evidence on the part of the police (i.e., reasonable suspicion). What becomes critical, then, is determining the amount of intrusion that exists. If a court decides that the interaction was not a mere stop, and that, instead, the intrusion had moved up a level to that of custody, then the level of evidence needed to justify the intrusion has to be PC so as to match that level of the intrusion. Otherwise, the encounter is illegal and any information or evidence obtained by the police is in jeopardy of being inadmissible.

Instead of defining the nature of a stop the Supreme Court has developed a definition of a seizure, which makes sense since that is the word used in the Fourth Amendment. According to the Court, a person has been seized when ***a reasonable person*** would believe he/she is ***"not free to leave."*** The Court identified a number of situations in which a reasonable person could believe he/she has been seized, such as when multiple police constitute a *threatening presence,* when an officer *displays a weapon, physically touches* a person, or uses a *tone of voice* or *language* that indicates there is no choice but to comply to the officer's requests

(*U.S. v. Mendenhall*, 446 U.S. 544, 1980). Similar to the Court's formula for finding an expectation of privacy, it is the belief of a reasonable person rather than a subjective view that determines whether a seizure has taken place.

WHEN A DETENTION IS TOO INTRUSIVE OR TOO LONG AND THUS BECOMES CUSTODY

As we will see, below, the Supreme Court has pretty consistently expanded the investigative powers initiated via *Terry v. Ohio* for nearly four decades. These powers have been enhanced in numerous ways, requiring a lengthy consideration. Nevertheless, before launching that discussion it is important to note that the Court has refused to provide the police with complete autonomy during their investigations. The police are subject to constraints in terms of the nature of the detention (such as transporting the detainee to another location) and its duration. Taking detention too far in either capacity can end up in being categorized as custody, requiring minimally PC.

Many years ago, the Supreme Court put to rest any notion that someone could be "brought in" to a police station ***on suspicion*** (for questioning, perhaps). That saying was popular, "back in the day." Regardless of the history this activity may have enjoyed at one time, the Court declared that to transport a suspect against his/her will to a police station for questioning required probable cause (*Dunaway v. New York*, 442 U.S. 200, 1979). The Court observed that the detention associated with this method of police investigation was too intrusive to be justified upon reasonable suspicion only (i.e., this is well beyond the temporary stop/seizure permitted under *Terry*). When the detention reaches this level of interference into someone's life, the Court insisted that police have probable cause to justify the action.

Similarly, during an investigation into a suspected drug courier in an airport, the police confiscated a traveler's airline ticket and driver's license and moved him, with his consent, to a room that was 40 feet away from the initial encounter (*Florida v. Royer*, 460 U.S. 491, 1983). Although the police may have had reasonable suspicion for the original stop, they lacked the probable cause this amount of detention required, according to the Court. The Court held (5–4) that the consent was invalidated due to the suspect's being effectively in custody. As the Court explained:

> What had begun as a consensual inquiry in a public place escalated into an investigatory procedure in a police interrogation room, and respondent, as a practical matter, was under arrest at that time (*Id.*, at 492).

In *Kaupp v. Texas* (538 U.S. 626, 2003), the accused had been awakened in his bedroom around 3AM. He said "okay" to police after they had told him "we need to go and talk." Simply because the suspect had said okay, that did not make the trip to the station voluntary in the eyes of the Court. It also did not negate the custodial nature of the interaction in the bedroom; he was not free to leave there or during the later transportation to the station. The police lacked PC at the suspect's house, and had actually been denied a warrant. The lack of PC made the "arrest" illegal and the ensuing confession they acquired at the station was inadmissible as illegally seized as well (a *fruit of the poisonous tree* product).

Also interesting is that the Court examined whether a passenger (as well as driver) in a car stopped by cops is seized (*Brendlin v. California*, 551 U.S. 249, 2007). The Court's response was telling:

> We resolve this question by asking whether a reasonable person in Brendlin's position when the car stopped would have believed himself free to 'terminate the encounter' between the police and himself. We think in these circumstances any reasonable passenger would have understood the police officers to be exercising control to the point that no one in the car was free to depart without police permission (*Id.*, at 254).

Certainly the Court's characterization is not surprising to anyone who has experienced a traffic stop. According to the Court, a traffic stop simply means everyone, driver and passengers alike, know they are not free to leave and thus have been seized. This ruling may make sense, but it can cause confusion as well since the Court has also ruled that the detention (or seizure) accompanying a traffic stop does not require PC to justify it (see the section on Traffic Stops, below), and, even more important, perhaps, that *Miranda* does not need to be given to the driver before any questioning that occurs during that stop (see Chapter 9). So, distinguishing a seizure from custody can be immensely difficult, but no less important; the former requires mere reasonable suspicion and no warnings before asking the suspect questions, while the latter requires both PC and *Miranda*, if there is any interrogation.

The length of the stop, even without any movement, per se, can raise a problem, too. In *U.S. v. Place* (462 U.S. 696, 1983), the Court held that a 90 minute detention, absent exigent circumstances, was too long when the police had only RS. Without some type of emergency, then, detentions of this length transform into a form of custody that requires PC in order to be viewed as reasonable.

Even a very brief seizure can be problematic if not supported by RS. Recently, the Court held that a mere seven to eight minute detention so as to bring a drug sniffing dog to a traffic stop was unconstitutional due to a lack of RS to support that detention (*Rodriguez v. U.S.*, 575 U.S. ___, 135 S.Ct. 1609, 2015). We will revisit this case in the traffic stop section, below.

ENHANCING *TERRY*-ORIENTED INVESTIGATORY POWERS

Contrary to the indications of the previous section, the Supreme Court has been much more consistent in enhancing police investigatory powers during the last four decades. This enhancement has been motivated mostly by a desire to assist the police in the War on Drugs and has occurred through two measures. First, the Court has classified arguably intrusive police actions as equivalent to mere stops, which reduces the types of behaviors that could be considered full-fledged seizures (thereby extending *Terry* into other realms of investigation by requiring only RS to be legal). Second, the Court has removed one-by-one the circumstances that were once considered reasonable and necessary for a *Terry* stop and frisk.

Narrowing the Parameters of the Definition of Seizure

One obvious way in which to further the cause of police investigation is to identify certain civilian interactions with the police as mere stops and not as examples of a seizure (let alone custody) that would be subject to Fourth Amendment limitations, particularly the need for PC. In these instances, *Terry* has been applied to encounters other than police walking up to and stopping/frisking suspects on the street (or a driver in a vehicle) as was the situation in the original *Terry* case.

One of the earliest cases that dealt with eliminating the prospect of a seizure is of particular relevance today: questioning someone to discover his/her immigration status. In *Immigration and Naturalization Service v. Delgado* (466 U.S. 210, 1984), the Court ruled that *questioning* by agents, in and of itself, does not constitute a seizure. Rather, the Court posited that for a seizure to exist there must be some restraint on liberty or a police showing of physical force or authority such that there would be intimidation sufficient for a person to believe he/she is not free to leave without answering questions. The Court found no seizure had occurred in this case even though the questioning had come about via what is known as a *factory survey*. A factory survey typically occurs near the border where the intent is to determine the immigration status of the workers. In *Delgado*, numerous INS agents went through the factory asking workers pertinent questions, removed suspected aliens in handcuffs for further investigation, and guarded all exists during the survey.

More interesting, police following a suspect was not regarded as a seizure so police did not need PC to justify their actions in *Michigan v. Chesternut* (486 U.S. 567, 1988). In this case the suspect began to run as a cop car approached him. As police pulled alongside Chesternut he threw away packets that he had pulled from his pocket; the packets contained drugs. The suppression judge had ruled that Chesternut had been seized before he discarded the drugs, ruling that any pursuit is a seizure. However, the Supreme Court determined that the cops were in an investigatory pursuit and that during the chase Chesternut still had freedom of movement so no seizure had occurred; the police had not activated the siren or blocked his path. The police had and needed only RS to justify the chase. The Court did note that seizure can occur before actual apprehension if a reasonable person would not feel free to leave the situation.

Taking *Delgado/Chesternut* one step further, the Court explained that there is no seizure when police seek to arrest a suspect through a show of authority, but no physical force was actually applied by the police. In *California v. Hodari D.* (499 U.S. 621, 1991), the suspect did not willingly submit to the police (so there was no actual or constructive seizure), and instead ran off. During that flight he threw away a small rock of crack cocaine. The police did not need to have RS to justify the chase, here, because the Court determined that an arrest (which would require PC, of course) needs to involve some measure of physical force or "submission to an assertion of authority," neither of which occurred in this case.

In the same year as *Hodari D.*, the Court issued an important ruling in *Florida v. Bostick* (501 U.S. 429, 1991), that bus sweeps are not seizures; (the case also reinforced the idea that seizure does not occur simply because police ask a few questions). Police conduct bus sweeps typically in search of illegal immigrants and/or drugs. The Court posited that the critical aspect in determining the presence of a seizure is whether the passengers on the bus feel free to leave? In this case, police boarded a bus and asked Bostick for his identification and bus ticket. They asked him if it was okay to search his bag, telling him he could refuse. Bostick gave consent and the police found cocaine. In *Bostick*, the Court explained that a seizure occurs only when a reasonable passenger would not feel free to refuse the officer's request (to search a bag) or to terminate the encounter. More recently, the Supreme Court extended the *Bostick* holding. Unless they specifically ask, the police are not required to inform bus passengers that they are free to not answer questions and can refuse consent to search their luggage (*U.S. v. Drayton*, 536 U.S. 194, 2002).

Removing the Need for *Terry* Circumstances

One by one, the Supreme Court has eliminated any requirement that the numerous circumstances that made *Terry v. Ohio* a "reasonable" decision be present in investigatory stops. As in the situations in which the definition of seizure has been reduced, eliminating *Terry*-related conditions has greatly expanded the investigatory powers of the police.

Not the Officer's Observations

The first circumstance that was modified was the source of the RS or information giving police grounds to be suspicious about a person's behavior. The *direct and sustained* observation by a *seasoned cop* was thought to be critical to the *Terry* decision. Within four years, however, the Court held that an informant known to a police officer can be the source of incriminating information. In *Adams v. Williams* (407 U.S. 143, 1972), the officer knew the informant and had received information from him in the past, albeit nothing that had resulted in an arrest or conviction. In this case, the officer approached the suspect who had been seated in a car and found a weapon in the suspect's waistband, which is precisely where the informant had said it would be located. The Court upheld this minimal *Terry*-authorized intrusion.

Several years later, the Court took *Adams v. Williams* one step further by allowing an anonymous tip to serve as the source for a *Terry* stop. In *Alabama v. White* (496 U.S. 325, 1990), while the Court allowed the anonymous tip it also required that the tip be corroborated to some extent by the officer. The Court opined that the corroborating exercise can show the reliability of the informant and the accuracy of the information if it discloses an ability of the informant to predict the suspect's behavior. This reliability and accuracy, in turn, can lead the officer to believe the anonymous source is honest and well informed, and serves as enough to justify the stop.

Accordingly, the Court refused to give police carte blanche in this context. In *Florida v. J.L.* (529 U.S. 266, 2000), the Court held that an anonymous tip that suspect is carrying a gun, without any more information or corroboration, does not suffice to provide police with the authority to stop and frisk in pursuit of that alleged weapon. The Court believed the tip in this case lacked "sufficient indicia of reliability to provide reasonable suspicion." The Court saw no predictive information coming out of this tip and thus there was no way for the police to test the informant's knowledge or credibility. Most interesting is that the Court refused to accept a so-called "firearms exception" to *Terry*. Dicta in the opinion, however, suggested that the Court might grant validity to a "bomb" exception to *Terry*.

Focus of the Investigation

Perhaps the most significant modification of the *Terry* "elements" is that the Court has allowed the focus or target of the investigation to go well beyond the interruption of an imminent violent crime (or to protect the life of the officer and others). While *Terry* involved an armed robbery, the *Terry* doctrine has been extended to a variety of other situations and inquiries. As we just saw in the section that addressed police activities that are not considered seizures, interrogating people to determine immigration status, chasing suspects in likely drug possession situations, and conducting bus sweeps in hopes of finding illegal immigrants or drugs have all expanded the investigatory powers of the police in contexts having no connection to preventing a violent crime that is about to occur.

Drug investigations aimed at both pedestrians and motorists have been enhanced by the Court's treatment of *Terry* stops. Besides bus sweeps, we've seen how (under the plain smell area) drug-sniffing dogs have enhanced investigatory traffic stops. The *Illinois v. Caballes* decision permitted an officer to bring a drug-sniffing dog to a traffic stop without needing either RS or an articulable suspicion required to justify it. Caballes had argued that the dog sniff both extended the length of the stop (the Court was not impressed by the length of the extension) and converted the traffic stop into a drug investigation (the Court essentially ignored that contention). In response, the Court noted:

> In our view, conducting a dog sniff would not change the character of a traffic stop that is lawful at its inception and otherwise executed in a reasonable manner. . . (*Id.*, at 408).

Similarly, *Florida v. Harris* permitted an officer to subject the trunk of a vehicle involved in a routine traffic stop to be subjected to a drug-sniffing dog to detect the presence of drugs.

In a very recent case, however, the Supreme Court revealed how important it would be if a traffic stop was overtly converted into a drug investigation in the absence of RS. In *Rodriguez v. U.S.*, the Court determined that a seven to eight minute delay following the completion of a traffic stop in order to employ the services of a drug sniffing dog required RS to justify the seizure. In *Caballes*, the dog activity slightly extended the traffic stop, but the dogs had arrived *prior to* the completion of the traffic stop. In *Rodriguez*, however, the driver would not consent to permitting the original officer from walking his drug sniffing dog around the vehicle. That refusal necessitated the summoning of a second officer to arrive at the scene to secure it while the original officer walked around the car with his dog. The traffic stop had run its course. That albeit short time period was thus blatantly associated with a drug investigation, requiring RS according to a 6–3 majority of the Court.

Past decisions have allowed police to investigate past or future crimes (as well as present ones). In *Berkemer v. McCarty* (468 U.S. 420,

1984), the Court ruled that police with only RS that a "person has committed, is committing, or is about to commit a crime, may detain that person briefly in order to 'investigate the circumstances that provoke suspicion' " (*Id.*, at 439). The next year, the Court determined that police can conduct a stop with RS that a suspect committed a robbery 12 days earlier; firearms were found in the car (*U.S. v. Hensley*, 469 U.S. 221, 1985).

A very controversial and recent decision, *Utah v. Strieff* (we discussed in the attenuation doctrine aspect of the Fruit of the Poisonous Tree Doctrine in Chapter 2), opens the door for widespread stops for investigatory purposes, perhaps mere fishing expeditions. The case can be considered an extension of *Berkemer v. McCarty*. In *Strieff*, an officer had been suspicious that there was drug activity in a residential building due to having received an anonymous tip. The officer observed the building, off and on, for a week. The observation seemed to confirm his suspicions because of the heavy traffic in and out of the house, all of which involved very brief visits. Officer Fackrell stopped Strieff as the latter left the building, but lacked RS since he was not aware of how long Strieff had spent inside the building. Fackrell told Strieff of his interest in the activity inside the house and then asked for identification. The officer called dispatch with Strieff's information and discovered there was an outstanding arrest warrant for a traffic violation. Strieff was then arrested and a search incident to arrest (see Chapter 6) disclosed drugs and drug paraphernalia. It could be said that the discovery of the outstanding warrant forced the officer's hand, in that an arrest at that point seems not only warranted, but necessary; the finding of the drugs flows naturally from the "lawful" arrest. The controversy stems from the temptation the decision creates to simply stop any "suspicious" character, even without any reasonable suspicion, and then call dispatch to see whether any warrants are outstanding for the stopped individual. The Court's decision can be regarded as retroactively "cleaning up" the illegal stop and permitting the admission of any evidence found on the suspect. A spirited dissent argued that the decision will end up disproportionately adversely affecting minorities.

In a related vein, the Supreme Court has also upheld "stop and identify" (S&I) statutes, provided there is RS for stopping the suspect for some violation (*Brown v. Texas*, 443 U.S. 47, 1979). The Court would not accept every version of S&I type statutes, however. One case involved a California statute that allowed the detention of someone who loiters or wanders about, and permitted arrest for those who refused to identify themselves. The Court held that this statute violated due process in that it vested too much discretion in the police officer (*Kolender v. Lawson*, 461 U.S. 352, 1983).

In *Hiibel v. Sixth Judicial District Court of Humboldt County, et al.* (542 U.S. 177, 2004), nevertheless, the Court said that a suspect can be stopped (and ultimately arrested and convicted) for refusing to identify self during a *Terry* stop. The identification activity authorized under the S&I statute does not implicate any Fourth Amendment rights, according to the Court. As the Court saw it, "(k)nowledge of identity may inform an officer that a suspect is wanted for another offence, or has a record of violence or mental disorder (*Id.*, at 186)." The 5–4 decision also contained a disagreement about any Fifth Amendment issue presented by the S&I statutes. While the majority said disclosing one's name and identity presents no reasonable danger of incrimination, the dissent claimed there was an incriminatory problem and that *Berkemer v. McCarty* had already held that a person should not have to respond.

What can also be considered an extension of *Terry* is the authority of police to seize and detain *property* for investigative purposes. The Court declared in *U.S. v. Place* (which we just saw had declared a lengthy detention of an individual as custody):

> When an officer's observations lead him reasonably to believe that a traveler is carrying luggage that contains narcotics, the principles of *Terry* and its progeny would permit the officer to detain the luggage briefly to investigate the

circumstances that aroused his suspicion, provided that the investigative detention is properly limited in scope (462 U.S. 696–697, 1983).

Watered-Down Estimates of RS (Perhaps Entire Area of Drug Courier Profile)

Due to the change in the investigatory focus (i.e., looking for drugs) there has arguably also been a change in the *amount of evidence* required of the police in order for them to investigate. The official amount of evidence required is still labelled reasonable suspicion, but what will suffice to constitute that has been watered down considerably from the *Terry* scenario. The RS present in *Terry* was on the verge of satisfying probable cause and seems considerably more substantial than that upheld in *Illinois v. Wardlow* (528 U.S. 119, 2000) where a 5–4 majority found a combination of a high crime area and an unprovoked flight constituted RS. Even still, a mere refusal to cooperate with the police does not amount to RS (*Florida v. Royer*, 460 U.S. 491, 1983).

Today, the drug courier profile developed by the Drug Enforcement Administration (DEA) is a tool utilized most frequently in airports (but elsewhere as well) so as to provide DEA agents with indicators that should suggest there is RS to believe the person fitting the profile is allegedly transporting drugs. DEA agents have testified in various court cases that the following laundry list of factors has been used by them in different times/situations in determining the existence of a drug courier. The profile indicators are as comprehensive as they are contradictory:

- Arrival at the airport (early in the morning, afternoon, late at night);

- Deplaning (first, middle, last);

- Purchasing ticket (at airport, on short notice);

- Ticket bought (coach, first-class, one-way, round-trip);

- Paying for ticket (cash, small or large denomination currency);

- Phone calls after deplaning (local telephone call, long distance call, pretended to make a call);

- Travel from (New York, LA, Detroit, Fort Lauderdale, Atlanta, Miami, Cleveland);

- Travel to (New York, Chicago, Detroit, Atlanta, Austin, Birmingham, Charlotte, Chattanooga, Dayton, Indianapolis, Kansas City, Newark, Tulsa);

- Travel through (Dallas/Fort Worth, Atlanta, Detroit, San Diego, LA, New York, San Juan);

- Travel route (non-stop or direct to and from source city, circuitous routes or changing airlines/flights to and from source cities);

- Luggage (none, brand new, small tote bag, medium sized bag, two bulky garment bags, two heavy suitcases, four pieces of luggage);

- Relationship to baggage (overly protective of luggage, staring at luggage after checking it, failing to claim luggage, having a companion claim luggage, disassociated self from luggage);

- Relationship to briefcase (holding briefcase firmly, disassociated from briefcase);

- Travel associates (none, with a companion);

- Behavior (acted too nervous, acted too calm, made eye contact with officer, avoided eye contact with officer, perspiring profusely, shortness of breath, appearing nervous during ID stop, appearing cool, exhibiting calm demeanor);

- Dress (wore expensive clothing and gold jewelry, casually dressed, sloppily dressed, smartly dressed);

- Conduct after deplaning (went to restroom, walked rapidly through airport, walked slowly through airport, walked aimlessly through airport, walked in an unusual pattern, leaving in a hurried or nervous manner);

- Departure from airport (left by taxi, limousine, private car, hotel courtesy van, public transportation);

- Demographics (Hispanic, black female, black male, female, young);

- Appearance (Fu Manchu mustache, collar-length hair).*

To the extent that someone needs to accumulate only a few of these factors in order to fulfill the profile, it is difficult to image any obstacle to DEA agents or other police from alleging the existence of a drug courier in any particular traveler. As one critic noted, the drug courier profile "provides an all-purpose checklist to justify stopping anybody the law enforcement officer selects. The police are left to rely on hunches and stereotypes, often racial in nature. . . ." (Cole, 1999: 1079).

In *U.S. v. Sokolow* (490 U.S. 1, 1989), the defendant purchased two plane tickets for a flight from Honolulu to Miami with cash, a thick roll of $20 bills; he appeared nervous while purchasing the tickets. Neither he nor his companion checked a bag. Sokolow also bought a return flight ticket for three days later. These characteristics meant that Sokolow fit the drug courier profile. DEA agents stopped the two travelers and escorted them to an office. A drug sniffing dog alerted to one of the bags the men were carrying. The agents secured a warrant, but the search revealed no drugs. The dog then alerted to a second bag. Sokolow was released while the agents pursued a second warrant. That

---

* These factors constituting the drug courier profile were derived from two sources: David Cole, "Foreword: Discretion and Discrimination Reconsidered: A Response to the New Criminal Justice Scholarship." 87 *Georgetown Law Journal* 1059–1093 (May 1999), pp. 1077–1078; and, Charles C. Becton, "The Drug Courier Profile: All Seems Infected That Th'Infected Spy, as all Looks Yellow to the Jaundic'd Eye." 65 *North Carolina Law Review* 417–480 (1987), pp. 438–54. There was no attempt made to update to see how many more factors have been added to the profile in the last 20 years or so.

search disclosed 1000 grams of cocaine. The Supreme Court upheld the initial seizure of Sokolow and his companion as satisfying the RS standard of *Terry*.

In establishing the presence of RS (the same as in finding PC), the Court employs a Totality of Circumstances (TOC) test. The circumstances or factors can each be legal, but yet cumulate to form RS. In *U.S. v. Arvizu* (534 U.S. 266, 2001), the police had seven factors, all of which were legal in nature:

- The time the car drove on the road was during a shift change for border patrol;

- The road was remote and was not well suited for Arvizu's vehicle;

- The vehicle slowed down dramatically when the police were observed;

- The driver would not look at the police;

- The children had their feet propped on some cargo in the back seat;

- The children waved "mechanically" at the police; and,

- The vehicle made turns that avoided the checkpoint.

Feeling that he had RS, the officer stopped the vehicle, and found drugs after Arvizu consented to a search. The U.S. Court of Appeals suppressed the evidence, citing an absence of RS since almost all of the factors were legal. The Supreme Court reversed, however, holding that RS is not determined by considering each factor but rather whether the TOC amounts to RS.

Frisk for Drugs

Not only has the focus of the stop been altered so as to allow various types of investigations, the *target of the frisk* has changed as well. Contrary to *Terry*'s limited frisk for weapons, *Minnesota v. Dickerson* (508 U.S. 366, 1993) permitted a pat down that found crack cocaine. Under what we already saw as a plain feel authorization, "officers may seize nonthreatening contraband detected during a protective pat down search of the sort permitted by *Terry* (*Id.*, at 373)." The Court declared that this frisk is permitted as long as it is conducted within the bounds of *Terry*. The Court believed this frisk involves no greater invasion of privacy than that allowed for weapons. Moreover, according to the Court, "(i)f the object is contraband, its warrantless seizure would be justified by the same practical considerations that inhere in the plain view context (*Id.*, at 367)." The frisk in *Dickerson* was not allowed, however, because the officer had squeezed and manipulated the item in the suspect's pocket before knowing it was cocaine. The Court regarded this action as a continued exploration of the pocket. Even still, if the officer feels an object "whose contour or mass makes its identity immediately apparent (*Id.*)" that the item is contraband or a weapon there is no invasion of privacy beyond what was authorized in terms of a frisk for weapons, in the Court's view.

Not a Brief Detention

Today, the length of a *Terry* stop can certainly well exceed the less-than-one-minute threshold that had been authorized in the original decision. We discovered in *U.S. v. Place* that a 90-minute detention was considered excessive by the Court and that it could not be sanctioned under *Terry*. Nevertheless, certainly a *Terry* stop can last many minutes. In *U.S. v. Sharpe* (470 U.S. 675, 1985), the Court found a stop of 20 minutes was reasonable. The case involved an automobile stop and suspected transportation of drugs. The delay was due to waiting for additional officers to arrive. As the Court explained the answer to any question involving the length of a stop has to be answered via a *totality of circumstances test*. There are three factors in the test employed in this context: purpose of the stop; reasonableness of the time lapsed; and, reasonableness of the method of investigation. The Court also offered that police diligence is critical to determining if the detention is too long. Interesting, the Court suggested that 30–40 minutes may not be too long depending upon circumstances (especially if suspect caused some or all of the delay). Of course, we already saw where there can be lengthy detentions lasting hours in the securing or executing of a search warrant (but see *Rodriguez v. U.S.*, section below).

TRAFFIC STOPS

Early on the Supreme Court announced that its examination of traffic stops would be guided by the principles established in *Terry v. Ohio* (see *U.S. v. Cortez*, 449 U.S. 411, 1981).

Most important, the Supreme Court determined in 1979 that stopping cars on a whim or gut instinct was not constitutional (*Delaware v. Prouse*, 440 U.S. 648). The Court's holding prevents police from using purely discriminatory reasons for pulling cars over. Instead, the Court insisted that police have RS in order to effect a traffic stop. This puts traffic stops on a par with *Terry*-oriented stops. In fact, in *Berkemer v. McCarty* (468 U.S. 420, 1984), the Court noted that a traffic stop was a limited detention for investigatory purposes permitted by *Terry*.

As with *Terry*, the RS requirement for a traffic stop must be based on objective factors as particularized or applicable to the vehicle in order to justify the intervention. In other words, looking at the TOC where is the RS to stop this particular car? Also similar to *Terry* (via its extensions), an anonymous 911 phone call/tip can serve to provide RS for a traffic stop, provided there is enough information for the police to corroborate its validity and reliability (*Navarette v. California*, 572 U.S. ___, 134 S.Ct. 1683, 2014). In *Navarette*, police had received a 911 call that a truck had run another vehicle off the road. The cops found the truck, and decided to do an investigative stop. They smelled marijuana, searched the truck and found 30 pounds of marijuana. The Court felt that the tip had disclosed a dangerous activity and that was enough to justify the investigative stop.

A traffic stop can involve two different circumstances: purely investigatory (as in the above example, a suspected DUI or drug transporter) or there could already be grounds for a citation/arrest (as in a defective tail light, speeding, weaving, out of date inspection/

registration, failure to keep right, failure to wear a seat belt). (Here, we'll cover only detentions conducted so as to investigate. In the next chapter we will return to the auto under warrantless searches.)

The latter situations are already "known" to the police since the misconduct had been discovered prior to the traffic stop. It is possible, however, that this "justified" stop is actually a pretext stop or one in which the police were hoping to uncover other (perhaps more significant) wrongdoing (such as DUI or transporting drugs or illegal immigrants). In *Whren v. U.S.* (517 U.S. 806, 1996), the Supreme Court endorsed pretext stops. The Court noted that all the police need to stop a vehicle is a legitimate traffic violation. The violation makes the seizure of the car reasonable. The reasonableness of a traffic stop, in turn, does not depend upon the actual motivations of the police (as in finding a more serious wrongdoing) in stopping the car. In *Whren,* after some initial suspicious behavior, the motorist had made a right turn without using a signal and then sped away. The cops stopped Whren's truck and found drugs in his hands. (Pretext arrests were later sanctioned in *Arkansas v. Sullivan*, 532 U.S. 769, 2001—see Chapter 4).

Even if the police did not initiate the stop under a pretext, they are allowed to combine a legitimate vehicle stop (such as for speeding) with an exploratory investigation on their own (such as discovering contraband in the passenger compartment via plain view) or through the analysis provided by drug sniffing dogs. (We will see in Chapter 6 that police can conduct a warrantless search of the entire vehicle provided they have PC). We saw in *Illinois v. Caballes* (543 U.S. 405, 2005) that while one officer was involved with the motorist he had stopped for speeding (and was issuing a warning) a second officer arrived with a drug detecting dog that indicated the presence of drugs in the trunk of the car. The interesting aspect of *Caballes* is that the Illinois Supreme Court found the search illegal because the dog sniffing test was performed without any "specific and articulable facts" to suggest drug activity; this court focused on the nature of the investigation. The U.S. Supreme court, however, reversed the state court and focused more on the duration of that stop, which was accomplished in less than 10 minutes (see *Rodriguez v. U.S.*). Prolonging a stop "beyond the time reasonably required" to issue a warning ticket would be unlawful, according to the Court. That did not happen in this case. The Supreme Court stressed that the use of a well-trained narcotics-detection dog during a traffic stop generally does not implicate legitimate privacy interests (see *U.S. v. Place*).

The *Caballes* holding revealed an interesting divide in the Court. The usually liberal Justice Stevens wrote the decision (and was joined by the usually liberal Justice Breyer) while Justices Souter and Ginsburg wrote poignant dissents; both were concerned about the character/ nature of the investigation. Justice Souter observed:

> (T)he Court took care to keep a *Terry* stop from automatically becoming a foot in the door for all investigatory purposes; the permissible intrusion was bounded by the justification for the detention. Although facts disclosed by enquiry within this limit might give grounds to go further, the government could not otherwise take advantage of a suspect's immobility to search for evidence unrelated to the reason for the detention. That has to be the rule unless *Terry* is going to become an open-sesame for general searches, and that rule requires holding that the police do not have reasonable grounds to conduct sniff searches for drugs simply because they have stopped someone to receive a ticket for a highway offense 543 U.S. at 415).

Similarly, Justice Ginsburg said she would apply

> *Terry's* reasonable-relation test . . . to determine whether the canine sniff impermissibly expanded the scope of the initially valid seizure of Caballes (*Id.*, at 420).

For her duration was not the issue. Rather, she believed this stop involved an

> unwarranted and nonconsensual expansion of the seizure here from a routine traffic stop to a drug investigation (that)

broadened the scope of the investigation in a manner that . . . runs afoul of the Fourth Amendment (*Id.*, at 420–421).

Interesting is the fact that the Supreme Court did focus on the nature of the investigation rather than the duration of the detention in *Rodriguez v. U.S.* (575 U.S. ___, 135 S.Ct. 1609, 2015). In *Rodriguez,* the detention was extended due to the need for a second officer to arrive on the site of a traffic stop. The second officer did not arrive until *after the traffic stop had been terminated* via the issuing of a written warning. The termination of the traffic stop meant that RS was required to prolong the detention, according to a 6–3 majority of the Court. This was the case even though the added detention was a mere seven to eight minutes long. There was simply no obscuring the fact that the traffic stop had turned into an investigation for the presence of drugs when there had been no RS to believe there were drugs in the vehicle; the Court viewed this as being beyond the permissible scope of *Terry*. The lesson from *Rodriguez* (and *Caballes* as well as *Arizona v. Johnson*, below) is that the authority for a seizure (as in a traffic stop) lasts only for as long as the tasks associated with a traffic violation reasonably need to be completed; besides issuing a warning or ticket, ascertaining the driver's sobriety, checking the driver's license, determining whether there are outstanding warrants, and verifying the automobile's registration and proof of insurance are tasks the police are authorized to conduct.

The target of an "expanded" investigation could be critical. While a pursuit of drugs may not appear warranted via traffic stops for other reasons, the employment of bomb-sniffing dogs could lead to a different conclusion as suggested in dicta in the *Caballes* opinion.

POLICE INTERACTIONS DURING TRAFFIC STOPS

Police can order the driver out of a car even when only a citation (as opposed to an arrest) is involved and even without RS. Assuming there is RS to believe that the driver poses a threat or is armed, the police can frisk him/her as well (*Pennsylvania v. Mimms*, 434 U.S. 106, 1977). Twenty years later, the forcible exit aspect of *Mimms* was extended to passengers since they can pose even a greater threat than a single driver, especially when there are multiple passengers (*Maryland v. Wilson*, 519 U.S. 408, 1997). The Court's theory was that since all those inside the car are already stopped, requiring them to exit the vehicle is no big deal. More recently, the Court determined that passengers can be detained for the duration of the stop, and with RS, can be frisked as well; both of these actions were considered reasonable by the Court (*Arizona v. Johnson*, 555 U.S. 323, 2009). In this case, there were three passengers in the car and one of them, Johnson, had a police scanner in his pocket, was wearing clothing consistent with gang membership (i.e., the infamous Crips), and admitted to both being from a town that was home to the Crips and having been in prison. The police suspected Johnson might have a weapon; the frisk verified that (a gun was found).

Inasmuch as *Terry* had given police clear authority to frisk detained suspects it was not a quantum leap when the Court extended this authority to frisk the passenger compartment of a vehicle when there is a traffic stop and RS to believe the driver or passengers pose a threat (*Michigan v. Long*, 463 U.S. 1032, 1983). The Court explained that a pouch can be frisked, too, since a weapon could have been inside. A frisk was authorized for any location in which a weapon could be found; any contraband found in plain view along the way could be used against the suspect as well.

SOBRIETY CHECKPOINTS

Highway sobriety checkpoints have been granted constitutional sanction by the Supreme Court for nearly three decades. In *Michigan v. Sitz* (496 U.S. 444, 1990), the Court upheld the stopping of all vehicles for a brief duration without any suspicion. In *Sitz*, there were 126 vehicles that had been stopped (an average of 25 seconds per car) and two DUIs were discovered. The case encouraged the Court to employ a *balancing test*: measuring the amount of damage/pain/suffering cause by automobile accidents versus the amount of intrusion resulting from the checkpoints. The Court reasoned that there was a suspicionless seizure, but a reasonable one. For one thing, the use of a vehicle is heavily regulated. That could allow one to regard sobriety checkpoints as regulatory enforcement only (i.e., not having a blatant crime control purpose). Moreover, at checkpoints the intrusion was slight compared to a very substantial interest (i.e., public safety). Interesting, all three levels of state courts had found the checkpoint to be a Fourth Amendment violation (and violative of the state constitution, too). These courts conceded there was a legitimate interest in public safety, but believed that the checkpoints were ineffective and don't further that interest. Nevertheless, the majority equated sobriety checkpoints with those erected to find illegal immigrants (see *U.S. v. Martinez-Fuerte*, 428 U.S. 543, 1976 in Chapter 6), in that both involved slight intrusion and were needed to ensure highway safety. The Court also noted the non-discriminatory character of sobriety checkpoints in that all vehicles are stopped. There is no discretionary or possible discriminatory selection of motorists to be examined for DUIs (or other possible violations).

DRUG CHECKPOINTS

The Supreme Court put on the brakes (so to speak) when the issue of drug checkpoints arose. These are not permissible, according to the Court (*City of Indianapolis v. Edmond*, 531 U.S. 32, 2000). These checkpoints differed from sobriety ones in that they promote crime control or, as the Court stated, "to uncover evidence of ordinary criminal wrongdoing (*Id.*, at 41)." This contravenes the Fourth Amendment and the majority feared they could lead to additional roadblocks for other crime control purposes. Justice Thomas did not see any reason to distinguish drug stops from other permissible roadblocks and dissented, accordingly. Interesting is that he thought the Framers would have problems with all forms of checkpoints since *all* of them involve "indiscriminate stops of individuals not suspected of wrongdoing (*Id.*, at 56)." He makes a good point.

An interesting question is whether the Court would allow drug sniffing dogs to be placed at sobriety checkpoints. The answer is probably *no* since that would combine a law enforcement (or crime control) objective with a regulatory one. One advantage to this combination approach is that it would remove any discriminatory potential that accompanies selective/individual application of the dogs. Even more intriguing, perhaps, is what would be the Court's response to multiple tag-team tandems of cops using the scenario that was approved by the Court in *Caballes*. In other words, if a jurisdiction sent out drug sniffing dogs to most/all of the stops initiated by traffic enforcement police, would the Supreme Court sanction the results? *Caballes* is certainly adequate precedent to suggest the answer would be *yes*. But such a blatant exploitation of the Court's allowance could lead the Justices to reconsider their position.

INFORMATION SEEKING CHECKPOINTS

As long as the crime control objective is not personal, the Court seems inclined to authorize checkpoints. In *Illinois v. Lidster* (540 U.S. 419, 2004), a 70-year-old bicyclist was killed by a hit and run driver. Police set up a checkpoint at the location and time period of the incident to see if anyone would report having seen the accident. The Court allowed this activity because the checkpoint's "primary law enforcement purpose was not to determine whether a vehicle's occupants were committing a crime, but to ask vehicle occupants, as members of the public, for their help in providing information about a crime in all likelihood by others (*Id.*, at 423)." As Lidster approached the checkpoint, he swerved his car, almost hitting an officer. He was directed to another area where he failed a sobriety field test. The Court did not believe a checkpoint with this type of mission violated the Fourth Amendment. Checkpoints that would seek information for other emergencies (such as kidnapping, bomb threats) would also likely pass constitutional scrutiny, too.

ONE LAST VEHICLE OBSERVATION

One last comment about traffic stops is necessary. States differ as to whether traffic violations will end with a citation or an arrest. States are free to choose between the two; the decision is critical because the searching authority of the police differs greatly between the two outcomes. As we will see in Chapter 6, arrest authorizes the police to search the car without a warrant, provide there is PC to believe the car contains evidence of some crime. A citation does not confer that authority.

Box 5-1: Special Case of Seizure

In *Brower v. County of Inyo* (489 U.S. 593, 1989) the Court ruled that for a seizure to occur there has to be "governmental termination of freedom of movement *through means intentionally applied* (*Id.*, at 597, italics in original). In this case the police had set up a roadblock with an 18-wheeled truck straddling the road. There was a police car in front of the truck with its lights on so as to blind the suspect. The effect was precisely as intended and the suspect rammed the truck and died. The Court said this was a seizure for Fourth Amendment purposes. While this answered the constitutional question it did not resolve the question of the civil liability of the police and any potential litigation for wrongful death.

Box 5-2: The Various Ways to Examine an Automobile

Automobile searches can occur:

- Incident to arrest, but no trunk (see Chapter 6)
- Inventory inspections, including trunk (see Chapter 6)
- Frisk for weapons, but no trunk
- Checkpoints (with PC), but no trunk
- Probable cause on the highway, including trunk

Box 5-3: Traffic Stops Run the Gamut of Evidence Requirements as to When and Why

1) They can be PC for an observed violation (and can then be a pretense for further investigation)

   - Speeding
   - Weaving
   - Tail light
   - Registration
   - Failure to keep right
   - Running red light

2) They can be *Terry*-like investigations with only RS

   - DUI

3) They can be regulatory w/o any evidence of wrongdoing

   - Sobriety checkpoints

CHAPTER 6

Searches That Do Not Require a Warrant

So far we haven't discussed *searches* per se. We've covered Public Domain or areas in which the lack of a reasonable expectation of privacy means there is no search occurring, which means there is no Fourth Amendment control at all. We also considered the category of stop and frisk, in which there are limited intrusions not amounting to full-blown arrests or searches. This converts to making the Fourth Amendment relevant, but still less than fully controlling such that neither probable cause nor a warrant is required to "investigate" the suspect; reasonable suspicion is necessary, however. Now we turn our attention to actual searches, but these types of interference nevertheless require no warrant, and demand that police have only probable cause or less.

Box 6-1: Warrantless Search Categories and Evidence Required

Requiring PC

- Incident to Arrest (at least for the arrest itself)
- Automobile
- Exigent Circumstances

Requiring Less than PC

- Consent (no evidence)
- Border (no evidence)
- Regulatory/Administrative/Business
- Inventory
- Special Needs

INCIDENT TO ARREST

Anyone arrested is subject to a search of his/her person (and belongings) with no further evidence (beyond the PC needed to arrest) required to conduct that search. This has long been the understanding of police authority in this context. Originally, the justifications for this activity were to protect the officer and to prevent the destruction of evidence. And, considering the intrusion already resulting from an arrest, any added intrusion experienced via a search was not seen as unreasonable or unlawful. More than four decades ago, the Court eliminated the need for the original justifications; no longer would officer safety or evidence preservation be required to uphold a warrantless search incident to arrest.

In *U.S. v. Robinson* (414 U.S. 218, 1973), the Court upheld a search incident to arrest of a motorist taken into custody for driving with a revoked license. In Robinson's situation there would be no reason to fear for the officer's safety or to think there was evidence to preserve. Nevertheless, the Court determined that the heroin the officer found via a search of a cigarette pack in Robinson's pocket was admissible at trial. The officer's conduct was more intrusive than a frisk (the cigarette pack was searched) and would not have been lawful under *Terry* (the officer conceded that he knew the object was not a weapon). For the heroin to be admissible, then, only a search incident to arrest could justify the discovery of the drugs. The Supreme Court called the search exactly that. According to the Court, "(a) custodial arrest of a suspect based on probable cause is a reasonable intrusion under the Fourth Amendment; that intrusion being lawful, a search incident to arrest requires no additional justification (*Id.*, at 235)."

In this decision the Court established a *bright-line rule*: any and all arrests authorize the police to conduct a search incident to that arrest. The severity or nature of the crime was not relevant; protecting the officer and preserving evidence were no longer considerations here.

In subsequent decisions the Court ruled:

- An inventory search of the arrestee's personal effects, such as a shoulder bag, was lawful as part of the booking procedure (*Illinois v. Lafayette*, 462 U.S. 640, 1983);

- The search of the arrestee can occur hours later where the person is held in detention (*U.S. v. Edwards*, 415 U.S. 800, 1974); and,

- The search can immediately precede the arrest as long as there is PC for the arrest (*Rawlings v. Kentucky*, 448 U.S. 98, 1980).

Perhaps the most interesting and critical ruling on this issue is the very recent *Birchfield v. North Dakota* (579 U.S. ___, 136 S.Ct. 2160, 2016). In *Birchfield*, the Court determined that requiring a breath test on a suspected DUI driver was permissible without a warrant as incident to arrest. The Court employed a balancing test and found the intrusion on privacy to be minimal, while the government and societal interest in deterring drunk driving to be substantial. Breath tests simply do not "implicate significant privacy concerns." In the Court's eyes, the physical intrusion is "almost negligible." Equally interesting, however, is that the Court held that blood tests for the same driver were not permissible without a warrant despite the arrest. Absent an exigent circumstance, the police need a warrant to secure blood from a DUI suspect.

Scope of the Search Incident to Arrest

There is no doubt that the person of an arrested suspect is subject to being searched incident to that arrest, but (the scope of or) exactly how far that search may go depends upon the location of the suspect. If the suspect is on the street, that answer is the suspect's person and belongings, if any. If a vehicle is involved, the answer lies in the next section, below.

The exact scope of this type of search when the arrest occurs in a room/house was somewhat uncertain until 1969 when the Supreme Court issued *Chimel v. California* (395 U.S. 752, 1969). The answer is what became known as the *Chimel Doctrine*, namely that the search is limited to the area within the immediate control of the arrestee or the "area from which he might gain possession of a weapon or destructible evidence (*Id.*, at 763)." In this case, the police had searched through a three-bedroom house, garage, attic and workshop without a warrant and under the notion that this search was incident to the arrest. The Supreme Court declared the search unlawful and implemented the "immediate control" limitation that is now standard for these searches.

The police are not allowed to let the arrest serve as an excuse to enter and search a house. In *Vale v. Louisiana* (399 U.S. 30, 1970) the police had arrested Vale on his front steps and then followed him into his house and searched without a warrant. The Court ruled that this development did not serve as grounds for a warrantless search since no one else was home and thus the house was under the control of the police, meaning no emergency or other justification existed for the search (such as removal of or destruction of evidence).

Chimel Extensions

However, police are allowed to accompany an arrestee into an apartment or house when the latter went into his room in pursuit of identification after the police had asked him for ID (*Washington v. Chrisman*, 455 U.S. 1, 1982). The arrestee had said the identification was in his room and both he and the officer entered the room upon which the officer saw drugs in plain view. The Court upheld the legality of the "search."

Police are also allowed to conduct a protective sweep for dangerous persons when they enter a private residence (*Maryland v. Buie*, 494 U.S. 325, 1990). With RS that there could be other suspects present, police are permitted to look in closets and other spaces adjoining the place of the arrest, including any area in which a person could be found and from which an attack could be launched. This search involves a cursory inspection of those plausible areas. In *Buie,* the suspect emerged from a basement. The police conducted a protective sweep of that area and in plain view found a red running suit that was used to convict Buie. Since *Buie* allows police to look wherever someone is hiding in the house it is an extension of *Chimel.*

INCIDENT TO ARREST AND THE AUTOMOBILE

In 1981, the Supreme Court established a bright-line rule for the search of a vehicle when one is involved with the arrest of a suspect. In *New York v. Belton* (453 U.S. 454, 1981), the Court determined that an arrest connected to a car means the entire passenger compartment may be searched, including a closed or open glove compartment as well as the contents of any containers, such as receptacles, boxes, bags, and clothing. The only section of the vehicle that was off-limits (via incident to arrest at least) was the trunk of the car. For the time being, *Belton* served as a workable formula and constituted an extension of *Chimel* (into the passenger compartment). One important limit the Court placed on *Belton* was that there had to be an *actual arrest* in order for a search of this type to be allowed. This meant that if only a citation were involved with the traffic stop, a search incident to arrest was not permissible (*Knowles v. Iowa*, 525 U.S. 113, 1998).

The Court took *Belton* one step further in *Thornton v. U.S.* (541 U.S. 615, 2004). In this case police saw that the tags attached to a vehicle did not belong to the car Thornton was driving. The police followed Thornton and arrested him after he had stopped the car and had walked away from it. The police searched the passenger compartment incident to arrest, which the Supreme Court upheld under that principle. The Court explained that this search was permissible provided that the driver was a "recent occupant." The suspect has to have been connected to the vehicle, which applied to Thornton.

Somewhat surprising was the Court's partial overruling of *Belton* in *Arizona v. Gant* (556 U.S. 332, 2009). The police had arrested Gant for driving with a suspended license, had handcuffed him, and had put him in the back of the police car. They then searched the car and found drugs and a gun. A 5–4 majority of the Court effectively performed a partial retreat from *Belton/Thornton* (but didn't characterize it as such) by proclaiming henceforth that a search of the passenger compartment incident to arrest is permitted only if: 1) the arrestee is unsecured and within reaching distance of the passenger compartment or 2) it is reasonable to believe that evidence relevant to the crime of arrest might be found. Thus, a search of the vehicle following an arrest for a car-related offense would seem to be permissible only if the suspect is still unsecured. Presumably, the arrestee would have to be reasonably believed to be a threat to the officer's safety, and even then only a limited search/frisk of the passenger compartment would be allowed.

A good theoretical question is whether the Supreme Court will ultimately apply *Gant* to a comparable search incident to arrest involving a suspect and his/her house.

AUTOMOBILE EXCEPTION

The automobile has been treated differently than other possessions in a number of contexts as we have already seen. The car has been included as well among the areas in which a warrant is not required for a search, provided there is PC for the search. This exception to the warrant requirement is nearly 100 years old, having begun during the days of prohibition in the 1920s. Historically, dispensing with the warrant requirement has been justified, here, due to the inherent movability of the vehicle and the lesser expectation of privacy one has in a car (as opposed to a house). Another way of highlighting the lesser privacy of the vehicle is to focus on the pervasive regulation it experiences via licensing and inspections (*South Dakota v. Opperman*, 428 U.S. 364, 1976).

The automobile exception was initiated in *Carroll v. U.S.* (267 U.S. 132) in 1925. The pressures of enforcing prohibition certainly contributed to the Court's determination that the automobile is not entitled to the same Fourth Amendment protection as a residence, but the Court has not varied from its stance regarding movable objects. As the Court noted, there is "a necessary difference between a search of a store, dwelling house, or other structure in respect of which a proper official search warrant readily may be obtained and a search of a ship, motor boat, wagon, or automobile for contraband goods, where it is not practicable to secure a warrant, because the vehicle can be quickly moved out of the locality or jurisdiction in which the warrant must be sought (*Id.*, at 153)."

Decades later the Supreme Court explained that the PC alternative to a warrant in searching cars travels with the vehicle to the police station. In *Chambers v. Maroney* (399 U.S. 42, 1975), a suspect was arrested in a car on a robbery charge. The officer did not search the car until later after it had arrived at the station. Thus, it was not a situation in which there could be a search incident to arrest. Nevertheless, he did not secure a warrant. The Supreme Court upheld the search because there was PC to believe guns and money were present in the car due to the robbery. The Court explained that PC means police can search right away at the scene or later at the station. In other words, PC travels with the car to the police station, and a warrant is unnecessary even if one could have been obtained.

Perhaps the most complicated aspect of a vehicle search upon PC is what should be done about containers located in a car or recently removed from one. The Court's initial reaction to containers was to require a warrant before a search of them. In *U.S. v. Chadwick* (433 U.S. 1, 1977), the Court ruled that police cannot search a movable container (here, a 200 pound footlocker) without a warrant unless there is an emergency. Similarly, the Court refused to allow a warrantless search of a closed container found in a car when there was PC for the container, but not for the car (*Arkansas v. Sanders*, 442 U.S. 753, 1979). The reasoning was that the container was not mobile but rather was firmly in police custody so there was no exigency that would prevent the pursuit of a warrant. For years the Court appeared to go back and forth on this issue, with no steady and clear direction to the police as to when a warrantless search of containers would be permissible. That finally came to an end in 1982.

In that year, the Supreme Court delivered *U.S. v. Ross* (456 U.S. 798, 1982). The *Ross* decision made it explicit that with PC police can search any part of a vehicle likely to hold the focus/target of the PC without a warrant. That search included any containers. While a search incident to an arrest does not let a cop search the trunk, *Ross* does and establishes a bright-line rule in this context. *Ross* was later reaffirmed in *Pennsylvania v. Labron* (518 U.S. 938, 1996), which held that no warrant is needed for an automobile search when there is PC even if there is time to secure a warrant, at least if the car is "readily mobile."

Ross Extensions

Ross was not only reaffirmed, it was also extended to other contexts. Possibly the most critical *Ross* extension was that experienced in *California v. Carney* (471 U.S. 386, 1985). The California case involved a mini-motor home in which the suspect was exchanging drugs for sex. The Supreme Court ruled that a motor home, if readily mobile, was to be considered an automobile for Fourth Amendment purposes. Factors that are considered in determining whether a mobile home is a residence and not a vehicle include location, ready movability, connection to utilities, and convenient access to a public road. It is a vehicle if it is found "in a place not regularly used for residential purposes." *Carney* held that the mobile home in question was a vehicle due to its movability. It established a bright-line rule for "homes" of this nature. The Court did not want to get bogged down in addressing the size of the vehicle and noted a fear that to hold otherwise was to encourage drug trafficking via these vehicles. The dissent pointed out that this was the first time the highway-oriented vehicle exception was applied to a vehicle parked in a lot that coincidentally was located near a court house where a warrant could have been obtained.

In the same year as *Carney,* the Court revisited the container category in *U.S. v. Johns* (469 U.S. 478, 1985). *Johns* involved the seizure of some packages from two vehicles that Customs agents had PC to believe contained contraband. The packages were not searched until several days after they had been removed from the vehicles and sent to a DEA warehouse; the agents did not secure a warrant. Both the District Court and the U.S. Court of Appeals ruled the search was illegal and that the agents needed a warrant to conduct the search. The Supreme Court disagreed and held that since the agents had PC to search the packages under *Ross* at the time of the seizure that authority simply continued until the agents finally got around to searching the packages. Coincidentally, the agents claimed they detected the distinct odor of marijuana as they approached the packages, which provided them with PC to believe the vehicles contained drugs. Justices Brennan and Marshall dissented and wanted the agents to pursue a warrant.

The Court returned to the container category a few years later in *California v. Acevdeo* (500 U.S. 565, 1991). *Acevedo* involved two searches, involving a knapsack and a brown paper bag, placed in two vehicles by two defendants. In neither situation did the police have PC to believe there were drugs in the cars, but in both they did have PC to believe the containers held marijuana. The Court ruled that PC to believe the containers held drugs was sufficient, without a warrant, to justify the searches. The majority commented that "the Fourth Amendment does not compel separate treatment for an automobile search that extends only to a container within the vehicle (*Id.*, at 576)." Moreover, the majority simply felt that the warrant requirement served no purpose in this situation; the police certainly had PC and would have been able to secure a warrant anyway. In addition, the police also would have been able to search the containers as a search incident to arrest (consistent with both *Belton* and *Gant*). In a concurring opinion, Justice Scalia observed that he would not require a warrant for containers located in the public sector, independent of the automobile exception, provided there is PC. The dissent did not like that this decision leads to a conclusion that "the privacy interest that protects the contents of a suitcase or a briefcase from a warrantless search when it is in public view simply vanishes when its owner climbs into a taxicab (*Id.*, at 598)."

Between *Johns* and *Acevedo* containers currently or formerly connected to vehicles are subject to warrantless searches as long as there is PC to believe they contain contraband.

The Court extended the *Ross* holding one step further in *Wyoming v. Houghton* (526 U.S. 295, 1999). *Houghton* permitted the warrantless search of all containers in a vehicle, regardless of ownership, if police have PC. In *Houghton*, the police had PC to believe the driver of a car had used drugs and currently possessed same in his vehicle. The police found a purse on the back seat, which a passenger, Houghton, claimed was hers. The police found drugs in the purse. The Wyoming Supreme Court reversed her conviction because the police knew or should have known that purse did not belong to the driver of the car and there was no PC to believe there were drugs in the purse (as opposed to the car). The U.S. Supreme Court reversed that decision, however. The Court explained the Fourth Amendment's requirement of reasonableness is based not on whether the owner of property is suspected of crime but rather there is PC for a seizable item, such as drugs. In addition, passengers as well as drivers of cars "possess a reduced expectation of privacy with regard to property that they transport in cars, which 'travel public thoroughfares (*Id.*, at 303).'" The majority believed that if passengers were granted a greater expectation of privacy, all contraband would be held by the passenger. The three dissenters (Stevens, Souter, Ginsburg), insisted that the officer had to have but lacked PC to believe there were drugs in the purse, which invalidated the search.

INVENTORY SEARCHES

Another way in which to search an automobile without a warrant is through the inventory exception to the warrant requirement. Simply put, any vehicle that has been impounded is subject to being searched for inventory purposes. The Supreme Court recognized this exception more than forty years ago in *South Dakota v. Opperman* (428 U.S. 364, 1976). In *Opperman*, a car had been ticketed twice for illegal parking; the car remained in the spot for seven hours, overnight. The vehicle was "inspected" and towed to an impound lot. At the lot the police observed a watch on the dashboard and other personal items on the back seat. They opened the locked doors and using a "standard inventory form" and, following procedures, the officer inventoried the contents. An unlocked glove compartment also was opened and drugs were found. Opperman was prosecuted for drug possession; he lost a motion to suppress the evidence. The Supreme Court found the activity reasonable. Moreover the search had to be allowed:

1) To protect the owner's property while in police custody;

2) To protect the police against a false claim of lost or stolen property; and,

3) To protect the police from physical danger.

More than a decade later the Court re-emphasized the need for standardized procedure, detailing when and how an inventory of an impounded vehicle can take place (*Colorado v. Bertine*, 479 U.S. 367, 1987). In *Bertine*, a suspect had been taken into custody for a DUI. Before the tow truck arrived another officer inventoried the content of the driver's van in accordance with department policy, which required a detailed inspection and inventory of impounded vehicles. In a backpack the backup officer found drugs and drug paraphernalia. The Court upheld the search and noted that standardized procedures were preferred so there would be no bad faith and to prevent pure investigatory searches.

More recently, the Court reiterated and demonstrated the need for "standardized criteria or established routine" for inventory searches to be valid (*Florida v. Wells*, 495 U.S. 1, 1990). In *Wells*, the police had found drugs in a locked suitcase that had been found in the trunk of the car. The Court invalidated the search. The Court specified that without a department policy for opening closed containers the police are not permitted to conduct this type of search via an inventory rationale. The absence of policy left the decision to search in the officer's hands, which allowed too much discretion, according to the Court. In short, policy matters.

CONSENT SEARCHES

The police need no evidence to pursue a person's consent to search. Consent means a person is waiving his/her Fourth Amendment right to not be subject to search and seizure without PC or a warrant. In a nutshell, consent needs three elements to be valid:

1) Voluntary;

2) Within the scope given; and,

3) Properly authorized.

Before examining these elements it is important to address what is not consent. Consent is not a failure to object, but it can be implied. In other words, a suspect's mere silence does not mean that he/she has consented to a search. However, prolonged silence while observing a police search of one's property could reasonably lead the police to infer that consent has been granted.

If the police announce an intention to search, that is not consent, but rather is coercion (*Amos v. U.S.*, 255 U.S. 313, 1921). Thus, if a cop tells a driver to open the trunk of the car, consent has neither been sought nor granted. Coercion will also be said to exist if a suspect has been illegally detained; an illegal detention invalidates consent as we saw in *Florida v. Royer* (460 U.S. 491, 1983). Moreover, police cannot have a false claim to authority to search, as in offering a bogus warrant to justify a search. In that case, deception explains the access to the property searched and not consent (*Bumper v. North Carolina*, 391 U.S. 543, 1968).

Voluntary (and Knowledgeable?)

To be sure, consent must be voluntary and not the product of coercion as we just discussed. Probably the most critical question in this area is whether, in order to be truly voluntary, must the consent be knowledgeable as well? The parallel to this area is the *Miranda* requirement (see Chapter 9) that a voluntary statement from a suspect must be an informed one as well. Thus, we have the obligation for police to provide suspects with *Miranda* warnings before being able to interrogate them.

The Supreme Court would answer this question in the negative in *Schneckloth v. Bustamonte* (412 U.S. 218, 1973). In this case, a police officer had pulled over a car for a burned out headlight. The driver had no license. One of the passengers (Alcala) had a license and claimed the car was his brother's. The officer ordered everyone out of the car and asked Alcala for consent to search it. Alcala gave permission and even opened the trunk and glove compartment. The cop found three stolen checks implicating Bustamonte. The Supreme Court said the search was lawful and that no warnings to refuse consent for the search were necessary.

The Court noted that consent must be voluntary but that voluntary does not equate with a "knowing choice." The Court declared that the validity of a consent search was ruled by a totality of circumstances, including: age, education, intelligence, warning of rights, length of detention, nature of questioning, physical punishment, and deprivation of food or sleep. The Court explained that informed consent, while relevant, was not determinative and thus was not a necessary element of voluntary consent. Moreover, the Court pointed out that consent searches, unlike interrogations, do not typically occur in custody and are very different from other waiver situations, such as waiving a right to trial. Knowing and intelligent waivers are linked to trial-related rights and not those rights associated with the Fourth Amendment, the Court explained. One could make an argument that warnings are even more necessary in the consent search arena compared to the interrogation area. While vast numbers of people are familiar with *Miranda*, especially through books and movies, not as many people are aware that they can refuse the request of an officer to search parts of the their car.

In dissent, Justice Marshall said he did not agree that "one can choose to relinquish a constitutional right—the right to be free of unreasonable searches—without knowing that he has the alternative of refusing to accede to a police request to search (*Id.*, at 277)."

Although the Supreme Court emphasized that not being in custody was a factor in deciding there were no warnings needed for consent searches, three years later the Court ruled that suspects in custody when giving consent also did not need to be warned of their right to refuse (*U.S. v. Watson*, 423 U.S. 411, 1976).

Schneckloth Extensions

The Supreme Court has demonstrated that it will not expand the contexts in which people need to be advised of their rights beyond *Miranda*. Two decades after Schneckloth the Court ruled that drivers do not need to be told during a traffic stop that they're free to leave. In *Ohio v. Robinette* (519 U.S. 33, 1996), the driver exited the car upon request and was issued a verbal warning for speeding. The officer asked the driver if he was carrying any weapons or drugs. The driver said no.

The cop then asked if he could search car. Robinette gave consent and the officer found some drugs.

Interesting, the Ohio Supreme Court said there was continued detention, and the driver was never told he could leave. The Ohio court surmised that Robinette probably thought he couldn't leave and had to answer questions. The court opined: "Most people believe that they are validly in a police officer's custody as long as the officer continues to interrogate them. The police officer retains the upper hand and the accouterments of authority. That the officer lacks legal license to continue to detain them is unknown to most citizens, and a reasonable person would not feel free to walk away as the officer continues to address him (*Id.*, at 41)." Accordingly, the Ohio court held that motorists must be told they are free to leave before any consensual interrogation can exist; the drugs were suppressed.

Nevertheless, the U.S. Supreme Court reversed this decision and determined that the encounter between Robinette and the officer was voluntary and that there was no need for warnings of the right to leave the traffic stop and to terminate the conversation with the officer.

Even more interesting, on remand the Ohio Supreme Court said the consent given by Robinette was not voluntary since he never had any indication that he was free to leave. In fact, just the opposite was true in the court's eyes since "the circumstances surrounding the request to search made the questioning impliedly coercive (*Ohio v. Robinette*, 80 Ohio St. 3d 234, 245, 1997)."

Several years later, the Supreme Court held in *U.S. v. Drayton* (536 U.S. 194, 2002) that two bus passengers who had encountered three cops from a drug interdiction team did not need to be advised that they could refuse both to answer questions and to refuse consent to search their belongings.

Scope of Consent

The scope of the search will usually be consistent with the scope of the consent that has been given to the police. Occasionally, however, a dispute can arise as to whether the officer has gone too far and has exceeded the scope of consent. That was the issue in *Florida v. Jimeno* (500 U.S. 248, 1991). An officer stopped a car due to a violation. Jimeno was asked permission to search the car and he said okay. The cop found drugs in a brown paper bag. The trial court and both levels of appellate courts in Florida ruled for the defendant. The theory was that consent to search a car doesn't go as far as to include closed containers.

The U.S. Supreme Court reversed the lower courts' holdings. The Supreme Court declared that the standard for determining the scope of consent is "objective reasonableness." That standard means what a typical reasonable person would interpret was understood to have been the consent given to the officer. In *Jimeno*, there was no explicit limitation placed on the scope of the search by the driver. Thus, it was objectively reasonable for the officer to infer that he had permission to search the container in which he found the drugs. Moreover, contrary to what the Florida courts had determined, the U.S. Supreme Court insisted that police do not need specific and separate permission to open each container they come across in a vehicle. The Court explained that "(a) criminal suspect's Fourth Amendment right to be free from unreasonable searches is not violated when, after he gives police permission to search the automobile, they open a closed container found within the car that might reasonably hold the object of the search (*Id.*, at 248)."

The dissent would have invalidated the search "(b)ecause an individual's expectation of privacy in a container is distinct from, and far greater than, his expectation of privacy in the interior of his car (*Id.*, at 254)." For the dissent, the cop should have secured additional consent to search the paper bag in this case.

Parallel to *U.S. v. Ross*, which gives police the authority to thoroughly search a car when there is PC, *Jimeno* gives police the authority to thoroughly search a car when there is consent to the search. It is important to note that the consent once given can be retracted by the person granting the consent.

The request to search usually should contain its own limits due to what was asked to be searched. For example, a request to search for drugs—if granted—would allow an extensive and intrusive search whereas a search for a person would have much greater limits attached.

Authority and Third-Party Consent

Ordinarily, the person giving consent is authorized to grant that consent, and is the only person present to decide whether consent should be given. That person has a temporary or permanent right of possession of the property to be searched and thus is authorized to surrender Fourth Amendment rights and to give permission to search to the police. Important, it must appear to the officer that the person giving consent is actually authorized to give the consent.

Several decades ago the Supreme Court ruled that that right of possession applied to those renting a property such that the actual owners of the property would not be authorized to give consent to search. Thus, hotel clerks, among others, could not give consent to the police to search the room of a hotel guest (*Stoner v. California*, 376 U.S. 483, 1964).

What complicates an understanding of the law in this area is when more than one person has possession or at least appears to be in that position. Joint possession means there can be more than one person authorized to grant consent. It also means there could be a disagreement as to whether consent should be given. The rule is that the police need only one party to consent for jointly occupied premises (*U.S. v. Matlock*, 415 U.S. 164, 1974). The absence of a second party is not an obstacle to securing consent from the party that is present. Thus, a wife can consent against the husband (or vice versa), and parents can give consent against their children (but not the reverse). Essentially, co-habitation means that one surrenders a right to privacy (or REP) at least to all the areas shared with another (so this applies to roommates as well). Shared areas means shared authority to consent. But, non-shared areas also means no shared authority to consent. The wife's having a private office in the house results in the husband's lacking authority to give consent to search there. Children generally have no REP vis-à-vis their parents, but parents do not lose their REP to their children, except, perhaps, in jointly used areas, such as living and dining rooms, etc.

Of course, the more interesting scenario is when there is disagreement between the co-owners. In *Georgia v. Randolph* (547 U.S. 103, 2006), the wife had called to report a domestic disturbance, and, after the police arrived, accused her husband of drug use. The police asked the husband for consent to search and he said no. The wife then gave consent. The Supreme Court determined that the latter consent was invalidated by other co-owner's refusal to consent since this involved co-equal tenants. *Randolph* is considered a "narrow exception" to the one-tenant consent rule.

Also important is that *Randolph* doesn't hold if police enter to help one person collect belongings and get out of a residence safely or if domestic violence has happened or is about to occur. In *Fernandez v. California* (571 U.S. ___, 134 S.Ct. 1126, 2014), the police became aware of a domestic violence situation as they observed that the woman answering the door was bleeding. An officer asked her to come outside the apartment so they could conduct a protective sweep. Fernandez objected. The police arrested him, suspecting an assault against the woman (he was also independently identified as a robbery suspect by another witness). Fernandez was taken to police station. One officer returned to the apartment an hour later and secured the woman's consent to search. He found robbery items and drugs. The question in this case was whether *Randolph* applied here when joint authority goes opposite ways and the cops have removed the one objecting to the search. In this case, there was a legitimate reason to remove the objecting party. The Supreme Court refused to extend *Randolph* to this scenario, and upheld the search.

Apparent Authority Doctrine

Police can make mistakes in securing consent. The most likely mistake is assuming the person giving consent actually has the authority to give that consent. This mistake is included within the good faith exceptions to the exclusionary rule we covered in Chapter 2. The mistake will not bar the use of evidence provided the police had a reasonable belief that the person possessed common authority over the premises. In *Illinois v. Rodriguez* (497 U.S. 177, 1990), the police encountered a former girlfriend who had moved out of her boyfriend's house a month before the search; she still had a key.

As the Court had noted elsewhere, the police don't always have to be correct, but always have to be reasonable in their mistake. The Court held that they were here in this instance. The Court insisted that "(t)he Constitution is no more violated when officers enter without a warrant because they reasonably (though erroneously) believe that the person who has consented to their entry is a resident of the premises, than it is violated when they enter without a warrant because they reasonably (though erroneously) believe they are in pursuit of a violent felon who is about to escape (*Id.*, at 186)." The Court explained that the Fourth Amendment protects against unreasonable searches; it "does not demand that the government be factually correct in its assessment. . . (*Id.*, at 184)."

The dissent countered that there was no exigency here so the police should have gone for a warrant. As the dissent saw it: "Police officers, when faced with the choice of relying on consent by a third party or securing a warrant, should secure a warrant, and must therefore accept the risk of error should they instead choose to rely on consent (*Id.*, at 193)."

BORDER SEARCHES

Customs and Immigration officials are authorized to search for items for which the owner owes duty or anything that constitutes contraband. That search applies to any vehicle, person or beast, provided there is merchandise that fits description above. The authorities can board any vessel or vehicle, and search every part of them, including any person, trunk, package, or cargo. The agents can also interrogate any suspected alien as to a right to be in country.

The authorities can also board any vessel, railway car or conveyance "within a reasonable distance" of any external border so as to search for persons. Federal agents also conduct "area control" operations, which include traffic control and factory surveys (to discover workers). These are conducted so as to identify aliens who have entered the country illegally (*Immigration and Naturalization Service v. Delgado*, 466 U.S. 210, 1984). In the interior there are permanent checkpoints, temporary checkpoints and roving patrols that serve to detect illegal immigrants and merchandise.

Decades ago, the Court announced in *U.S. v. Ramsey* (431 U.S. 606, 1977): "That searches made at the border, pursuant to the longstanding right of the sovereign to protect itself by stopping and examining persons and property coming crossing into this country, are reasonable simply by virtue of the fact that they occur at the border, should, by now, require no extended demonstration." (*Id.*, at 616).

One of the more serious encounters between Customs agents and a foreign individual at the border occurred in *U.S. v. Montoya de Hernandez* (473 U.S. 531, 1985). In this case, a woman had make eight recent trips to Miami or Los Angeles from Columbia. She spoke no English, and had no family in the states. She said she came to the U.S. to purchase goods for her husband's store in Bogata. The agents thought she was a "balloon swallower" (had consumed drugs secreted in numerous balloons that she had swallowed to get by customs). The agents sent the suspect to a private area for a patdown and strip search. The agent at that location felt the woman's abdomen and felt firm fullness. The agent found no contraband but noticed she "was wearing two pair of elastic underpants with a paper towel lining the crotch area (*Id.*, at 534)." The suspect was asked and originally agreed to submit to an X-ray. However, she later said she was pregnant and withdrew the consent. After 16 hours she still had not defecated or urinated so customs officials sought a court order, which they received. They tested her for pregnancy, and the test disclosed she wasn't. A physician then conducted a rectal exam and removed a balloon containing drugs. The suspect was arrested. After 28 hours the suspect passed six similar balloons, while over the next four days she passed 88 balloons containing 528 grams of "80% pure cocaine hydrochloride."

The Supreme Court upheld this search, citing the historical reasoning behind and broad congressional authority granted to routine border searches that can be conducted without RS, PC or a warrant. Moreover, an extended detention at the border requires only RS, which the Court believed existed in this case. The two dissenting Justices (Brennan and Marshall) wanted a warrant for the search and PC to extend detention for so long.

More recently, the Supreme Court sanctioned extensive searches under the routine suspicionless category of border searches, including the authority to remove and take apart (and then reassemble) a vehicle's gas tank (*U.S. v. Flores-Montano*, 541 U.S. 149, 2004). The lower federal court had said this was beyond a routine border search. In this case, the suspect was asked to leave car while it was subjected to a secondary inspection. The customs agent tapped the gas tank and it sounded too solid. Then agents removed the gas tank and found 37 kilos of marijuana. The Court upheld the search.

Roving Patrols at the Border

Once a vehicle is located well within the interior of the country, however, it assumes the same legal status as a car on any other highway. In *Almeida-Sanchez v. U.S.* (413 U.S. 266, 1973), a car driving on Highway 78 in California, 25 miles north of the border, was stopped and searched by border patrol agents; regulations set by the Attorney General had identified 100 air miles as the permissible area for routine searches. Although the Court of Appeals had upheld the agents' actions, the Supreme Court, in a 5–4 decision, didn't think border enforcement justified such a search and said (consistent with *Ross*) that PC or consent was necessary for a vehicle search this far inside the country or the search is unreasonable.

Also consistent with "regular" traffic stops, the Court held in *U.S. v. Brignoni-Ponce* (422 U.S. 873, 1975) that the border patrol need to have RS to conduct a stop on I-5 in the San Clemente area. Similarly, the Court determined that agents having RS are authorized to stop cars and question drivers (*U.S. v. Cortez*, 449 U.S. 411, 1981). In *Cortez*, border agents had RS to believe the suspect was illegally transporting illegal immigrants and stopped his vehicle on Highway 86 in Arizona. The Court upheld the search.

Fixed Checkpoint at the Border

The Supreme Court applied *Almeida-Sanchez* to fixed checkpoints and demanded that PC or consent is needed to search vehicles even at fixed checkpoints (*U.S. v. Ortiz*, 422 U.S. 891, 1975). The border patrol had found three aliens in the trunk of the car, but the Court invalidated the search due to a lack of PC to believe illegal aliens would be found.

Important, however, is that a vehicle may be stopped at a fixed checkpoint for a brief questioning without any evidence (*U.S. v. Martinez-Fuerte*, 428 U.S. 543, 1976). With RS the border agents would then refer the vehicle to a secondary checkpoint for a more thorough investigation. The Ninth Circuit Court of Appeals had wanted RS to justify the initial stop. The Supreme Court disagreed and stressed that the initial stop was brief with limited intrusion. Beyond that, the Court also determined that "it is constitutional to refer motorists selectively to the secondary inspection area at . . . the checkpoint on the basis of criteria that would not sustain a roving-patrol stop. Thus, even if it be assumed that such referrals are made largely on the basis of apparent Mexican ancestry, we perceive no constitutional violation. . . . (*Id.*, at 563)." To search, the border agents still needed PC or consent.

The two dissenting Justices (Brennan and Marshall) posed a good question. They wanted to know why since appearance does not provide

RS sufficient to stop vehicles via a roving patrol, why can it serve as the basis for secondary referred point at fixed checkpoint.

EXIGENT CIRCUMSTANCES

Exigent—or emergency—circumstances will allow police to search without a warrant. The situations covered under this exception to the warrant requirement include:

- Hot pursuit;

- Preventing the destruction of evidence; and,

- Danger of physical harm to the police or public

The hot pursuit exception was established in *Warden v. Hayden* in 1967 (387 U.S. 294). In this case the police were in active pursuit of a robbery suspect and were told he had entered a house. The police secured consent from Hayden's wife to search the house. Inside the police found and arrested Hayden and later discovered in plain view a pistol, a shotgun and clothing that matched the description of clothing worn by the robbery suspect; the latter discoveries would today be said to have been found via a protective sweep. The Court upheld this search and established the hot pursuit exception to the warrant requirement. This case also initiated the "mere evidence" rule wherein items that corroborate the commission of a crime (such as clothing worn by the perpetrator) can be seized by police even though these items are not contraband or products of a crime.

The appropriateness of the destruction of evidence exception (also known as *evanescent* evidence) began a year earlier in *Schmerber v. California* (384 U.S. 757, 1966). *Schmerber* involved the potential loss of incriminating evidence and is better known for its connection to securing blood samples and will be examined in Chapter 10 (on identifying procedures).

The case that actually launched the exception was delivered in 1973. In *Cupp v. Murphy* (412 U.S. 291, 1973), an estranged husband was being questioned at the police station concerning the death of his wife.

During that conversation the police noticed what appeared to be a blood spot on the husband's finger. The husband was asked to provide scrapings from under his fingernails, refused to cooperate, and began to rub his hands behind his back. The police believed he was attempting to wipe off the blood stain and, without consent or a warrant, took fingernail samples. The samples turned out to have the victim's blood, skin, and clothing fabric in them. The Supreme Court ruled that PC exited for a search, no warrant was necessary due to the destructibility of the evidence and the limited nature of the intrusion. The Court concluded this after applying a totality of circumstances test.

A more recent case sort of combined hot pursuit and preventing the destruction of evidence exceptions. In *Kentucky v. King* (563 U.S. 452, 2011), the police were chasing a drug dealing suspect who escaped into an apartment complex. The police knew the suspect had escaped into one of two apartments, but had left their cars before the officer involved in the drug sale had radioed them that the apartment on the right was the correct one. The police approached the apartments and smelled marijuana emanating from the left one. They knocked on the door, announced their identity, heard what they thought was the destruction of evidence, and ultimately kicked in the door. King and others were found in the apartment smoking marijuana, and a subsequent protective sweep disclosed more drugs and cash. Although the trial court ruled against the motion to suppress, citing exigent circumstances, the Kentucky Supreme Court reversed the conviction, claiming the police should have known that their conduct would have encouraged the occupants of the apartment to destroy evidence. The U.S. Supreme Court held that exigent circumstances allowed the warrantless search. Since no one answered the knock on the door, and the police heard what they thought was the destruction of evidence, the warrantless entry and search were constitutional. Important, however, was that the police did not create an impermissible exigency or the search would not have been upheld, the Court explained. Here, there was a legal basis for the police actions, which were reasonable.

Crime scene investigations can qualify for the exigent circumstances category if conducted properly. No warrant is needed at the time of or immediately following the investigation of the causes of a fire (*Michigan v. Tyler*, 436 U.S. 499, 1978). But, as the Court noted in *Michigan v. Clifford* (464 U.S. 287, 1984) a warrant was needed for a search of a private residence conducted hours after a fire had been extinguished. The Court reaffirmed *Tyler* in *Mincey v. Arizona* (437 U.S. 385, 1978). Nevertheless, the Court invalidated this search of a homicide scene because it involved a four-day extensive search of the apartment from which two to three hundred objects were seized. The Court explained that the seriousness of the crime doesn't create its own exigency. The Arizona Supreme Court had created a "murder scene exception" to the warrant requirement as an addendum to the exigency exception. The U.S. Supreme rejected this doctrine and determined that the police may do an immediate inspection of a murder scene to see if there are other victims or if the offender is present (and anything seen in plain view is ok), but a search of this dimension requires a warrant.

It is difficult to determine the exact scope and requirements for the preventing danger to police/public aspect of the exigent circumstances category. A recent case detailed the Court's willingness to allow police to protect the public without waiting for a warrant to be issued. In *Brigham City, Utah v. Stuart et al.* (547 U.S. 398, 2006), police heard screams from inside a house. Inside were juveniles illegally drinking and engaging in a fight. The police heard screams and entered the residence. The Supreme Court upheld an "emergency aid exception" to the warrant requirement, believing it is a reasonable search and seizure. The Court observed: "One exigency obviating the requirement of a warrant is the need to assist persons who are seriously injured or threatened with such injury. . . . Accordingly, law enforcement officers may enter a home without a warrant to render emergency assistance to an injured occupant or to protect an occupant from imminent injury (*Id.*, at 403)." The Court also declared that it didn't matter that there might be a subjective motivation of the police to gather evidence, too. The police do not have to wait outside for a more serious blow to be inflicted, according to the Court.

ADMINISTRATIVE INSPECTIONS/ SEARCHES OF LICENSED PREMISES

The requirements of the Fourth Amendment tend to be relaxed when a non-law enforcement governmental action takes place. This is particularly applicable to various inspections carried out via code enforcement. Originally, the Supreme Court put no constitutional limits on health inspections (*Frank v. Maryland*, 359 U.S. 360, 1959). This was modified somewhat several years later in *Camara v. Municipal Court* (387 U.S. 523, 1967). In *Camara*, the Court ruled that warrants were required for nonemergency housing inspections, but that PC to believe there was a code violation was not necessary. These administrative inspections are not aimed at the discovery of crime (but that discovery is possible, of course), and there is limited invasion of privacy. This led the Court to hold that a modified warrant, explaining that an area is due for inspection, is all that is needed by the authorities. This warrant should limit the opportunity for the government to discriminate against any individuals and to demonstrate the legitimacy of the government action. In the same year, the Court applied this standard to a fire inspection of a commercial warehouse as well (*See v. City of Seattle*, 387 U.S. 541, 1967).

Historically, the Court has recognized several businesses that involve a high government interest (referred to as "closely regulated") and qualify for reduced or no REP. These businesses fall under the modified warrant category for inspections. They include liquor dealers (*Colonnade Corp. v. U.S.*, 397 U.S. 72, 1970), pawn shops that sell guns (*U.S. v. Biswell*, 406 U.S. 311, 1972), and automobile junkyards (*New York v. Burger*, 482 U.S. 691, 1987). As the Court noted in *Biswell*: "When a dealer chooses to engage in this pervasively regulated business and to accept a federal license, he does so with the knowledge that his business records, firearms, and ammunition will be subject to effective inspection (*Id.*, at 316)."

Typically, businesses of this nature require a license to operate, and the license is premised on an agreement to consent to search the premises of the business without a warrant or probable cause.

In *N.Y. v. Burger*, the Court held that warrantless inspections of junkyards are permitted even when there is a law enforcement purpose. The Burger Court developed criteria to determine whether a business would fall within the scope of this allowance:

- There must be a substantial government interest;

- The warrantless inspection must be necessary to further a regulatory scheme; and,

- The statute's inspection program must provide a "constitutionally adequate substitute for a warrant (*Id.*, at 692)." (i.e., "advise owner that the search is being made pursuant to the law and has a properly defined scope and it must limit the discretion of the inspecting officers." *Id.*, at 703).

The *Burger* Court characterized the automobile junkyard as a "pervasively regulated industry," and admitted that the purpose of administrative inspection was to deter criminal activity. New York City police conducted 5–10 inspections of vehicle dismantlers, junkyards, and related businesses daily. They copied down VIN numbers of several cars and parts, finding some to be stolen. The trial court denied the motion to suppress but the New York Court of Appeals (the state's highest court) reversed that decision and granted the motion because the purpose of the inspection was to find criminal activity. The NY court considered this to be a Fourth Amendment violation because the warrantless search was not geared to enforce a regulatory scheme. Nevertheless, the U.S. Supreme Court reversed the state court and determined this inspection satisfied the criteria it had established to gauge this type of search. The Court added that in such a closely regulated business there is no REP. The dissent in *Burger* disagreed and said the NY statute for junkyards authorized searches solely to uncover evidence of crime, and suggested the inspections were a mere pretext to search without PC.

SPECIAL NEEDS AREA

The *special needs* category was first mentioned in a concurring opinion by Justice Blackmun in *New Jersey v. TLO* (469 U.S. 325, 1985). The case involved searches conducted against juveniles by school personnel. The New Jersey Supreme Court had invalidated the search because the associate vice-principal lacked reasonable suspicion for the search. TLO had been accused of smoking in the girls' lavatory with a friend. Students at this time were permitted to carry cigarettes and even to smoke on campus, but in designated areas only, and the lavatory was not one of them. Consequently, TLO was accused of committing a violation of school rules. The associate vice-principal wanted to corroborate the accusation and thought that finding cigarettes in TLO's purse would sustain the allegation against her. Finding cigarettes on her person would not have corroborated the accusation, of course. Corroboration would have required finding DNA evidence linked to TLO on the spent cigarette in the lavatory. Without any evidence to support the presence of cigarettes in TLO's purse, nevertheless, the school official, against TLO's wishes, simply examined the contents of the purse and found cigarettes; removing the cigarettes led to his finding marijuana. The state court was ready to dispense with PC and a warrant, but wanted at least a reduced level of evidence (RS) for a search to be justified in a school setting.

The U.S. Supreme Court ruled that school searches required neither a warrant nor PC. In fact, even RS was not required to authorize a search of a student's private belongings (i.e., a school bag or purse and not a locker). Instead, the Court relied on the idea that school searches had to be reasonable in themselves. The Court said that the school official had *acted reasonably*. The search was upheld and the adjudication was reinstated.

In his concurrence, Justice Blackmun observed that school searches were "exceptional circumstances in which special needs, beyond the normal need for law enforcement, make the warrant and probable-cause requirement impracticable. . . (*Id.*, at 351)."

All special needs situations involve a balancing test of the intrusion on a person's privacy versus the special needs at hand. This means that these are not normal law enforcement situations such that some searches can be justified without either PC or a warrant. Purportedly, if the search is too closely related to a criminal justice purpose, the exception to the warrant requirement will not be recognized.

Not surprisingly, then, searches of employee workplaces by a public employer for work-related reasons have been upheld when only RS was present (*O'Connor v. Ortega*, 480 U.S. 709, 1987). More recently, the Supreme Court upheld a warrantless audit of a police department-owned pager. The audit captured text messages between two police officers that were sexually explicit. The officers were disciplined by the department and then sued the city but lost. The Ninth Circuit Court of Appeals then ruled that the search violated the officer's Fourth Amendment rights, even though it was conducted for a work-related reason. A unanimous U.S. Supreme Court, however, reversed the Ninth Circuit Court and held that this constituted a work-related search. Although the Court acknowledged that the officer had a REP, the search was reasonable under the special needs analysis (*City of Ontario, California v. Quon*, 560 U.S. 746, 2010).

The Supreme Court has applied the special needs warrant exemption to a variety of cases. In *Griffin v. Wisconsin* (483 U.S. 868, 1987), the Court upheld a warrantless search of a probationer based on RS only due to the special need to supervise a probationer. The probation officer conducted the search, which had been authorized by the conditions of Griffin's probation.

The Court reaffirmed *Griffin* in 2001 (*U.S. v. Knights*, 534 U.S. 112). Knights had been put on probation in California for a drug offense. A condition of his probation was to submit to a search of his person, car and property by a PO or LEO without a search warrant. A sheriff detective had RS to believe that Knights was involved in an arson of a Pacific Gas & Electric (PG&E) power transformer. The detective searched Knights' apartment and found arson and bomb-making materials together with a PG&E padlock. Knights was prosecuted in federal court. Most interesting, and puzzling, is that the District Court granted the MTS, finding that the detective's search was for "investigatory" and not "probationary" purposes. The Court of Appeals affirmed that decision. Inasmuch as not committing another crime is invariably a condition of probation, it is perplexing how investigating a possible crime does not fall within a "probationary" purpose. The paradox was eliminated by a unanimous Supreme Court that ruled the presence of RS and the condition of probation authorized the search in question. The Court also noted that a probationer was more likely to engage in crime that a non-offender.

In 1984, the Supreme Court determined that prison inmates lack a REP and thus there are no Fourth Amendment controls over the searches of their lockers or cells (*Hudson v. Palmer*, 468 U.S. 517, 1984). That case does not concern us since it involves searches conducted by corrections officers and not by LEOs. Nevertheless, the reasoning of that case was extended to parolees in *Samson v. California* (547 U.S. 843, 2006). *Samson* upheld a suspicionless search of a parolee by an LEO. The Court noted that, as in the prison environment, searches of parolees do not require RS or a warrant. In the Court's eyes, parolees have less REP than probationers since parole is "more akin to imprisonment than probation (*Id.*, at 851)." Parolees thus have diminished constitutional rights and do not have a REP. Moreover, Samson had signed an agreement that specified he could be searched by a parole officer or LEO "with or without a search warrant and with or without cause (*Id.*, at 843)."

Drug tests of various individuals have been approved within the special needs category, including:

- Railway employees involved in train accidents (*Skinner v. Railway Labor Executives' Association*, 489 U.S. 602, 1989);

- United States Customs Service employees seeking promotion to certain sensitive positions (*National Treasury Employees v. Von Raab*, 489 U.S. 656, 1989);

- High school students participating in interscholastic sports (*Vernonia School Dist. 47J v. Acton*, 515 U.S. 646, 1995); and,

- Middle and high school students participating in extracurricular activities (*Board of Education v. Earls*, 536 U.S. 822, 2002).

Interesting is that the Court determined that drug tests of candidates for designated state offices were unreasonable and were not entitled to inclusion in the special needs category (*Chandler v. Miller*, 520 U.S. 305, 1997). Not long after that decision the city of Charleston mandated urine tests for pregnant women seeking medical care if they were suspected of using cocaine. If they tested positive, they were threatened with prosecution if they did not participate in a treatment program. The Supreme Court invalidated that provision, declaring that it had too much of a law enforcement purpose and did not constitute special needs (*Ferguson v. City of Charleston*, 532 U.S. 67, 2001).

Box 6-2: Special Case Exception to Incident to Arrest: The Cell Phone

In a very recent case, the U.S. Supreme Court put very important brakes on the search incident to arrest category. The search involved searching the digital record of an arrestee's cell phone. In *Riley v. California* (and *U.S. v. Wurie*, 573 U.S. 783, 2014) the Court announced: "The police generally may not, without a warrant, search digital information on a cell phone seized from an individual who has been arrested (*Id.*, at 434)." The Court explained that there is a huge difference between a typical search of an arrestee incident to arrest and the search of a cell phone. In the latter there is an amount of information that is simply too immense, complex, and private. Riley was involved in a traffic stop. His car was impounded because of traffic violations. The police conducted an inventory search and found weapons for which he was arrested. His smart phone provided information that implicated Riley in a gang-related shooting so he was charged accordingly. Wurie was observed making a drug sale. He was arrested and taken to the police station. The police found a flip phone on his person that provided information that served as a basis for securing a warrant. The police served that warrant and found crack and other drug paraphernalia and weapons. The Supreme Court ultimately demanded warrants for these types of search, despite the fact that the phones were discovered incident to arrest. The Court noted the original purposes of allowing this warrantless search (i.e., protection of the officer and preservation of evidence) and offered: "The digital data stored on cell phones does not present either *Chimel* risk (*Id.*, at 435)." Emphasizing the uniqueness of the cell phone search the Court observed that there are "privacy concerns far beyond those implicated by the search of a cigarette pack, a wallet, or a purse. (*Id.*, at 446)" The Court understood the costs this ruling had on policing, but countered: "We cannot deny that our decision today will have an impact on the ability of law enforcement to combat crime. Cell phones have become important tools in facilitating coordination and communication among members of criminal enterprises, and can provide valuable incriminating information about dangerous criminals. Privacy comes at a cost. (*Id.*, at 451)."

CHAPTER 7

Electronic Surveillance

There is relatively little constitutional law surrounding the area of electronic surveillance. Most of the regulations and restrictions have emerged from legislative statutes, typically prohibiting the interception and divulging of communications between and among non-consenting parties.

It should also be noted from the outset that the Fifth Amendment's protection against self-incrimination offers no help to someone objecting to his/her overheard comments since the remarks will not be the product of an interrogation or questioning by police authorities (see Chapter 9).

Meanwhile, the Fourth Amendment was originally depicted by the Supreme Court as not relevant to the major method of electronic surveillance, namely, wiretapping. In *Olmstead v. U.S.* (277 U.S. 438), delivered in 1928, the Court declared that there must be a trespass into a "constitutionally protected area" for the Fourth Amendment to be violated. In other words, a physical intrusion of some sort had to be involved. The wiretapping involved in this case occurred outside the suspect's home so there was no physical intrusion into a protected area. Moreover, there was also no physical seizure, which the Fourth Amendment required. All that was seized was a conversation and words are not physical items. Here the Supreme Court was adopting a literal and Eighteenth Century-focused view of the Amendment, not allowing for any evolution in the ways in which "evidence" could be "seized" by the government.

The Court maintained its physical orientation in Fourth Amendment matters for several decades. While the use of a detectaphone by federal agents to overhear a conversation in an adjoining apartment was permissible without a warrant (*Goldman v. U.S.*, 316 U.S. 129, 1942), inserting a "spike-mike" through a wall so that federal agents could hear what was said in the next room was invalid, due to the literal penetration involved with the device (*Silverman v. U.S.*, 365 U.S. 505, 1961). The government was also allowed to use radio transmitters so that federal agents could hear statements made to an undercover agent by an unknowing suspect since no trespass was involved (nor was there any fraud) (*On Lee v. U.S.*, 343 U.S. 747, 1952); hidden recording devices were also given a green light (*Osborn v. U.S.*, 385 U.S. 323, 1966).

The Supreme Court put an end to the unregulated capture of private conversations in 1967. In *Katz v. U.S.* (389 U.S. 347, 1967), the Court held that any type of electronic surveillance can amount to a violation of an expectation of privacy; trespass was no longer necessary. In *Katz*, federal agents had attached a listening device to the outside of a phone booth; the suspect was using the phone to transmit wagering information across state lines. The Court famously noted that the Fourth Amendment "protects people rather than places." Of course, it protects both as we have seen. Henceforth, policing authorities would need a warrant in order to intercept conversations conducted in most contexts. As we have seen, Justice Harlan's concurring opinion, stressing the need for the expectation of privacy to be "reasonable" (as opposed to being merely subjective) has actually been adopted by a majority of the Supreme Court as the surviving principle set by the *Katz* decision.

Since *Katz*, Congress has established the critical legislation concerning electronic surveillance in Title III of Omnibus Crime Control and Safe Streets Act of 1968. The Act stipulates that there can be no wiretapping or interception of wire communications (or use of any electronic devices to intercept communications) unless the police secure a court order or the consent of one of the parties; state law must also authorize it.

As noted earlier, current law in the electronic surveillance area is dominated by legislative enactments; warrants issued by judges, pretty strictly controlling the gathering of evidence via that medium, is the norm today. Since *Katz*, most of the rulings in the electronic surveillance area have gone "against" the use of monitoring devices.

U.S. v. Knotts (460 U.S. 276, 1983) was a victory for law enforcement, however. In *Knotts*, the Supreme Court allowed police to place a beeper in a car that travelled on a public highway. The Court considered this activity to not be a search because there was no REP. Here, cops learned nothing other than what they could have learned via visually observing the car's travels; all the monitoring occurred in a public place. Important is that the beeper was placed in a container and that the owner had given permission for the beeper to be inserted in the container before the defendant came into possession of it. The beeper revealed only the car's location.

The location of the monitoring proved critical in *U.S. v. Karo* (468 U.S. 705, 1984). Police had also inserted a device in a car in this case, this time it was a homing device in a can. The surveillance lasted several months and agents followed the can's movement (within the car) to a variety of locations, including houses and commercial facilities. The agents then secured a warrant for one of the houses. The Court determined that this warrant violated the Fourth Amendment. The Court observed: "The monitoring of a beeper in a private residence, a location not opened to visual surveillance, violates the Fourth Amendment rights of those who have a justifiable interest in the privacy of the residence (*Id.*, at 706)." In this situation the device surreptitiously gave agents access to a person's house since it verified the presence of the can there. Karo's conviction was not reversed, however, since the Court believed there was sufficient legally seized evidence (apart from the illegal search) to uphold the conviction.

We saw in Chapter 4 that the Court disallowed the use of a thermal imaging device in *Kyllo v. U.S.* (533 U.S. 27, 2001). The police had used the device to detect heat emanating from a house in order to detect the presence of a grow house. The device disclosed that the roof over the garage was much hotter than other parts of the roof (the same applied to a side wall of house. The police used this information as well as utility bills (and information from informants) to secure a search warrant; they found more than 100 marijuana plants. The Court said using this device constituted a search within the Fourth Amendment. The Court considered use of the device without a warrant was impermissible since it was not in general public use and allowed the authorities to examine details of the house that only a physical intrusion would disclose. The majority explained that it thought "that obtaining by sense-enhancing technology any information that could not otherwise have been obtained without physical intrusion into a constitutionally protected area constitutes a search, at least where (as here) the technology in question is not in general public use (*Id.*, at 34)." The dissent saw no constitutional problem in the case because the thermal imaging device disclosed only heat emanating from the external part of house, did not involve an entry into the house, and did not detect private activities within the house.

Chapter 4 also detailed the limitations of the use of GPS tracking devices in *U.S. v. Jones* (565 U.S. 400, 2012). The police had a search warrant for a GPS tracking device, which was placed on the vehicle of the suspect's wife while it was parked in a public lot; the vehicle's movements were tracked for 28 days beyond the time permitted via the warrant. The GPS disclosed that the jeep had been driven to a drug house where large amounts of drugs had been found. Interesting is that the Court (unanimously) found a search had occurred due to there being a physical intrusion by the police. It didn't matter whether there was a REP, according to the Court. Important was that the police had physically intruded on the defendant's property, and that they did this to find something or obtain information. Here, there was an intrusion on the owner's property. Writing for the majority, Justice Scalia believed this physical intrusion would have been considered a search when the Fourth Amendment was adopted (an originalist perspective).

Another interesting facet of the case is that three of the more liberal Justices (Ginsburg, Breyer and Kagan) agreed with the outcome but only because the length of the GPS monitoring was too long. They made a cogent point: "If the police attach a GPS device to a car and use the device to follow the car for even a brief time, under the Court's theory, the Fourth Amendment applies. But if the police follow the same car for a much longer period using unmarked cars and aerial assistance, this tracking is not subject to any Fourth Amendment constraints (*Id.*, at 931)." These Justices (together with Justice Alito) see the length of surveillance as what constituted a search. Now with Justice Scalia gone the future viability of this decision remains unclear.

CHAPTER 8

Undercover Investigations and Entrapment

UNDERCOVER INVESTIGATIONS

The constitutional law in the use of secret agents is also relatively sparse. As mentioned in Chapter 4, there is no Fourth Amendment protection when an undercover LEO or an informant is permitted access by a suspect into his/her home. The U.S. Supreme Court put it succinctly in *Hoffa v. U.S.* (385 U.S. 293, 1966): "Neither this Court nor any member of it has ever expressed the view that the Fourth Amendment protects a wrongdoer's misplaced belief that a person to whom he voluntarily confides his wrongdoing will not reveal it (*Id.*, at 302)." Invitation, here, amounts to consent in terms of entering the house or business, and whatever the agent/informant sees in plain view has been discovered without a search or any constitutional violation having occurred.

The undercover agent/informant can be wired too (*U.S. v. White,* 401 U.S. 745, 1971). As long as the agent is entitled to hear what is being heard, recording and/or transmitting the dialogue amounts to the same thing; taping is not equal to a search. Interesting, the dissent did not like the recording aspect and wanted agents to have a warrant in order to perform that function.

The Fifth Amendment is of no help as well. The conversation between the suspect and the agent while it may be considered an interrogation, it is certainly not compulsory; the conversations are voluntary (*Hoffa v. U.S.*, 385 U.S. 293, 1966).

The same applies even when the suspect and the agent are in jail. The Supreme Court considers the jail to not be a police-dominated atmosphere; no compulsion was employed by the agent in eliciting the conversation (*Illinois v. Perkins*, 496 U.S. 292, 1990). As the Court saw it, the situation represented simply an incarcerated person speaking freely to someone he thought was a fellow inmate. The Court remarked: "*Miranda* forbids coercion, not mere strategic deception by taking advantage of a suspect's misplaced trust in one he supposes to be a fellow prisoner (*Id.*, at 297)."

The one constitutional right that can have relevance to this area is the right to counsel, but even this right is limited in nature. To be sure, there is no right to counsel while any conversations or transactions between the suspect and the agent/informant are underway. Where the right to counsel attaches is when the suspect has become a defendant and has already been charged/indicted. Early on the Supreme Court ruled that post-indictment contacts with a defendant who had already hired an attorney were a violation of the Sixth Amendment (*Messiah v. U.S.*, 377 U.S. 201, 1964). The Court later reaffirmed this position in *U.S. v. Henry* (447 U.S. 264, 1980) where a government informant elicited evidence from a cellmate. The Court found this behavior to be unconstitutional even though the informant had been instructed to simply listed to the inmate and not ask any questions. Although the informant followed those instructions, the Court ruled the statements were inadmissible because there was too much conversation between the two parties. The dissent thought the informant had acted properly since he had not *prompted* the inmate.

The exception to this is that the Court has allowed statements to be obtained from a defendant when the informant is completely passive or when the statements are spontaneous and unsolicited (*Kuhlman v. Wilson*, 477 U.S. 436, 1986). And although an informant certainly can't ask about any crime that is in the post-indictment stage, it is okay to elicit information on other non-charged crimes (*Maine v. Moulton*, 474 U.S. 159, 1985).

ENTRAPMENT

Entrapment involves a crime that would not have occurred without the assistance of the government. The government's assistance is necessary since, contrary to popular thought, perhaps, it is not possible to be entrapped into committing a crime by a fellow civilian (unless that person is a government informant or any person acting under the control or direction of a LEO). The pivotal questions center around how much assistance the government rendered, and what type of person is the defendant. Although the defense is not of constitutional dimension, it could be a violation of *due process* (or an unfairness) to be entrapped into committing a crime by the government.

There are two possible tests to determine the plausibility of an entrapment defense. The first is *subjective* and focuses on the *character of the defendant*. The second is *objective* and examines the *behavior of the government agent*.

The critical question is where did the intent to commit the crime originate? Did the idea emanate from the mind of the offender or was it the creative activities of a LEO.

The subjective test appears to have the stronger acceptance by the U.S. Supreme Court (*U.S. v. Russell*, 411 U.S. 423, 1973; *Hampton v. U.S.*, 425 U.S. 484, 1976). Simply put, if the defendant appears to have a predisposition to commit the crime at hand, an entrapment defense is very unlikely to prevail. As the Court sees it, if an accused has a history (or perhaps reputation) of dealing in crime, any instigation on the part of the government in setting up this criminal incident merely provided the defendant "another" opportunity to engage in crime. The government, in effect, did not create something out of nothing. Often, the government will set up a sting (perhaps to ferret out police corruption or misbehaviors by judges or politicians) and will film the interactions between the target and the agent. If the former discloses a propensity to engage in the proposed criminal actions, he/she has not been entrapped; at most, he/she has been enabled. Those supporting the subjective test will insist that the only way to unearth certain crimes (especially "victimless" crimes like bribery, drug sales) is to get down and dirty with predisposed offenders and to allow a crime to unfold. Otherwise, these offenders and their illegal behaviors remain hidden. As the Court sees it, undercover stings are the only way to suppress the drug trade, and police behavior here does not violate fundamental fairness or amount to a shocking of the conscience.

Moreover, the Court has upheld convictions of those appearing to be predisposed even when the government supplied a legal but indispensable ingredient for committing the crime (an essential chemical for manufacturing methamphetamine) (*U.S. v. Russell*), and also when the government supplied an illegal ingredient (heroin) to complete the crime (a drug sale) (*Hampton v. U.S.*).

On the other hand, if the defendant truly had no predisposition discernible via a criminal record or reputation and does not reveal him/herself on film as anxious to commit the proposed crime, an entrapment defense can lead to exonerating the accused. In fact, federal law requires the government to show predisposition before launching a sting.

The objective test is supported by those who believe the government should not at all be engaged in the business of manufacturing crime; if the government had not instigated this crime, no crime would have occurred. Here, the question is whether the police conduct amounts to improper use of government power. The U.S. Supreme Court has indicated that it would extend an entrapment defense even to a predisposed offender when the government's behavior was outrageous (*Jacobson v. U.S.*, 503 U.S. 540, 1992). Were this to happen the Supreme Court would most likely find the police officer's behavior to be a violation of due process rather than entrapment per se.

CHAPTER 9

Miranda and Custodial Interrogations

The U.S. Supreme Court has been concerned about suspect's tendering involuntary statements for more than 125 years, long before the infamous *Miranda* decision of 1966 attempted to regulate the police interrogation stage of the criminal justice process.

INITIAL CONCERNS FOR INVOLUNTARY CONFESSIONS: THE VOLUNTARINESS TEST

The Court's first focus on the admissibility of a confession centered on its voluntariness. This was a standard inherited from common law. The thinking back then (and still today) was than an involuntary confession is unreliable (*Hopt v. U.S.*, 110 U.S. 574, 1884). A coerced confession was regarded as incompetent and federal cases were evaluated directly under the command of the Fifth Amendment such that individuals may not be compelled to be witnesses against themselves (*Bram v. U.S.*, 168 U.S. 532, 1897).

When state cases were first examined by the Supreme Court the Fourteenth Amendment Due Process Clause was the focus and not the Fifth Amendment because the latter had not yet been incorporated (*Brown v. Mississippi*, 297 U.S. 278, 1936). The reliability of the statement was still the major concern. But it was coercion that violated due process. Brown was hanged, whipped, beaten multiple times and was told this would continue until he confessed; he finally did. The Supreme Court adopted a *fundamental rights* approach, such that the right to be free from coercion in police interrogation was critically important, a fundamental right made applicable to the states via the Fourteenth Amendment. The Court characterized the police tactics in *Brown* as shocking to the conscience. The Court would employ this criterion eventually to searches they invalidated on a case-by-case basis prior to the *Mapp* decision (see Chapter 2).

Eventually, the Court launched a voluntariness test that would evolve and expand by adding factors to the test. As the 1930s yielded to the 1940s and 1950s, the Court became increasingly inclined to assume control over and to supervise the way both federal and state police operated in general and interrogated people in particular.

EXPANDING THE VOLUNTARINESS TEST

Before the major criminal justice renovations performed by the Warren Court in the 1960s, the Justices revealed a change in perspective towards involuntary confessions:

> The abhorrence of society to the use of involuntary confessions does not turn alone on their inherent untrustworthiness. It also turns on the deep-rooted feeling that the police must obey the law while enforcing the law; that in the end life and liberty can be as much endangered from illegal methods used to convict those thought to be criminals as from the actual criminals themselves. (*Spano v. New York*, 360 U.S. 315, 320–321, 1959).

So it became clear that reliability was not the only concern regarding involuntary confessions. The Court expressed displeasure with what might be called "offensive police tactics." In *Rogers v. Richmond* (365 U.S. 534, 1961) the police were trying to get the suspect to confess so they lied to him about their intent to interrogate his wife.

He confessed and the statement was ruled admissible by the trial judge due to its apparent truthfulness. The police had not secured an unreliable confession, according to the state court. The U.S. Supreme Court reversed this decision, however, stating that truth and accuracy are not sufficient to render admissible what is *not a fully voluntary* confession. The Court announced that henceforth its analysis of suspects' statements would focus

> on the question whether the behavior of the State's law enforcement officials was such as to overbear petitioner's will to resist and to bring about confessions not freely self-determined—a question to be answered with complete disregard of whether or not petitioner in fact spoke the truth (*Id.*, at 544).

The Court explained that we have an accusatorial system of justice, not an inquisitorial one.

Two years later, in *Townsend v. Sain* (372 U.S. 293, 1963), the police obtained a confession from a suspect who had been given a drug by the police that had had the effect of truth serum; the police were unaware of the drug's effects. Nevertheless, the Court disallowed the confession despite its potential accuracy and reliability (and the absence of knowingly wrongful police conduct).

The next year, the Court ruled that the judge needed to determine the voluntariness of a confession and not the jury. The Court feared that a jury could be so influenced by the accuracy of a confession that it would refuse to find an involuntary confession to be such (*Jackson v. Denno*, 378 U.S. 368, 1964).

FEDERAL RULES AND THE VOLUNTARINESS REQUIREMENT

While the Supreme Court was developing the voluntariness test through state cases, the federal system had been observing the same voluntariness test plus what was known as the *McNabb-Mallory Rule*.

McNabb involved a case in which a federal agent had been killed (*McNabb v. U.S.,* 318 U.S. 332, 1943; see, also, *Upshaw v. U.S.,* 335 U.S. 410, 1948). Several McNabb family members were held for 14 hours in detention and then interrogated for two days without having been arraigned by a federal magistrate. The police secured confessions that were instrumental in convicting the McNabbs of murder charges.

Similarly, the issue in *Mallory v. U.S.* (354 U.S. 449, 1957) was an interrogation that lasted more than seven hours prior to the suspect's being arraigned. The Court ruled in both cases that the confessions had to be suppressed because they had been obtained in violation of federal law that prohibited a period of unnecessary delay in bringing the accused before a federal magistrate in order to be arraigned.

The Supreme Court was gradually expanding its control over and management of the police interrogation process in both the state and federal systems.

PRELIMINARY WORK ON A RIGHT TO COUNSEL AT INTERROGATION

While the voluntariness test was evolving the Supreme Court was also starting to recognize a right to counsel at the police interrogation stage. In *Cooker v. California* (357 U.S. 433, 1958), the Court held a confession to be voluntary and admissible despite the fact that the accused's request to consult his lawyer had been denied. Cooker had agreed to talk to the police, but only in the presence of counsel. While the ruling was not surprising at this time, the more important historical feature was that four Justices (Douglas, Warren, Black, Brennan) dissented in the case, claiming that a suspect who wants to confer with an attorney following arrest should be allowed to do so.

The next year, the Court found that an 8-hour interrogation of a suspect had produced an involuntary confession and ruled it must be suppressed (*Spano v. New York*, 360 U.S. 315, 1959). More important, however, Justice Stewart joined the group of Justices that believed that statement was secured in violation of a right to counsel since Spano had already been indicted at this time.

THE FINAL PRE-*MIRANDA* DEVELOPMENT: THE FIFTH AND SIXTH AMENDMENTS MEET AT INTERROGATION IN *ESCOBEDO*

For quite some time the Fifth Amendment right to not self-incriminate was perceived as a trial-related right with little or no applicability to the police station. As we just saw, the interrogation phase in state prosecutions was originally regulated via the Fourteenth Amendment Due Process Clause since the Fifth Amendment had not been applied to the states. All this changed with critical decisions delivered by the Warren Court.

The Fifth Amendment self-incrimination provision was finally incorporated into state law in 1964 in *Malloy v. Hogan* (378 U.S. 1). The voluntariness test, based as it was on the Fourteenth Amendment Due Process Clause, was ripe for being replaced.

Leading up to the infamous *Miranda* decision, while the Court was still developing the voluntariness test, the Court also resolved the denial of counsel at interrogation shortly before *Miranda* in *Escobedo v. Illinois* (378 U.S. 478, 1964). Escobedo specifically and repeatedly asked for counsel, one he had retained (so not a public defender), was denied that request, and ultimately confessed. The Supreme Court handed down a decision that anticipated *Miranda*. The Court declared that denying Escobedo an opportunity to consult counsel was a Sixth Amendment violation, which invalidated the confession. The Court employed a TOC test to evaluate the confession:

- The investigation had begun to focus on Escobedo;

- Escobedo was in police custody;

- The interrogation had aimed to elicit incriminating statements;

- Suspect had requested and was denied access to his lawyer; and,

- The police had not effectively warned him of his absolute right to remain silent.

This led the Court to conclude that Escobedo had been denied assistance of counsel in violation of the Sixth Amendment, and that no statements could be used against him even though they were voluntary. The Supreme Court had obviously abandoned the narrow contents of the voluntariness test. Strictly speaking, the Fifth Amendment prohibits only "compelled" testimony. The Court went beyond these words in invalidating voluntary statements. Moreover, the Court strongly suggested that the validity of future confessions would be evaluated, in part, by whether the suspect had been warned of a right to silence at interrogation (prior to *Miranda).* That *Malloy v. Hogan* had just incorporated the Fifth Amendment a week earlier and that *Gideon v. Wainwright* (372 U.S. 335, 1963) had just incorporated the Sixth Amendment a little more than a year earlier probably facilitated the Court's decision in *Escobedo.*

It is interesting that *Escobedo* had a Sixth Amendment foundation (the ruling was he was denied effective assistance of counsel) that ended with a Fifth Amendment add-on (police better warn suspects of a right to silence). Within two years, *Miranda* would accomplish the reverse.

MIRANDA AND THE MARRIAGE OF 5TH AND 6TH AMENDMENT RIGHTS AT INTERROGATION

Ernesto Miranda was arrested and charged with rape and kidnapping. He was interrogated for two hours, gave an oral confession and then signed a written confession. Although the statement was submitted on a form that mentioned an acknowledgement that statements could be used against the signer, there had been no warnings given to Miranda concerning a right to silence or counsel. The confession was admitted at his trial, he was convicted and given a 20–

30 year sentence in prison. The state appellate courts upheld his conviction (the confession was considered voluntary) and Miranda appealed to the U.S. Supreme Court, which reversed the conviction (*Miranda v. Arizona*, 384 U.S. 436, 1966).

Miranda had not requested to speak with an attorney, and the decision does not have a Sixth Amendment foundation, per se; if not questioned, the suspect does not have to be provided counsel. The Supreme Court reached its 5–4 decision due to a perceived violation of the Fifth Amendment; the Court's movement away from sole reliance on the voluntariness test to examine suspects' confessions furthered by *Escobedo* reached fulfillment in *Miranda*. The dissent lost its argument that the Fifth Amendment prohibited only compelled statements. Essentially, the Court determined that any confession tendered without the suspect's having been given explicit warnings as to a right to both silence and counsel would be considered presumptively invalid. The Court noted:

> The Fifth Amendment privilege is so fundamental to our system of constitutional rule and the expedient of giving an adequate warning as to the availability of the privilege so simple, we will not pause to inquire in individual cases whether the defendant was aware of his rights without a warning being given. . . . (*Id.*, at 468).

Miranda ended any the idea that confessions tendered at the police station were not covered by the Fifth Amendment, holding that custodial interrogation directly triggered Fifth Amendment concerns and protections. The thinking here would be that the Fifth amendment right not to be compelled to testify against yourself (decidedly a trial-related provision) does one little good if the police can accumulate evidence from the accused via an illegal interrogation. In other words, to be effective, the trial-oriented protection needed to be "walked back" to the interrogation stage. In fact, the Court saw the Amendment's protection as more critical in the police station than in the courtrooms "where there are often impartial observers to guard against intimidation or trickery (*Id.*, at 461)."

Although strictly speaking *Miranda* is a Fifth Amendment case, the Court also developed a Sixth Amendment right to counsel at interrogation, which was designed to protect the Fifth Amendment right to silence. As the Court offered, "the right to have counsel present at the interrogation is indispensable to the protection of the Fifth Amendment privilege. . . . (*Id.*, at 469)." To make the rights to silence and counsel effective the Court believed the accused needs to be apprised of having those rights in the first place.

Altogether, *Miranda* commanded police to issue four warnings before interrogating a suspect who is in custody: two apply to a right to silence (the right to silence and any statements can be used against the accused in court), and two apply to a right to counsel (the right to the presence of an attorney and one will be appointed, if the suspect is indigent).

CONSTITUTIONALITY OF *MIRANDA* RESOLVED 34 YEARS LATER IN *DICKERSON V. UNITED STATES*

As we saw *Miranda* was delivered in 1966. Two years later, Congress passed a law that stated confessions secured by federal law enforcement had to be voluntary, but without any need to comply with *Miranda* (Omnibus Crime Control and Safe Streets Act of 1968; see Title 18 USC Section 3501(a)). That law sat dormant for decades because federal LEOs observed *Miranda* and there had not been a confession obtained without *Miranda* that was justified by the government as being voluntary and admissible even though *Miranda* had not been given. There was finally an appeal by a defendant directly challenging that law in 2000.

Between 1966 and 2000 the Supreme Court issued numerous rulings narrowing and limiting *Miranda*, especially form the mid-1970s on. This was due to the Court's being more conservative and law and order oriented. The Justices dominating the Court during those years mostly perceived *Miranda* as an obstacle to effective police interrogation. Most of the remainder of this chapter will detail the many ways in which the Court reduced the impact of *Miranda* during those years (and afterwards as well). In the midst of this restructuring of *Miranda*, and after the Court had questioned the constitutionality of *Miranda* on numerous occasions, the Court was required to answer, once and for all, whether *Miranda* enjoyed constitutional status.

The Court of Appeals handling the matter prior to its reaching the Supreme Court had "concluded that the protections announced in *Miranda* are not constitutionally required (*Id.*, at 438)." Thus, the Supreme Court had been handed an opportunity to simply agree with and uphold a lower court's decision. It had to surprise many pundits when the Court held, in a 7–2 decision, that *Miranda* was, indeed, of constitutional dimension. Perhaps most surprising is that Chief Justice Rehnquist, long considered as the most vocal opponent of *Miranda,* wrote the decision. That surprise had to have been tempered, somewhat, when the decision was read and the Court's very lukewarm support of *Miranda* was revealed. If there was ever going to be a "killing with soft praise" or a "left handed compliment" among Supreme Court rulings, the *Dickerson* decision was it. Essentially, the Court explained there were four reasons why *Miranda* must be constitutionally based. First, Rehnquist explained that *Miranda* and two companion cases that had involved three states (Arizona, California, and New York) and the Court has consistently applied the *Miranda* rule to state prosecutions, which can happen only when a constitutional principle is present. As we noted in the first chapter, the Supreme Court can dictate to the states only when a constitutional law/right is involved. If the matter is not constitutional in origin, the Court has no authority over the states. Moreover, the Court observed that in *Miranda* there are numerous occasions in which the majority was announcing what it considered to be a constitutional rule. Chief Justice Rehnquist then noted that a constitutional rule cannot be superseded by an act of congress. So, if the Justices portray it as constitutional it must be. Not exactly a ringing endorsement or strong declaratory statement of the need for and status of Miranda.

Second, the Court acknowledged that *Miranda* was probably the most effective way in which to prevent coerced confessions. This was the most (and only) positive remark concerning *Miranda* in the decision.

Third, Chief Justice Rehnquist noted that the Court adheres to *stare decisis*, meaning deference is given to established precedents and reversing previous decisions is not a maneuver taken lightly or often, and only when very necessary or when there is some "special justification." The Court saw none here and observed that *Miranda* had actually become part of our culture. In an attempt to square the many limitations on *Miranda* the Court had created over three decades (at that point) with a constitutional principle, the Court wrote that its "cases have reduced the impact of the *Miranda* rule on legitimate law enforcement while reaffirming the decision's core ruling that unwarned statements may not be used as evidence in the prosecution's case in chief (*Id.*, at 443–44)."

Finally, in what might be perceived as a self-serving way, the Court offered that employing a totality of circumstances test (or voluntariness test) for all confessions (the alternative to *Miranda*) would be unmanageable for both police and the courts. Although each confession must be voluntary, requiring *Miranda* means that an involuntary confession is that much more unlikely. In other words, successful and faithful employment of *Miranda* allows each confession to enjoy a presumption of validity and removes the need to carefully scrutinize each and every confession.

The dissent (Justices Scalia and Thomas) criticized the ruling as expanding the constitution such that the Court was effectively amending the constitution by adopting *Miranda* warnings as constitutional law.

MIRANDA: CRITICAL QUESTIONS AND ESSENTIAL INGREDIENTS

There are *four critical questions* that can be raised via litigation regarding all custodial interrogations:

- Were warnings necessary and were they given prior to interrogation;

- Did the offender understand the warnings;

- Did the offender invoke or waive the rights; and,

- Was the waiver voluntary and intelligent?

There are *four ingredients* that are *all necessary* for *Miranda* to be relevant. From the beginning the Court has required

- the *police*

- to conduct an *interrogation*

- concerning a *crime*

- of a suspect in *custody*.

The four questions have not changed since the *Miranda* ruling was handed down. What has happened is that the Court has modified, sometimes significantly, the elements of when and how *Miranda* must be administered. We will see, below, how the Court has modified the giving, invoking and waiving of *Miranda*.

Although the ingredients have not changed, either, there have been some adjustments of the original understanding of *Miranda's* applicability to these conditions. The modifications have gone both ways: The Court has moderately *extended* the cause of *Miranda* in terms of how the *police and crime* are necessary ingredients, and has both *extended and contracted* the reach of *Miranda* in terms of what constitutes *interrogation and custody*.

MODEST EXTENSIONS OF *MIRANDA*

The extensions of *Miranda*, with one notable exception, have been modest and can be covered quickly.

The *Where* Element of *Miranda* Warnings

The *Miranda* decision was influenced, in no small part, by the inherent intimidation of the police station. Even still the Court decided to take *Miranda* out of the station to *anywhere* there is custodial interrogation conducted by the police, including questioning for a few minutes in a suspect's bedroom (*Orozco v. Texas*, 394 U.S. 324, 1969); the questioning occurred at 4AM, however.

Warnings *for Whom* Element (i.e., The Crime Involved)

In *Berkemer v. McCarty* (468 U.S. 420, 1984), to the surprise of some, the Supreme Court extended *Miranda* to misdemeanor offenses. *Miranda* was held to apply to all crimes and not just major ones. Originally, it was thought that *Miranda* applied to major crimes only (much like search incident to arrest was thought to be) and not to DUIs as in *Berkemer*. *Berkemer* created a *bright line rule* such that all crimes that result in arrest/custody make *Miranda* relevant to any interrogation resulting from the arrest. Interesting is that *Berkemer* both extended *Miranda* and also restricted it by holding that traffic stops do not qualify as custodial situations (see Chapter 5 and section below).

Warnings *by Whom*

The Supreme Court has not strayed far from the original premise that *Miranda* needs to be given by police or by someone operating under the control or direction of police only. The only exception to this, thus far, was for a psychiatrist who interviewed a defendant raising an insanity defense. An issue arose as to the psychiatrist's testifying at the defendant's death penalty sentencing hearing. The psychiatrist testified that the defendant had no remorse and was a continuously dangerous person (an aggravating factor used to sentence the offender to death). The Supreme Court ruled that *Miranda* should have been given in this context (*Estelle v. Smith*, 451 U.S. 454, 1981). No warnings are necessary if the psychiatrist is offering standard testimony as to competency to stand trial or the insanity defense, however.

What Is Interrogation?

As to interrogation, one item that is very clear (and has been since the early days of *Miranda*) is that volunteered statements are not the product of interrogation. When an accused spontaneously offers a statement it is not necessary that the police had *Mirandized* the accused prior to the utterance in order to use the statement at trial.

One way in which *Miranda* has been expanded is "indirect" interrogation. The original case involved what became known, famously, as the "Christian Burial Speech" (*Brewer v. Williams*, 430 U.S. 387, 1977). Williams had been arrested and *Mirandized* regarding a homicide of a young girl. His lawyer instructed the police not to interrogate his client. During the transportation of the suspect, however, an officer talked with Williams about getting the child a proper Christian burial. Williams agreed to show the police where the body could be located; the body was found about two miles from where search teams had been looking (and became the foundation for the "inevitable discovery" exception to the exclusionary rule; see Chapter 2). The Supreme Court said that not just direct questioning is covered by *Miranda*. According to the Court, the officer here "deliberately and designedly set out to elicit information from Williams just as surely as— and perhaps more effectively than—if he had formally interrogated him (*Id.*, at 399)." This indirect question was just as much a violation of *Miranda* as explicit interrogation would have been.

What Is Custody?

There was another minimal extension in the custody element of *Miranda* in *J.D.B. v. North Carolina* (564 U.S. 261, 2011). The extension was slight in that the Court ruled here that age is a factor in a suspect's perception of whether he/she is in custody (making *Miranda* relevant). JDB was a 13-year-old student who was questioned at school about two burglaries by police and school officials. The questioning lasted 30–45 minutes in a conference room. *Miranda* had not been read to him nor was he offered an opportunity to speak to anyone or told he could leave the room. JDB gave a statement. Then the officer said JDB could refuse to answer and was free to leave. The youth said he understood and gave another statement and wrote one, too. The state court said the youth was not in custody and that age was not relevant. His adjudications were upheld through the appellate process until the Supreme Court reversed those rulings in a 5–4 decision. The Court said that age must be considered in determining whether an accused is in custody. The context in which the statements were given needed to be reexamined to determine if *Miranda* should have been given due to the JDB's possibly thinking he was in custody and not free to leave the interrogation.

The *Edwards* Rule: A Meaningful Extension of *Miranda*

By far the most important expansion of *Miranda* is what is known as the **Edwards** **Rule.** The *Edwards* rule stems from *Edwards v. Arizona* (451 U.S. 477, 1981) and involves what happens when, following *Miranda,* the suspect requests counsel. In *Edwards,* the suspect declared he wanted to consult with an attorney before deciding whether to accept a proposed deal the officers had offered. That request forced the negotiations to cease. The next day, while the suspect was still in jail, and before he had had a chance to talk with a lawyer, two detectives, who were colleagues of the arresting officer who had tried to interrogate Edwards and who were investigating the same crimes, insisted on seeing him. They *Mirandized* him, and told him they had a tape on which an alleged accomplice implicated him in the crime. Edwards said he was willing to talk, but only after he heard the tape.

Following that, he then made statements implicating himself in the crime.

The Supreme Court, after noting that *Miranda* holds that a request to consult counsel bars any further interrogation until an attorney is present, declared that Edwards' supposed waiver was not valid and thus the statement was not admissible. The Court held that a suspect has to initiate any further communication with police, and would have to waive counsel then.

Extensions of *Edwards*

Subsequently, the Court extended the *Edwards* Rule by applying it to a scenario where a second officer was investigating a crime unrelated to the offense for which the suspect was originally arrested and had invoked a right to counsel. In *Arizona v. Roberson* (486 U.S. 675, 1988), the suspect was arrested for an alleged burglary that took place on April 16, 1985. He invoked a right to counsel after being *Mirandized* and there was no interrogation on that charge. The suspect remained in jail and did not see a lawyer before another officer, unaware that Roberson had requested counsel for the April 16 burglary, approached him concerning an April 15 burglary. The second officer *Mirandized* Roberson and questioned him about only that burglary. The suspect waived his rights and admitted having committed the offense. Nevertheless, the Court held the statement was inadmissible as a *Miranda* violation (of the *Edwards* Rule).

Taking the *Edwards* rule yet one step further, the Court held in *Minnick v. Mississippi* (498 U.S. 146, 1990) that even when the suspect who requested counsel has been able to consult counsel the police may not attempt to conduct an interrogation unless counsel is present. The Court observed that "a fair reading of *Edwards* and subsequent cases demonstrates that we have interpreted the rule to bar police-initiated interrogations unless the accused has counsel with him at the time of the questioning (*Id.*, at 153)."

In *Oregon v. Bradshaw* (462 U.S. 1039, 1983) the Court elaborated on the *Edwards* rule. In *Bradshaw*, a suspect thought to be criminally liable for having caused a fatal car accident was *Mirandized* and requested counsel. The interrogation stopped. During a later transport to jail the suspect asked an officer what was going to happen to him. The officer reminded Bradshaw that he had asked for a lawyer and did not have to talk to the officer. The two talked and the officer explained where Bradshaw was headed and what the charges would be. The officer suggested Bradshaw take a lie detector test, which the suspect did the next day, after being *Mirandized* again. Bradshaw ended up making incriminatory statements following the lie detector test, which were admitted against him at trial. The state court regarded this admission as an *Edwards's* violation and reversed the conviction. The Supreme Court, however, reversed that decision, holding that the statements made without the advice of counsel were admissible because the suspect had approached (or had initiated the conversation with) the police.

The Court ruled that once suspects have invoked a right to counsel, the only way further interrogation can occur is if the suspects voluntarily approach the police, and, after being thoroughly apprised of their rights, including, of course, the right to consult a lawyer, make a statement. In other words, the police must be careful not to initiate the second conversation and the second *Miranda* better emphasize that the suspect still has a right to consult counsel.

Ultimately, the Supreme Court placed a 14-day time limit to the duration of an invocation of the right to counsel via the *Edwards* rule (see *Maryland v. Shatzer*, 559 U.S. 96, 2010; see next sections).

REINING IN *MIRANDA*

Not surprising, perhaps, considering the majority of the Supreme Court Justices' ideology of late, the Court has developed many more restrictions of *Miranda* compared to extensions during the last five decades. The reining in of *Miranda* has been both extensive and diverse.

This section will be presented as limits to or equivocations on *Miranda*. It needs to be pointed out that the reader reasonably could interpret some (and perhaps all) of these limitations as completely warranted and thus not as limits or equivocations but rather as explanations or clarifications of *Miranda*.

Miranda was devised by a liberal Supreme Court that considered *Miranda* a necessity and a valuable tool by which to reduce police coercion. *Miranda* was then interpreted for decades by a conservative Court that regarded *Miranda* as an obstacle to the finding of truth/ evidence by the police. In the 50 plus years since the *Miranda* decision the conservative Court has mostly reduced the impact of *Miranda* when possible.

There have been two major ways in which the Court has limited the impact of the *Miranda* decision. The first involves *reducing the chances of having a Miranda violation* occur. The second involves *limiting the negative consequences of a Miranda violation*.

Box 9-1: Reining in *Miranda*

Reducing the Chances of a *Miranda* Violation

- Narrowing Definitions of Custody, Interrogation, Voluntary/Intelligent

- Relaxing Rules on Giving *Miranda,* Invoking/Waiving *Miranda*

- Creating Exceptions to *Miranda*

Limiting the Negative Consequences of a *Miranda* Violation

- "Undoing" a *Miranda* Violation

- *Miranda* Violation Used to Impeach

- Ability to Admit Physical Evidence from *Miranda*-violated Statement

---

Reducing the Chances of a *Miranda* Violation

As Box 9-1, above, indicates, the Supreme Court has established *three methods* by which police can avoid a *Miranda* violation; the first involves limiting the situations in which *Miranda* must be given by *narrowing definitions* of custody, interrogation, and voluntary/intelligent.

Narrowing Definitions: Custody

An obvious and important way in which to restrict the reach of *Miranda* is to shrink the situations to which *Miranda* applies. A major way to shrink *Miranda* is to limit what counts as *custody*. The more interactions between civilians and police that do not count as custody increases the detention power of police by reducing the amount of evidence they need to detain (discussed in Chapter 5) and freeing the police from having to *Mirandize* suspects prior to questioning them.

Although the Court has found that custody can occur inside a suspect's home, as we just saw, the general rule is that most questioning that takes place outside a police station will be regarded as noncustodial because it will be in an atmosphere that is not isolated or dominated by the police.

Various tests have been identified for determining custody:

1) Focus of investigation;

2) Officer's intent to arrest;

3) Subjective estimate of being in custody; and,

4) Reasonable or objective estimate of being in custody.

Each of the four tests represents a different starting time of the beginning of custody. Focus of the investigation would start the clock the earliest. It could begin long before the suspect is anywhere physically near the police. So *Miranda* would theoretically be necessary at a first encounter with a suspect. The officer's intent to arrest could begin at the same time as the focus, but is likely to develop after some interaction with the suspect, making it likely to start after the focus would. A subjective estimate would require the presence of police, but would likely begin sooner than an objective perception that one is in custody, or, in the Court's words, is "not free to leave."

The Supreme Court has clearly rejected the first two tests as legitimate determinations of custody. The focus of the investigation was dismissed in 1976 in *Beckwith v. U.S.* (425 U.S. 341). IRS agents visited Beckwith in his house and interviewed him for three hours. He was not in custody and knew that. He made incriminating statements that were admitted at trial against him. Beckwith argued that because the tax fraud investigation had already focused on him before he was questioned, he should have been *Mirandized*. The Supreme Court rejected his claim, finding he was not in custody during the questioning.

Similarly, the Court dispensed with the officer's intent to arrest as the starting point for custody in *Berkemer v. McCarty* (468 U.S. 420, 1984), which we have seen in other contexts. The case involved a suspected DUI. The officer intended to arrest the driver early on, especially after the latter had trouble standing and failed a field sobriety test. Nevertheless, the driver was not told he was under arrest and answered the officer's questions by admitting to drinking a couple of beers and smoking some marijuana. The driver was taken into custody and was interrogated further at the police station, also without *Miranda*. Although the statements at the station were ruled inadmissible by the Supreme Court, the statements at the traffic stop were admissible. According to the Court, despite the officer's early intention to arrest the driver, *Miranda* was not necessary due to a lack of custody. The Court simply noted:

> A policeman's unarticulated plan has no bearing on the question whether a suspect was "in custody" at a particular time; the only relevant inquiry is how a reasonable person in the suspect's position would have understood his situation (*Id.*, at 421–422).

Of course, at the same time the Court was rejecting the officer's intent starting point, it was declaring its adoption of the reasonable/

objective estimate as being the appropriate test for custody, giving *Miranda* the latest possible starting point. The Court's lengthy account of how the traffic stop does not amount to custody for purposes of *Miranda* is illustrative:

> The roadside questioning of a motorist detained pursuant to a routine traffic stop does not constitute "custodial interrogation" for the purposes of the *Miranda* rule. Although an ordinary traffic stop curtails the "freedom of action" of the detained motorist and imposes some pressures on the detainee to answer questions, such pressures do not sufficiently impair the detainee's exercise of his privilege against self-incrimination to require that he be warned of his constitutional rights. A traffic stop is usually brief, and the motorist expects that, while he may be given a citation, in the end, he most likely will be allowed to continue on his way. Moreover, the typical traffic stop is conducted in public, and the atmosphere surrounding it is substantially less "police dominated" than that surrounding the kinds of interrogation at issue in *Miranda* and subsequent cases in which *Miranda* has been applied. . . . (*Id.*, at 421).

It is interesting that the Court questioned whether the traffic stop defendant feels enough pressure to self-incriminate and answered by saying only that there is *less* pressure than that experienced in the police station situated defendant due to: a shorter time period; in the public arena; and, fewer cops involved.

The Court did address two pivotal aspects of the traffic stop: the suspect is simply not free to leave and almost definitely will feel compelled to respond to the officer's questions, even if only to lie. The Court focused instead on the likely/possible outcome (probably not going to be an arrest) and the duration of the encounter (it usually is temporary and short) rather than on the actual nature of the encounter (you are, in fact, not free to leave, and you were, in fact, asked a specific question to which the officer is waiting for an answer).

Most interesting is that the Court acknowledged these realities and the custodial-like atmosphere presented by a traffic stop:

> It must be acknowledged at the outset that a traffic stop significantly impairs the "freedom of action" of the driver and the passengers, if any, of the detained vehicle. Under the law of most states, it is a crime either to ignore a policeman's signal to stop one's car or, once having stopped, to drive away without permission. Certainly few motorists would feel free either to disobey a directive to pull over or to leave the scene of a traffic stop without being told they might do so. . . . (*Id.*, at 436).

The Court also acknowledged that a traffic stop is a "seizure" for Fourth Amendment purposes, but, nevertheless, fails to satisfy the custody element required for *Miranda* warnings. Perhaps the most intriguing aspect of *Berkemer* is that Justice Marshall was the author.

After *Berkemer*, the Court ruled in *Pennsylvania v. Muniz* (496 U.S. 582, 1990) that, while stopped for a DUI, a suspect can also be asked routine questions without receiving *Miranda*. Viable questions include age, weight, eye color, height, date of birth, address and name so as to gauge intoxication. This material is all non-testimonial so the questions do not raise constitutional flags; videotaping is permitted as well.

The Supreme Court reaffirmed the inapplicability of the first three tests of custody in *Stansbury v. California* (511 U.S. 318, 1994). In *Stansbury*, a ten-year old girl had been raped and murdered. She had been seen talking to an ice cream truck driver. Four officers went to Stansbury's trailer home and asked if he would accompany them to the police station; he agreed to do so. Without being *Mirandized* he made incriminating statements, which were admitted at trial. The state court held the statements admissible because he had not become the focus of the investigation at that point. The Supreme Court said their "decisions make clear that the initial determination of custody depends on the objective circumstances of the interrogation, not on the subjective views harbored by either the interrogating officers or the person being questioned (*Id.*, at 323)."

In terms of defining custody, the Supreme Court seems committed to identifying only a true "restraint of movement" (if not a formal arrest) as a proper indicator of custody status. Consequently, a suspect who accompanied the police to the station, made incriminating statements in a thirty-minute interview, and was subsequently allowed to go home was not considered to be in custody for *Miranda* purposes; he had been told he was not under arrest (*California v. Beheler*, 463 U.S. 1121, 1983). The state court had invalidated the statements and reversed Beheler's conviction because the state had failed to show a lack of custody.

Even parolees (*Oregon v. Mathiason*, 429 U.S. 492, 1977) and probationers (*Minnesota v. Murphy*, 465 U.S. 420, 1984) who, by the Supreme Court's description, exist in a "coercive environment" are not viewed as being in custody for *Miranda* purposes by the Court and thus can be questioned without receiving warnings. The police request of Mathiason to appear at the station, and the PO's request of Murphy for a meeting were not custody situations *triggering Miranda*, according to the Court.

The Supreme Court took the lack of coercive environment idea one step further in 1990. We already considered the implications of using undercover agents (see Chapter 8). The Court held in *Illinois v. Perkins* (496 U.S. 292, 1990), that undercover agents can be utilized in a jail setting and can interview inmates without the need for *Miranda*. The absence of a "police-dominated atmosphere" is what led the Court to describe that setting as lacking a custodial element, making *Miranda* unnecessary. The "conversation" between the undercover agent and the inmate can still be problematic, however, if the latter has already been formally charged since that status triggers a right to counsel, independent of *Miranda* (see later sections of this chapter). Thus, the undercover agents would likely never to be able to discuss a charged crime for which the inmate has a right to counsel, but can talk about as-of-yet uncharged crimes without violating the right to counsel or *Miranda.* The statements in *Perkins* involved a homicide that was still under investigation so they were admissible in the eventual homicide prosecution.

Narrowing Definitions: Indirect Interrogation

The Supreme Court gave a narrow interpretation to *indirect* interrogation (or at least refused to extend its definition) in *Rhode Island v. Innis* (446 U.S. 291, 1980). Innis was given *Miranda* warnings three times, and the police were told not to question him. There were three officers in the car with the accused. One LEO said to another officer: "I frequent this area while on patrol and (that because a school for handicapped children is located nearby), there's a lot of handicapped children running around in this area, and God forbid one of them might find a weapon with shells and they might hurt themselves (*Id.,* at 294–95)."

The other officer responded that it was a safety factor and that the police should continue to search for the weapon. The accused interrupted the conversation, told them to turn the car around and that he would show them where the weapon was. After again being *Mirandized* he said he wanted to show the police where the weapon was because of the school kids in the area. The Court said the issue was whether the defendant was "interrogated," and that it was not limiting *Miranda* requirements to "express questioning." Instead it would include also its "functional equivalent." So, *Miranda* was held to apply "to any words or actions on the part of the police . . . that the police should know are reasonably likely to elicit an incriminating response from the suspect. . . (*Id.,* at 292)."

The Supreme Court, nevertheless, simply could not characterize the exchange between the police and the suspect as an interrogation, indirect or otherwise.

In dissent, Justice Stevens declared "the definition of 'interrogation' must include any police statement or conduct that has the same purpose or effect as a direct question. Statements that appear to call for a response from the suspect, as well as those that are designed to do so, should be considered interrogation. . . (*Id.*, at 311)." An interesting observation from Justice Stevens noted: "The Court's assumption that criminal suspects are not susceptible to appeals to conscience is directly contrary to the teachings of police interrogation manuals, which recommend appealing to a suspect's sense of morality as a standard and often successful interrogation technique. . . (*Id.*, at 315). Finally, Justice Stevens offered: "It is not inconceivable that two professionally trained police officers concluded that a few well-chosen remarks might induce respondent to disclose the whereabouts of the shotgun. This conclusion becomes even more plausible in light of the emotionally charged words chosen by Officer Gleckman ('God forbid' that a 'little girl' should find the gun and hurt herself (*Id.*, at 316)."

Arranged Spousal Communication Is Not Interrogation

The Supreme Court made it clear several years later that a conversation between husband and wife is not an interrogation. In *Arizona v. Mauro* (481 U.S. 520, 1987), a husband/father was arrested in connection with his son's death. He volunteered he had killed his son and led the police to the body. He was later advised of his rights at the station upon which he said he didn't want to talk with police until he had consulted a lawyer. Before Mauro consulted a lawyer his wife asked to speak with him; the wife had also been interrogated by other cops. The police allowed the spousal contact, but with a caveat that the police had to be present; a tape recorder was plainly visible in the room where the conversation transpired. The accused advised his spouse not to talk with the police until she had consulted a lawyer. The defendant eventually presented an insanity defense at trial, whereupon the state offered a recording of the spousal conversation as an indication that the shooter had been operating sanely. The defense challenged the recording arguing it amounted to an interrogation in violation of *Miranda* since the accused had invoked a right to counsel. The Court

(5–4) narrowly found no *Miranda* violation. The majority saw neither an interrogation nor any kind of "psychological ploy." They saw the statements as volunteered. "The purpose of *Miranda* . . . is to prevent the government from using the coercive nature of confinement to extract confessions that would not be given in an unrestrained environment. This purpose is not implicated here, since respondent was not subjected to compelling influences, psychological ploys, or direct questioning (*Id.*)."

The four dissenters believed the police had "employed a powerful psychological ploy; they failed to give respondent any advance warning that Mrs. Mauro was coming to talk to him, that a police officer would accompany her, or that their conversation would be recorded. . . (*Id.*, at 531)." As these Justices saw it, "the police took advantage of Mrs. Mauro's request to visit her husband, setting up a confrontation between them at a time when he manifestly desired to remain silent. Because they allowed respondent's conversation to commence at a time when they knew it was reasonably likely to produce an incriminating statement, the police interrogated him. . . (*Id.*)."

Narrowing Definitions: Voluntary

The Supreme Court has made it clear for decades that statements/ confessions must be voluntary on the suspect's part, independent of any *Miranda* considerations. We saw actual physical beatings by the police were found to be an unconstitutional use of force in extracting a confession in *Brown v. Mississippi* (see Chapter 2). And the Court has not actually required the spilling of blood in order to find coercion in police interrogation; coercion can be mental, too, as in the overbearing of the defendant's will, which is impermissible as well (*Blackburn v. Alabama*, 361 U.S. 199, 1960). The Court has explained that it will use a TOC test to determine whether the suspect's will has been overborne, analyzing factors, such as extensive questioning, delay in getting the accused before a judge, refusal to permit the accused to contact others, especially family and counsel, the length and conditions of detention, the police attitude toward the suspect, the latter's mental and physical state, and pressures that may have overwhelmed the suspect such that he/she has lost a capacity for self-determination (*Culombe v. Connecticut*, 367 U.S. 568, 601–02, 1961).

Nevertheless, another factor that the Court has demanded is that the coercion stems from the behavior of the police (or some government agent) and not from the accused. In *Colorado v. Connelly*, (479 U.S. 157, 1986), the accused was *Mirandized*, said he understood his rights and that he wanted to discuss the murder about which he had approached police. He was *Mirandized* a second time and again stated he understood his rights. Connelly not only gave a statement, he also led the police to the location of the crime. The defendant suffered from mental illness and later claimed that that condition compelled him to confess a murder to the police; he stated that God had commanded him to confess. There was some proof of an impaired mental condition as he had once been hospitalized after becoming disoriented. Nevertheless, he was found competent to stand trial. The state courts agreed with Connelly's position that the confession was involuntary and suppressed it. The Colorado Supreme Court said there was government action present when the trial court admitted the confession into evidence. Justices Brennan and Marshall echoed these sentiments and observed that the U.S. Supreme Court had never upheld the admission of a confession that had not been obtained through the exercise of free will.

A majority of the Court insisted, however, that a confession is not a free choice only when there is governmental coercion. Only then is due process violated. The Supreme Court worried that adopting Connelly's position would require courts to determine the motivations behind a confession and believed that excluding confessions in this context would not deter police. Implicit in the Court's holding was a fear that if subjective coercion were adopted as the standard for coercion, it would be open to abuse. An additional consideration is to question how a suspect's free will has been violated by the state when the coercion is internal. Simply put, self-coercion does not equal state coercion or a *Miranda* violation.

The Supreme Court has also refused to find police use of *trickery* as sufficient to render a confession involuntary in violation of *Miranda* (*Bobby v. Dixon*, 565 U.S. 23, 2011). Police are permitted to encourage suspects to admit wrongdoing, if for no other reason than an accomplice is already speaking to the police and might receive a better deal than an uncooperative suspect (see also *Frazier v. Cupp*, 394 U.S. 731, 1969). The Sixth Circuit Court of Appeals had found the confession to be involuntary due to the trickery, but this ruling was eventually reversed.

Similarly, the police can lie to a suspect as to finding his/her fingerprints at the scene of a burglary without compromising the voluntary nature of a confession (*Oregon v. Mathiason*, 429 U.S. 492, 1977).

Narrowing Definitions: Intelligent

Although the suspect has to be informed of and understand the constitutional rights connected to *Miranda* warnings, the same does not apply to the nature of the charges the suspect is facing. In *Colorado v. Spring* (479 U.S. 564, 1987), the accused was brought in under suspicion of transporting stolen firearms. The police asked about that offense and then proceeded to inquire about a homicide incident. The accused admitted committing the homicide, but he hadn't been told the interrogation was headed that way. Even still, Spring had been *Mirandized* twice and waived silence, after signing a statement that he understood his rights. The Colorado Supreme Court ruled the waiver was not voluntary and intelligent. The U.S. Supreme Court found no *Miranda* violation, however. According to the Court, the defendant understood his rights and the consequences of waiving them. Moreover, he could have stopped the interrogation at any time, particularly when the more serious offense was brought up. In the Court's view, being told of the more serious charges would "affect only the wisdom of a *Miranda* waiver, not its voluntary and knowing nature (*Id.*, at 565)."

More Reining in of *Miranda*

A second way in which the Supreme Court has assisted police in avoiding a *Miranda* violation is by relaxing the rules surrounding *Miranda*. The relaxation of rules has been varied and extensive, covering virtually every dimension of *Miranda*.

Box 9-2: Relaxing the Rules of *Miranda*

Giving *Miranda*

- Warnings need not be precise
- Warnings do not need to be repeated

Invoking Silence

- Must be explicit
- Is not permanent

Waiver of Silence

- Can be vague/implied
- Can be partial

Remaining silent

- Can be used at trial

Invoking counsel

- Must be explicit
- Cannot be anticipatory
- Must be made personally by the accused
- Is subject to a time limit (14 days for the *Edwards* rule)

Waiver of counsel

- Can be implied

Waiver of silence/counsel limited in scope

Waiver of silence/counsel can be proved by a preponderance of evidence

---

_____

Giving *Miranda*

From the early days of *Miranda* it was clear that the language employed by the police in issuing the warnings need not be a verbatim repeat of the decision (*California v. Prysock*, 453 U.S. 355, 1981). Most of what can be confusing about *Miranda* warnings is whether counsel will be appointed before trial and during questioning and be able to sit with the suspect at the station. Another ambiguity is whether if silence and/or counsel are initially waived, can one stop speaking (or request a lawyer) after they've started talking? Probably the "worst" move on the part of a suspect is to query, "*maybe I should keep quiet or talk to a lawyer?*"

Warnings Need Not Be Precise

Nearly three decades ago, the Supreme Court revealed it would allow *Miranda* warnings that appeared to be clear to the Justices, but others could interpret them as *vague or ambiguous*. In *Duckworth v. Eagan* (492 U.S. 195, 1989), the Court held that the following warning by the police sufficed to satisfy the warning requirements of *Miranda*:

> You have a right to talk to a lawyer for advice before we ask you any questions, and to have him with you during questioning. You have this right to the advice and presence of a lawyer even if you cannot afford to hire one. We have no way of giving you a lawyer, but one will be appointed for you, if you wish, if and when you go to court. . . (*Id.*, at 198).

In this case, the suspect had been arrested for a stabbing, was read the previous warning, and, 29 hours later, confessed to the stabbing after being warned again of his rights; he then took officers to the location where the police recovered physical evidence of the crime. The state courts and the U.S. District Court saw no *Miranda* violation and allowed his statements to be admitted against him. The Seventh Circuit Court of Appeals, however, had reversed the conviction due to the warning's being "constitutionally defective." According to this court, the warning denied the "accused a clear and unequivocal warning of the right to appointed counsel before interrogation and linked that right to a future event (*Id.*, at 195)." The U.S. Supreme Court found the warning sufficiently clear, nevertheless, and reinstated the conviction.

Warnings Do Not Need to Be Repeated

More recently, while discussing whether a suspect's waiver of the right to silence was adequate (see section, below), the Court stated, in no uncertain terms: "Police are not required to rewarn suspects from time to time (*Berghuis v. Thompkins*, 560 U.S. 370, 371, 2010)." Obviously, then, one reading of *Miranda* to a suspect is all that is constitutionally required, assuming, at least, that there are not multiple meetings between the police and the suspect.

Invoking Silence Must Be Explicit; Waiving Silence Can Be Vague/Implied

The Supreme Court originally suggested that invoking the rights provided for in *Miranda* did not need to be unequivocal or that the waiver of same had to be unambiguous. In *Miranda*, the Court held: "Once warnings have been given, the subsequent procedure is clear. If the individual indicates in any manner, at any time prior to or during questioning, that he wishes to remain silent, the interrogation must cease. . . (384 U.S. 436, 473–74, 1966)." Whether the Supreme Court has been faithful to that mandate is debatable.

Invoking a right to silence and its opposite, waiving a right to silence, are flip sides of the same coin, constitutionally speaking. What this means to us is that the Supreme Court has required the *invocation of the right to silence to be explicit* (or unambiguous) while the *waiver or surrendering of that right can be vague or inferred* from the actions of the suspect. The Court disclosed its satisfaction with inferring waiver from suspects' behavior long ago in *North Carolina v. Butler* (441 U.S. 369, 1979). In that case, Butler expressed a willingness to talk, but refused to sign any forms. The state court had said that a waiver of the right to silence needed to be "specifically made." The Supreme Court held that no per se express waiver rule exists in this context, however. Instead, the Court was willing to perceive "in at least some cases waiver can be clearly inferred from the actions and words of the person interrogated (*Id.*, at 373)."

Similarly and more recently, the Supreme Court permitted an "implied" waiver of silence. In *Berghuis v. Thompkins* (see above section), Thompkins refused to sign the *Miranda* form. He may or may not have confirmed that he understood his rights, and he never said he wanted to remain silent or to consult with an attorney. He was mostly non-communicative for nearly three hours. Although there were occasions when he answered "yeah," "no" or "I don't know," most of the time he gave no verbal response. The police asked Thompkins if he prayed to God and later he answered *yes* when the officer asked if he prayed for forgiveness for shooting the victim. That response was used against him at trial to convict him of murder. Not surprising, Thompkins argued he had not waived his right to silence. (Also at issue here, but not addressed by the Court, was whether there was a waiver of the right to counsel, which was implied at best).

The suspect alleged that his silence for an appreciable length of time was sufficient so as to indicate he was invoking a right to silence and that the interrogation should have ceased. The Court held that being non-communicative is not equivalent to invoking a right to silence. The Court drew a direct comparison to *Davis v. U.S.* (512 U.S. 452, 1994) (see sections, below), and offered that since invoking a right to counsel must be explicit so must invoking a right to silence: "There is no principled reason to adopt different standards for determining when an accused has invoked the *Miranda* right to remain silent and the *Miranda* right to counsel at issue in *Davis*. Both protect the privilege against compulsory self-incrimination by requiring an interrogation to cease when either right is invoked (560 U.S. at 371)."

The Court was not going to insist that a waiver of the right to silence be "express." "An implicit waiver of the 'right to remain silent' is sufficient to admit a suspect's statement into evidence (*Id.*, at 384)." Providing *Miranda* and showing the suspect understood the rights means that an uncoerced statement establishes "an implied waiver of the right to remain silent." *Miranda*, in the Court's eyes, "does not impose a formalistic waiver procedure that a suspect must follow to relinquish those rights (*Id.*, at 385)." Understanding the rights and continuing to talk constituted a knowing waiver of those rights.

In the end, the Court believed that police can't be forced to guess whether a suspect is invoking a right to silence and should not have to lose otherwise voluntary statements. The warnings were sufficient so the only question was whether a nonresponse constituted a waiver, which the Court answered, yes. Police referral to the suspect's religious beliefs also did not make the statement involuntary, according to the majority. The decision reaffirms two propositions: a request for silence must be clear and unambiguous (as with counsel), and waiver of the right to silence (as with counsel) need not be explicit.

The decision was a close 5–4 holding. The four dissenters saw the opinion as a retreat from *Miranda*, and as violating at least 5 precedents:

1) Courts are supposed to presume that a defendant did not waive his right(s);

2) The prosecution bears a heavy/substantial burden in proving there was a waiver;

3) A lengthy interrogation prior to obtaining statements is strong evidence against a finding of a valid waiver;

4) Mere silence in response to questioning is not enough to find there was a waiver;

5) Waiver may not be presumed simply from the fact that a confession was in fact eventually obtained (see *Id.*, at 396–410).

The dissenters saw the decision as making *Miranda* less clear and/or as a partial reversal of *Miranda*. They noted: "Criminal suspects must now unambiguously invoke their right to remain silent—which, counterintuitively, requires them to speak. At the same time, suspects will be legally presumed to have waived their rights even if they have given no clear expression of their intent to do so. . . (*Id.*, at 412)."

Invoking Silence Is Not Necessarily Permanent

What if a suspect clearly invokes a right to silence? We have already seen how sacred an invocation of the right to counsel has been treated (see *Edwards* rule, above). Although *Miranda* did not seem to treat the two rights differently (silence and counsel), the Supreme Court has treated them markedly differently.

In *Michigan v. Mosely* (423 U.S. 96, 1975), the suspect, after being arrested and *Mirandized*, stated he didn't want to talk about the robberies in which he was a suspect. More than two hours later, another officer advised him of his rights, and asked if it was okay to ask about a homicide in which he was also a suspect. Mosely was fully *Mirandized* again. This time he talked, however, and made incriminating statements. The Supreme Court noted that invoking a right to silence means the interrogation must stop, but that there was no guidance as to when, if ever, questioning could resume. Nevertheless, the Court held that requesting silence does not protect a suspect against other officers approaching the suspect later on and attempting to reinitiate an interrogation. The length of time between the two warnings/questionings will be critical as will be the number of times the suspect is reapproached.

What is perhaps most interesting is the marked difference between *Edwards* and *Mosely*. Whereas requesting counsel shuts virtually everything down, requesting silence seems to be a potential momentary interruption only, and while 14 days seem to be necessary in reapproaching a suspect who has requested counsel, a little more than 2 hours is enough when silence has been invoked.

Waiving Silence Can Be Partial (Unintelligent?)

In a case reminiscent of *North Carolina v. Butler* (see above section), the Court determined that a suspect, who had been *Mirandized* and had signed a statement indicating that he understood his rights, said he was willing to talk to the police, but would not give a written statement without the advice of counsel (*Connecticut v. Barrett*, 479 U.S. 523, 1987). Barrett was *Mirandized* a second time and for a second time signed the same waiver. On both occasions he gave an oral statement, but no written one. The oral confession was ruled admissible since there had been no coercion or trickery by the police. So, waiving a right to silence can be partial (oral but not written) and questionably intelligent by a suspect.

Failing to Invoke Silence/Remaining Silent Can Be Used at Trial

Interesting, a recent Supreme Court case established a principle that remaining silent can be used against a suspect at trial. In *Salinas v. Texas* (570 U.S. ___, 133 S.Ct. 2174, 2013), the investigation of two homicides led to the noncustodial questioning of Salinas. He was given no warnings, answered some questions, but stood mute when asked if ballistics would prove his gun would match the murder weapon. The state used his failure to answer the question as evidence against him. The Supreme Court said this was permissible since one must invoke the protection against self-incrimination in order to claim it. According to the Court, invoking silence does not occur "simply by standing mute." The Court explained that as "long as police do not deprive a witness of the ability to voluntarily invoke the privilege, there is no Fifth Amendment violation. (*Id.*, at 389)."

Invoking Counsel Must Be Explicit; Waiving Counsel Can Be Implied

Although the *Edwards* Rule certainly can stand between the police and a lawful statement and can constitute a valuable protection for the accused, the Court has limited *Miranda/Edwards* to some extent by requiring that defendant "unambiguously" request counsel. In *Davis v. U.S.* (512 U.S. 452, 1994) the Court, in a 5–4 ruling, explained that when

> a suspect makes a reference to an attorney that is ambiguous or equivocal in that a reasonable officer in light of the circumstances would have understood only that the suspect *might* be invoking the right to counsel, our precedents do not require the cessation of questioning (*Id.*, at 459).

Davis had been warned of his rights and waived them in both oral and written forms. An hour and a half into the interview, he observed, "Maybe I should talk to a lawyer." Davis was told that if he wanted a lawyer, the interview was over. He was asked to clarify whether he wanted a lawyer or was he merely commenting about one. He replied that he was not asking for a lawyer. After a short break, Davis was readvised of his rights and talked for another hour. Only then did he say that he thought he wanted to see a lawyer before he said anything else; the interview stopped. The statements he had already offered were admitted at trial. The Supreme Court upheld this decision. The Court insisted that the request to consult an attorney must "meet a level of clarity." Pointedly, the Court rejected the defendant's "invitation to extend *Edwards* and require law enforcement officers to cease questioning immediately upon the making of an ambiguous or equivocal reference to an attorney (*Id.*)."

In this case there were clarifying questions asked of the accused as to whether he was willing to proceed without counsel. Nevertheless, Court refused to adopt a *per se* "rule requiring officers to ask clarifying questions. If the suspect's statement is not an unambiguous or unequivocal request for counsel, the officers have no obligation to stop questioning him (*Id.*, at 461–62)."

Consequently, if police "reasonably do not know whether or not the suspect wants a lawyer," "the questioning may proceed without the presence of a lawyer to assist the accused (*Id.*, at 460)." Years later, in

Berghuis v. Thompkins (see above), the Court reaffirmed the idea that waiving counsel (as with waiving the right to silence) can be implied by the actions and words of the accused.

Invoking a Right to Counsel Cannot Be Anticipatory

Invoking the right to counsel is something that has to occur in the moment, so to speak. In other words, the defendant has to be in custody (*Bobby v. Dixon*, 565 U.S. 23, 2011). The suspect in this case was at the police station picking up an impounded car. He was approached by an officer who wanted to question him about a missing murder victim. Dixon was *Mirandized* and responded that he would answer no questions without a lawyer and then left the station. He had not been under arrest. Five days later he was arrested for the alleged homicide. Officers at first did not *Mirandize* Dixon but later did and at that time Dixon talked without requesting counsel. In a *per curiam* opinion, the Court ruled that the only person that can invoke counsel is one in custody being subjected to a custodial interrogation and that the right is not one that can be claimed "anticipatorily."

Invoking Counsel Must Be Done by the Suspect Personally

In *Moran v. Burbine* (475 U.S. 412, 1986), the suspect was *Mirandized* and waived his rights with written waivers; he confessed to a murder. Burbine's sister had secured the help of a public defender who called the police and asked if the accused was being interrogated (all the sister and counsel knew at this point was a breaking and entering charge and not about the homicide). The public defender was told by the Cranston police that they were not going to interrogate him that night. Meanwhile, Providence police were headed to Cranston to ask the suspect about the murder. The sister and the public defender knew none of this. Burbine was advised of his rights and three times signed a written waiver to an attorney and actually said he didn't want an attorney. He had access to a phone but did not know his sister had secured help for him; he signed three written statements admitting to the murder. The trial court found the waiver to be adequate and the defendant was convicted.

Burbine lost through state appellate system, but the First Circuit Court of Appeals reversed his conviction. The U.S. Sup Court accepted the case to decide if the confession should be suppressed "either because the police misinformed an inquiring attorney about their plans concerning the suspect or because they failed to inform the suspect of the attorney's efforts to reach him (*Id.*, at 420)." The First Circuit believed the police conduct negated the validity of the waiver. The Supreme Court, however, reversed the circuit court and declared that

> Once it is determined that a suspect's decision not to rely on his rights was uncoerced, that he at all times knew he could stand mute and request a lawyer, and that he was aware of the state's intention to use his statements to secure a conviction, the analysis is complete and the waiver is valid as a matter of law. . . (*Id.*, at 422–23).

According to the Supreme Court the intentions of the police are irrelevant in determining the intelligence and voluntariness of a waiver of counsel. Acknowledging that the police conduct may have been unethical, the Court nevertheless countered that "such conduct is only relevant to the constitutional validity of a waiver if it deprives a defendant of knowledge essential to his ability to understand the nature of his rights and the consequences of abandoning them. . . (*Id.*, at 424)." Even a "deliberate deception" of an attorney would not affect a waiver of rights by a suspect. According to the Court, the purpose of *Miranda*

> is to dissipate the compulsion inherent in custodial interrogation and, in doing so, guard against abridgement of the suspect's Fifth Amendment rights. Clearly, a rule that focuses on how the police treat an attorney—conduct that has no relevance at all to the degree of compulsion experienced by the defendant during interrogation—would

ignore both *Miranda's* mission and its only source of legitimacy (*Id.*, at 425).

The Court rejected the offer to establish a rule that the police must inform a suspect of the efforts of an attorney to reach the accused. Too many practical overriding considerations worked against adopting such a rule in the Court's eyes.

All the police have to do to satisfy *Miranda* is to inform the accused of his/her rights and to allow the accused to invoke those rights. The Court has not yet stacked the power in favor of the defendant such as requiring the lawyer to be present during warnings/interrogation. In the end, the inescapable message from the case is that suspects and counsel can be kept apart unless and until the suspect specifically asks to see counsel.

Time Limit to the *Edwards* Rule

In 2010, the Supreme Court finally put a time limit on the *Edwards* Rule in *Maryland v. Shatzer* (559 U.S. 96, 2010). Shatzer had been imprisoned for a conviction concerning a child molestation offense. Shatzer was approached by police on August 7, 2003 concerning another molestation charge. He invoked a right to counsel and the interrogation stopped. Nearly 31 months later, on March 2, 2006, he was revisited in prison (he was still serving a sentence on the first molestation conviction, but in a different prison) to investigate the offense that had prompted his request for counsel. Shatzer was *Mirandized*, waived his rights, and agreed to take a polygraph test. Five days later he took the polygraph and admitted committing the offense. While the state court believed there had been an *Edwards* violation, the Supreme Court found none. In *Shatzer* the Court developed a 14 day limit to the *Edwards* Rule, particularly (and likely only) if the suspect has been released from custody. That length of time away from custody was seen by the Court as sufficient to remove any coercion from a subsequent decision to talk with police without having consulted counsel. Although Shatzer had been in continuous custody due to his conviction, the Court believed his life in general population of prison was a break in custody as far as *Miranda/Edwards* was concerned. Whether a two-week time line would apply to suspects held continuously in pre-trial custody is extremely doubtful (due to a never-interrupted potential for coercion), but that or any possible limit can be answered only by the Supreme Court. There very well could be no time limit to *Edwards* for those who have not been released prior to trial. The concern most vividly expressed by the Court was any potential coercion experienced by a suspect who gives up a right to counsel without having secured it first; that coercion is most poignant for those in custody.

Waiver of Silence/Counsel Can Be Limited in Scope

The scope of a suspect's waiver can also be an issue. In *Wyrick v. Fields* (459 U.S. 42, 1982), the defendant agreed to take a polygraph without the presence of counsel (so he waived both silence and counsel). After the polygraph, the administrator informed Fields that there were indications of deceit and asked for an explanation. The suspect made incriminating admissions. He argued later that the statements should be suppressed and claimed that the waiver did not extend to the post-polygraph questioning. The Supreme Court disagreed and explained that

> it would have been unreasonable for Fields and his attorneys to assume that Fields would not be informed of the polygraph readings and asked to explain any unfavorable results. Moreover, Fields had been informed that he could stop the questioning at any time, and could request at any time that his lawyer join him. Merely disconnecting the polygraph equipment could not remove this knowledge from Fields' mind (*Id.*, at 47–48).

Waiver Needs to Be Proved by Only a
Preponderance of Evidence

The final relaxation of the rules surrounding *Miranda* involves what the state has to demonstrate to defeat a suspect's claim that a *Miranda* violation has occurred. In *Colorado v. Connelly* (479 U.S. 157, 1986), the state court had announced that the proof should be at a *clear and convincing* level. The U.S. Supreme Court disagreed, however, and determined that a *preponderance of evidence* is the appropriate level of proof to defeat such a claim. The Supreme Court explained that the level of proof should be the same as that existing to prove the voluntariness of a confession (see *Lego v. Twomey*, 404 U.S. 477, 1972).

Exceptions to *Miranda* (When *Miranda* Is Not Necessary)

Another way in which to limit the applicability of *Miranda* is to simply establish situations in which *Miranda* is inapplicable. Thus far, there are only three situations in which *Miranda* has been found to be unnecessary. Warnings are not required when one appears before *a grand jury*. The questioning that occurs there is not equivalent to custodial interrogation by the police (see *U.S. v. Mandujano*, 425 U.S. 564, 1976; *U.S. v. Wong*, 431 U.S. 174, 1977).

When a suspect is being *booked*, there is also no interrogation. The questions, provided they are of a routine booking nature, will not likely produce an incriminating response. Thus, the answers are not considered to be testimonial responses covered by Fifth Amendment protection (see *Pennsylvania v. Muniz*, 496 U.S. 582, 1990). This case involved a DUI stop in which Muniz had performed poorly during a field sobriety test. The police officer asked Muniz 7 questions that were not problematic, according to the Supreme Court. They included matters relevant to booking, such as name, address, height, weight, eye color, date of birth, and age. An eighth question was viewed as having gone too far and that was asking Muniz the date of his sixth birthday.

By far, the most controversial and important exception to *Miranda* is called the *public safety exception* that was established in *New York v. Quarles* (467 U.S. 649, 1984). In *Quarles*, a rape victim informed police that her assailant had just run into a grocery store with a gun. The police found Quarles inside the store and apprehended him. Upon arresting Quarles the police discovered an empty shoulder holster on him. Quarles was handcuffed, and, without being *Mirandized,* he was asked where the gun was. Quarles responded that the "gun is over there," and pointed out where the gun was. The state courts ruled in Quarles' favor and suppressed both his statement and the gun. By a 5–4 margin, however, the Supreme Court upheld the questioning of Quarles without the benefit of *Miranda* warnings due to the public safety issue at hand. Justice O'Connor held that the statement should be suppressed, but not the gun.

Limiting the Negative Consequences of a *Miranda* Violation

A Statement Violating *Miranda* Can Be Ignored in Securing a Second Statement

In *Oregon v. Elstad* (470 U.S. 298, 1985), the Supreme Court sustained the so-called two-step interrogation technique. This procedure involves failing to *Mirandize* a suspect at an initial contact and questioning, securing a statement (that violates *Miranda* and would not be admissible), and then *Mirandizing* the suspect while asking him/her if they would now repeat what they said the first time around (which statement would be admissible since *Miranda* was observed). That scenario was the progression that was upheld by the Court in *Elstad*. (I taught LEOs who announced in class that they purposely adopted this approach to interrogation). The Supreme Court had established an incentive to sidestep *Miranda*.

Most interesting, the Supreme Court retreated somewhat from its position in *Elstad* twenty-nine years later in *Missouri v. Seibert* (542 U.S. 600, 2004). In *Seibert*, the suspect was left alone in an interrogation room for 20 minutes, was then questioned for 40 minutes by an officer who purposely did not *Mirandize* her. The officer secured a statement. After a 20-minute break the same officer returned to the room and started a tape recorder. The officer *Mirandized* Seibert, secured a waiver, and obtained a signed waiver of rights. During the second session the officer repeated the statements from the first encounter and walked her through the account.

In a retreat from, if not repudiation of, *Elstad*, the Supreme Court ruled that the second statement was not admissible. *Elstad* had seemingly encouraged many police departments to adopt the two-step approach as a "conscious decision" in a purposeful avoidance of *Miranda*. The *Seibert* Court noted that the failure to first warn in Elstad was an oversight and not a purposeful design, a good faith *Miranda* mistake. In *Seibert*, the two-step had become "a police strategy to undermine the *Miranda* warnings (*Id.*, at 616)." The suspect had not been told that the original statement could not be used, but rather the officer just went right into repeating the first statement.

Between the four dissenters' views and the concurrence issued by Justice Kennedy there does seem to be room for a failure to first warn in good faith—as in *Elstad*—and then a proper statement could still be obtained after providing *Miranda*. Another possibility is that if there is a long time between the first and second statements, coupled with a warning that the first statement cannot be used, then perhaps a second statement would be found to be admissible.

The four dissenters did not object to the purposeful maneuver. They thought it might create a psychological effect such that a suspect thinks the "cat is out of the bag." This could encourage a suspect to confess who, otherwise, might be inclined to remain silent. But, as long as *Miranda* precedes the second statement, it would be admissible. This position demonstrates that there are Justices who still believe that the only "bad" statement is an involuntary one (i.e., one is compelled to testify against oneself), as opposed to a *Miranda*-violated one.

The possibility alluded to in *Seibert* (such that *Elstad* is not completely dead) happened in *Bobby v. Dixon* (see above section). Although *Dixon* did not involve the two-step procedure, there was an initial encounter in which the suspect was not *Mirandized* (purposely), but then he returned to the police station, was *Mirandized* a couple of times, and gave a second statement that the Supreme Court upheld as valid. The Supreme Court identified factors that distinguished this case from *Seibert* there were four hours between statements; Dixon had travelled from the police station to a jail and then back to the station; Dixon claimed to have talked with a lawyer and said he wanted to talk to the police; Dixon had learned that the police were talking to his accomplice; and, the police had found the victim's body. To the Court, this constituted a "significant break in time and dramatic change in circumstances (*Id.*, at 32)." Unlike *Elstad* and *Seibert*, the second statement in *Dixon* was a product of "a new and distinct experience (*Id.*, at 32)." All of these factors ended up ensuring that Dixon's first unwarned statement "did not undermine the effectiveness of the *Miranda* warnings he received before confessing to murder (*Id.*, at 32)."

A Statement Violating *Miranda* Can Be Used: To Impeach Defendant

The Supreme Court has permitted the state to use a statement that was voluntarily obtained but secured in violation of *Miranda* to impeach a defendant who takes the stand at trial (*Harris v. New York,* 401 U.S. 222, 1971; see also *Oregon v. Hass*, 420 U.S. 714, 1975). Not long after the *Miranda* ruling a New York-based defendant made a statement to police after there had been no warning of a right to counsel, thus constituting a *Miranda* violation. The statement could not be used at trial to convict the defendant, but he took the stand and offered an account that contradicted what he had said to the police. The Supreme Court allowed the original statement to be used to impeach him, paralleling what the Court has held with respect to evidence seized in violation of the Fourth Amendment (see Chapter 2). The majority in *Harris* believed there was sufficient deterrence (i.e., making police observe *Miranda*) in prohibiting the use of the *Miranda*-violating statement to convict the defendant (or during the prosecution's case-in-chief).

The Court emphasized that the statement has to be voluntary because then it is trustworthy, even if obtained illegally. If statement is ruled involuntary, then it cannot be used to impeach (*Mincey v. Arizona*, 437 U.S. 385, 1978). An interesting conflict exists here. On the one hand there is a *Miranda* violation that leads to forbidding any use of the statement. On the other hand, the state can't just sit back and knowingly allow the defendant to commit perjury. The solution (permitting impeachment), however, creates another potential problem since it can encourage police to refuse providing counsel after a suspect has made a request to consult a lawyer. Police can be tempted to continue the interrogation, meaning they will lose the statement (but warnings might have encouraged the suspect to remain quiet anyway), but they pretty much can guarantee the defendant will not be able to take the stand and testify on his/her own behalf. As we will see, below, the statement can also lead the police to physical evidence as well.

There may be some proof that police have done precisely this. In *Oregon v. Hass* (420 U.S. 714, 1975), the accused had asked to talk with counsel, but the officer continued the interrogation. Justice Brennan dissented and pointed out the possible temptation of police to skirt *Miranda*.

A Statement Violating *Miranda* Can Be Used: To Lead to Physical Evidence

The most controversial and significant use of a voluntary statement that violates *Miranda* was established in *United States v. Patane* (542 U.S. 630, 2004). *Patane* was a 5–4 decision that involved a suspect who was arrested, was not given *Miranda*, but was asked the location of his gun. Patane gave police permission to retrieve it from his bedroom. Three Justices saw no *Miranda* violation as long as police didn't try to use the statement, but, more important, five Justices said it was okay to admit the gun as physical evidence, even assuming a *Miranda* violation. According to the Court, this sequence did not constitute a violation of the *fruit of the poisonous tree doctrine* provided the statement was voluntary.

The Court posited that the fruit of the poisonous doctrine is limited to confessions/statements, and simply does not apply to physical evidence. The majority said admitting the gun

> does not run the risk of admitting into trial an accused's coerced incriminating statements against himself. In light of the important probative value of reliable physical evidence, it is doubtful that exclusion can be justified by a deterrence rationale sensitive to both law enforcement interests and a suspect's rights during an in-custody interrogation. . . (*Id.*, at 632).

The Supreme Court tied *Miranda* to the Fifth Amendment's self-incrimination clause and not to physical evidence:

> (T)he *Miranda* rule is a prophylactic employed to protect against violation of the Self-Incrimination Clause. The Self-Incrimination Clause, however, is not implicated by the admission into evidence of the physical fruit of a voluntary statement. . . . (T)he core protection afforded by the Self-Incrimination Clause is a prohibition on compelling a criminal defendant to testify against himself at trial (*Id.*, at 636, 637).

While the majority saw a *Miranda* violation's occurring only when an unwarned statement is admitted at trial, the dissent regarded *Patane* as an incentive to violate *Miranda*. According to the dissent, "(t)here is no way to read this case except as an unjustifiable invitation to law enforcement officers to flout *Miranda* when there may be physical evidence to be gained. . . (*Id.*, at 647)."

VOLUNTARINESS IN THE POST-*MIRANDA* ERA

We have seen that the *Miranda* decision is the major focus employed by courts in evaluating the way in which police secure statements from suspects. *Miranda* has, in some respects, swallowed the voluntariness test. Despite *Miranda's* dominance it is important to remember that the voluntariness of a confession is still a requirement and can still be the matter of constitutional challenge, even when *Miranda* is not at issue. In *Arizona v. Fulminante* (499 U.S. 279, 1991), a suspect in federal prison confessed to another inmate who was working as an FBI informant. The latter had promised to protect the suspect from physical harm while in prison. The suspect had felt he was under threat due to word getting out that he was a child murderer. In exchange for information regarding the homicide, the informant had promised to protect the suspect. The Supreme Court ruled the confession was coerced due to a fear of violence and that the violence does not have to come from the police. Important, however, was that the confession was secured in conjunction with a police operation (supplying physical protection to the suspect).

A claim by a defendant that his/her confession was involuntary must be countered by the prosecution with a *preponderance of evidence* that it was voluntary (*Lego v. Twomey*, 404 U.S. 477, 1972). The same standard has been applied to a claim of a *Miranda* violation (*Colorado v. Connelly*, 479 U.S. 157, 1986).

Another interesting facet in the admissibility of confessions is that they are treated differently compared to Fourth Amendment search and seizure claims. A defendant's failure to win suppression of illegally seized physical evidence means that the evidence will be admissible at trial unless the defendant's wins a reversal of the failed suppression motion on appeal. If a confession is ruled admissible, however, the accused is allowed to challenge the credibility of the confession before the judge and jury due to the way it was secured by the police (*Crane v. Kentucky*, 476 U.S. 683, 1986). Of course, the credibility of the statement in intricately tied to its voluntariness so the defendant is actually getting two chances to demonstrate that the police coerced the statement.

THE PROTECTION AGAINST SELF-INCRIMINATION IN THE POST-*MIRANDA* ERA

Simply because the *Miranda* decision has assumed prominence also does not mean self-incrimination issues at the policing stage have become completely irrelevant either. For example, the self-incrimination protection was raised by a defendant who had been stopped in a suspected DUI/DWI in South Dakota. He refused to provide a sample for a blood alcohol test. South Dakota law called for a revocation of a driver's license for such refusal. Moreover, the law also allowed the state to admit the driver's refusal as evidence of guilt in a criminal trial (*South Dakota v. Neville*, 459 U.S. 553, 1983). Neville challenged the introduction of the evidence, claiming a violation of the Fifth Amendment. The Supreme Court rejected his claim, holding that "a refusal to take a blood-alcohol test, after a police officer has lawfully requested it, is not an act coerced by the officer, and thus is not protected by the privilege against self-incrimination (*Id.*, at 564)." Justice Brennan's joining the conservative majority in this decision was interesting, to say the least.

Also interesting is that the Court has ruled that an unlawful confession must be admitted (or an attempt to admit must occur) at trial before the self-incrimination provision is violated (*Chavez v. Martinez*, 538 U.S. 760, 2003). This holding is important for civil suits against police. The Court determined: "Statements compelled by police interrogation may not be used against a defendant in a criminal case, but it is not until such use that the Self-Incrimination Clause is violated (*Id.*, at 760)." Chavez had interrogated Martinez while transporting him to a hospital after the latter had been shot by other officers in an altercation. Martinez admitted to a number of crimes, but he was never charged. Consequently, he lacked grounds to pursue a section 1983 suit against the officer.

A RIGHT TO COUNSEL ONCE CHARGED WITH A CRIME

Paralleling and supplementing *Miranda* protections that apply to custodial interrogation by the police, defendants have an independent right to counsel that is triggered by being charged with a crime. The right to counsel here is linked to protecting the defendant's trial-related rights, particularly the right to confront the state/adverse witnesses. As we will see in the next chapter, if there is significant confrontation occurring (as in a lineup), then the accused needs to have counsel present to ensure the confrontation is just (as in not having a suggestive lineup—such as four white guys and only one black guy there). If there's no confrontation, however, then there is no corresponding right to counsel. There is also no right to counsel if formal charges have not been filed. But what exactly do the words, formal charge, mean? An arrest could be considered a formal charge, but we know, for sure, that the right to counsel is not triggered by a mere arrest. We know this due to the Court's holding in *Moran v. Burbine* (see above section) that upheld a confession secured while the defendant was isolated from the lawyer that had been hired for him, but not by him. The Court was specifically asked, but said adversary proceedings had not yet begun in this case. So, the right to counsel is not independently triggered by arrest alone.

This is where the confusion starts due to the different terminology and different procedures employed by various jurisdictions. Arraignment can be different from one place to another and any one jurisdiction can have multiple arraignments (such as preliminary and formal), with varying significance attached to each. The Court has made it clear that the right to counsel exists at "the initiation of adversary judicial criminal proceedings—whether by way of formal charge, preliminary hearing, information or arraignment (*Kirby v. Illinois*, 406

U.S. 682, 689, 1972).” *Kirby* dealt with lineups, but again definitions matter and vary.

One of the initial cases dealing with this independent right to counsel, based on charging, was *Massiah v. U.S.* (377 U.S. 201, 1964). In *Massiah*, the Court ruled 6–3 that the statements of an indicted defendant were inadmissible. Massiah, who had been out on bail, was riding in his co-defendant's vehicle; he made incriminating remarks that were overheard by police via a radio transmitter that had been planted on the co-defendant. The Supreme Court held that the right to counsel recognized in *Spano* (i.e., post-indictment) applied to undercover police tactics as it had to an interrogation taking place in jail.

Early on, the Court seemed to hold that a nonadversary PC determination hearing does not require the presence of counsel (*Gerstein v. Pugh*, 420 U.S. 103, 1975). In this Florida case, the suspect was arrested without a warrant and was jailed on that basis. Most people are arrested this way (i.e., no warrant and only an officer's say so). Thus, only a police officer had determined the existence of probable cause. The *Gerstein* Court ruled that a judicial officer had to verify the existence of probable cause in order to justify a continued detention of the accused. However, the Court also noted that this proceeding did not need to afford greater rights to a suspect than those given to a person arrested with a warrant. Since the latter will have a warrant issued against him/her without any due process protections per se there are no rights (including counsel, of course) needed at a nonadversary PC determination hearing.

The Court reaffirmed the right to counsel in the post-indictment stage in *U.S. v. Henry* (447 U.S. 264, 1980). Henry had been indicted for a robbery and was jailed. A fellow inmate of Henry's was hired as an informant and was told to listen to Henry but not to initiate any discussions regarding his alleged robbery. Even still, the Court said the exchange between the two inmates amounted to a conversation. Thus, questions were implicit and this violated the suspect's right to a lawyer.

Similarly, in *Maine v. Moulton* (474 U.S. 159, 1985), the Court held, 5–4, that police are not allowed to obtain incriminating statements from an indicted defendant even though the police were investigating crimes not associated with the indictment. In this case, co-defendants were out on bail after being indicted for an auto theft charge. While released the co-defendant told police that he and Moulton had discussed killing a prosecution witness. The police then recorded several conversations between the co-defendant and Moulton. The recordings were admitted at trial helping to convict Moulton of the original charges and several other crimes revealed in the tape. Maine's highest appellate court reversed the convictions due to the absence of counsel and Moulton's status as an indicted defendant. The U.S. Supreme Court upheld the state court's decision. Subsequently, however, the Supreme Court declared that post-indictment defendants can utter admissible statements without counsel's presence, provided the informant hearing those statements is completely passive, such that no questions or inquiries are made by the informant (*Kuhlmann v. Wilson*, 477 U.S. 436, 1986).

The Supreme Court certainly appears committed to recognize the right to counsel that attaches upon being formally charged with a crime. The precise starting point may still seem somewhat uncertain, however. In *Rothgery v. Gillespie County* (554 U.S. 191, 2008), the Court said the Sixth Amendment right to counsel attached in a Texas case when the accused had been arrested, had a complaint filed by the police with the magistrate, had appeared before the magistrate, had been informed of the charges, had bail set and had been jailed until he posted bail. This was an initial appearance Texas-style. The contention in this case was that Texas would hold these hearings without the participation of prosecutors, leading to the state's claiming formal proceedings had not yet been launched. The Court firmly rejected this argument, and declared

> the right to counsel guaranteed by the Sixth Amendment
> applies in the first appearance before a judicial officer at

which a defendant is told of the formal accusation against him and restrictions are imposed on his liberty (*Id.*, at 194)."

AN *EDWARDS*-LIKE RULE FOR CHARGED CRIMES AND THE RIGHT TO COUNSEL

The Supreme Court at one time went pretty far in protecting a right to counsel for those charged with a crime. In *Michigan v. Jackson* (475 U.S. 625, 1986), the Supreme Court explained that arrest followed by arraignment triggers the right to counsel, but states can vary on the exact definition and meaning of arraignment. At the arraignment in this case the defendants requested counsel. That appointment did not occur at that time. The suspects were jailed and during that time they were approached by the police, were *Mirandized* and agreed to being questioned in the absence of counsel. The police acquired statements that were later declared inadmissible. Here, the Court established an *Edwards*-like rule (paralleling the request for counsel that would occur during *Miranda*). Nevertheless, the *Miranda*-based *Edwards* rule (based on the Fifth Amendment) ends up being more protective of defendants than the formal charge-based right to counsel (see *McNeil v. Wisconsin*, below). The *Jackson* Court suggested, however, that the protections emanating from the Fifth and Sixth Amendment rights were comparable:

> (T)he assertion (of the right to counsel) is no less significant, and the need for additional safeguards no less clear, when that assertion is made at arraignment and when the basis for it is the Sixth Amendment. If police initiate an interrogation after defendant's assertion of the right to counsel at an arraignment or a similar proceeding, as in this case, any waiver of that right for that police-initiated interrogation is invalid (*Id.*, at 636).

Reading *Jackson* might give the reader the impression that invoking a right to counsel after being charged formally would operate in the same way in which invoking counsel via *Miranda* (i.e., the *Edwards* rule) does in shutting down all conversations between the police and the accused.

NO *EDWARDS*-LIKE RULE FOR INTERROGATING CHARGED SUSPECTS FOR NON-CHARGED CRIMES

That did not prove to be the case, however, in *McNeil v. Wisconsin* (501 U.S. 171, 1991). In *McNeil*, the Court declared that the right to counsel attaches at the first formal proceeding against the accused. McNeil was arrested for an armed robbery and was represented by a public defender at a preliminary examination before a commissioner in Wisconsin. Subsequently, other officers approached him in jail regarding a robbery-homicide that had been committed in another Wisconsin city. McNeil was *Mirandized* and then made statements about that second robbery without counsel. The Supreme Court allowed this approach and questioning without the presence of counsel. The Court explained that the right to counsel in this context is "offense-specific." Unlike *Miranda* and the *Edwards* rule, invoking the right to counsel after being charged does not "shut down" all police inquiries. The Court explained that the right to counsel

> cannot be invoked for all future prosecutions, for it does not attach until a prosecution is commenced. . . . To exclude evidence pertaining to charges as to which the Sixth Amendment right to counsel has not attached at the time the evidence was obtained, simply because other charges were pending at that time, would unnecessarily frustrate the public's interest in the investigation of criminal activities (*Id.*, at 175).

Thus, only the offense for which the suspect has been formally charged is "off limits" for police questioning in the absence of counsel.

In *McNeil*, the two robberies were distinct and unrelated. Even when crimes are "interwoven" if one offense has not yet been charged, police can approach a defendant outside the presence of counsel on the "other" (non-charged) offense even though a related one has been formally charged and counsel has been appointed. In other words, it is okay for police to interrogate here because the right to counsel was derived through the "offense specific" right to counsel and not via *Miranda*.

In *Texas v. Cobb* (532 U.S. 162, 2001), the defendant was charged with a burglary and had counsel assigned. The burglary was connected to a homicide of a mother and daughter, who went missing after the burglary. The police approached the suspect and questioned him about the murders and he confessed. The state court would not allow the confession to be admitted because the homicides were factually close to the burglary to which counsel had been attached. Thus, the police should not have approached Cobb unless counsel had been present, according to the state court. The Supreme Court reversed this decision and allowed the statement to be used because the right to counsel is truly offense-specific, and burglary (for which counsel had been attached) is not homicide (for which counsel had not yet been attached) and homicide is not burglary. The only way for counsel to apply to both the original burglary and the subsequent homicide is if the two were considered the same offense (as in double jeopardy law). Otherwise the second offense (homicide) had not been charged and the right to counsel did not yet apply. It needs to be kept in mind, nevertheless, that this was a 5–4 decision.

The different rules for *Miranda*-based versus charge-based assertions of the right to counsel can produce interesting Supreme Court decisions. In *Fellers v. United States* (540 U.S. 519, 2004), the defendant already had been indicted when the police picked him up at his house with an arrest warrant. Fellers was questioned at his house, was then taken to the station and was *Mirandized*; he gave statements both times. Fellers challenged both statements as violations of the Fifth and Sixth Amendments. The Supreme Court explained that the second statement was okay by Fifth Amendment standards because there was no *Miranda* violation committed by the police. However, there was a Sixth Amendment violation since he had already been indicted. Obviously, a statement can violate one amendment and not a second one. Here, the defendant had been formally charged so counsel should have been present during police questioning.

NO SPECIAL WARNINGS FOR WAIVER OF COUNSEL FOR CHARGED CRIMES

In more recent times, the Court has somewhat limited the protective measure formal charging has over police interrogation, at least if the accused has not yet asked for or been appointed counsel. In *Patterson v. Illinois* (487 U.S. 285, 1988), the defendant was indicted for murder after having been arrested. The indictment required a transfer to the county jail. During the transfer the accused asked a police officer if a particular gang member had been charged yet with murder, and, after finding out that he had not been charged, declared that he should have been because he was the main participant. The officer *Mirandized* Patterson who read each of the warnings, initialed each and signed the waiver. He then gave a statement implicating himself in the murder. Patterson repeated his inculpatory statement to a prosecutor who had repeated the *Miranda* warnings and had the suspect sign a waiver that he understood his rights and the waiver. Patterson later claimed he did not knowingly and intelligently waive his right to counsel prior to giving both statements because the *Miranda* warnings did not adequately inform him of his right to counsel. Patterson wanted the right to counsel waiver to require more than the typical *Miranda* waiver. The Supreme Court responded that there is no "superior" right to counsel because one has already been charged with a crime. In the Court's view, the *Miranda* warnings and their waiver adequately covers both Fifth and Sixth Amendment rights and their surrender, even post-indictment. The Court observed that it has never adopted petitioner's suggestion that the Sixth Amendment right to counsel is "superior" to or "more difficult" to waive that its Fifth Amendment counterpart. . . (*Id.*, at 286).

Patterson had wanted a separate waiver of counsel since he had been indicted; a warning apart from *Miranda* was called for in his eyes. The Supreme Court rejected this argument. The Court made specific reference to the fact that the defendant had not retained or accepted the appointment of a lawyer to represent him at these interrogations. The Court explained:

Once an accused has a lawyer, a distinct set of constitutional safeguards aimed at preserving the sanctity of the attorney-client relationship takes effect (*Id.*, at 300, fn 3).

The Court determined that Patterson had sufficient notice of the right to counsel as contained in the *Miranda* warnings. *Patterson* was another 5–4 decision. The dissent wanted a rule that after formal adversary proceedings begin, no further interrogation by the police or the prosecutor can occur until counsel has made available to the accused, unless the defendant initiates the conversation.

THE RETREAT FROM *JACKSON* IS COMPLETED VIA ITS REVERSAL

The Court evidenced a willingness to retreat even further from the *Jackson* decision in *Montejo v. Louisiana* (556 U.S. 778, 2009). In fact, *Jackson* was overruled in *Montejo*. Montejo was charged with murder and appeared at a preliminary hearing, at which he was appointed counsel. The defendant made no comment regarding counsel. While in jail Montejo was approached by the police. He agreed to accompany them so as to locate the murder weapon. He was *Mirandized* prior to reaching this agreement. Montejo then penned a letter of apology to the victim's widow while being transported in the police car. Montejo finally met with his attorney following his excursion with the police. His apology letter was admitted at trial over his lawyer's objection. He was convicted and sentenced to death.

The Supreme Court allowed this police contact with the defendant, together with obtaining the letter of apology. According to the Court, the defendant had not asserted his right to counsel at the preliminary hearing. When that occurs police may initiate discussions with the accused, provided *Miranda* warnings have been given. The failure to request an attorney is what permitted the police contact. When a defendant asserts a right to counsel, via either *Miranda* or the right to counsel that applies to those formally charged with a crime, the police may not approach the defendant without counsel's being present or unless the defendant initiates the contact with police and expresses a willingness to proceed without counsel.

A STATEMENT VIOLATING THE SIXTH AMENDMENT RIGHT TO COUNSEL CAN BE USED: TO IMPEACH THE DEFENDANT

As we saw in Chapter 2, *Harris v. New York* permitted the state to use a *Miranda*-violated statement so as to impeach a defendant who takes the stand and commits perjury regarding the charged offense. In *Kansas v. Ventris* (556 U.S. 586, 2009), the Court applied the same ruling to a voluntary statement obtained in violation of a right to counsel. In *Ventris*, the police had used a jail inmate/informant to secure incriminating information on Ventris who already had been charged with a crime. The state could not use the statement to convict Ventris, but when Ventris took the stand and testified that the co-defendant was the actual shooter, the judge allowed the informant to testify so as to impeach Ventris. The U.S. Supreme Court upheld this impeachment use of the illegally obtained statement.

Assumedly, any physical evidence obtained via a right to counsel-violated but voluntary statement would be admissible at trial, just as a *Miranda*-violated statement allows (see *U.S. v. Patane,* above).

AFTER THE INTERROGATION

Besides complying with *Miranda* police will also need to be cognizant of requirements that they deliver the accused for a prompt presentation before a magistrate. We already discussed that this prompt appearance is geared to prevent coercive police tactics in interrogation. Earlier in this chapter we noted that in the federal system this prompt presentation requirement is called the *McNabb-Mallory* rule, named after two Supreme Court cases (*McNabb v. U.S.*, 318 U.S. 332, 1943; and, *Mallory v. U.S.*, 354 U.S. 449, 1957). Any unnecessary delay could render inadmissible any statement secured during that time period. The rule has not been imposed on the states, but states tend to have parallel rules of their own. If a state defendant asks the Court to suppress a confession the amount of time taken to obtain the statement would likely be a factor in a totality of circumstances test of the voluntariness of the confession.

Federal agents have a six-hour timeframe around which to be concerned about the admissibility of confessions; any statement secured within 6 hours is presumably okay, assuming voluntariness is not an issue. Those statements obtained beyond six hours must be examined by the court to decide whether there was unnecessary or unreasonable delay in the presentation, and, if so, the confession must be suppressed (*Corley v. U.S.*, 556 U.S. 303, 2009).

Similarly, we recently examined how all suspects arrested without a previous judicial finding of PC (i.e., no warrant) or indictment (which means a simple arrest decision by a police officer, which is the norm) are entitled to a nonadversary PC determination hearing before a judge (*Gerstein v. Pugh*, 420 U.S. 103, 1975) within 48 hours (*County of Riverside v. McLaughlin*, 500 U.S. 44, 1991) so as to determine the existence of PC. Whether a statement obtained after that time limit would be admissible at trial is uncertain (*Powell v. Nevada*, 511 U.S. 79, 1994), but would likely be analyzed by a TOC voluntariness test.

GOING FORWARD TO THE COURTROOM

Earlier we saw that a Fifth Amendment complaint by a defendant differs from a Fourth Amendment claim. If the latter is unsuccessful with a suppression judge, the matter is finished (except for a possible appeal to an appellate court). With a confession, however, the defendant, who loses initially before a judge, can relitigate the matter at the trial level. In some states the jury gets to evaluate the voluntariness and credibility of the statement given by the accused.

If the suspect has elected to remain silent after being *Mirandized*, that silence cannot be used against him/her, including for impeachment purposes (*Doyle v. Ohio*, 426 U.S. 610, 1976). Nor can a post-*Miranda* silence be used to challenge a defendant's claim of insanity (*Wainwright v. Greenfield*, 474 U.S. 284, 1986). Nevertheless, pre-arrest silence when there has been no *Miranda* connection, can be used to impeach (*Jenkins v. Anderson*, 447 U.S. 231, 1980), and it also can be used to challenge an exculpatory version of what had happened in the incident (*Fletcher v. Weir*, 455 U.S. 603, 1982).

What is necessary is that the silence of the accused is not linked to the exercise of constitutional right, such as operationalizing the rights identified in *Miranda*. Such a connection would eliminate the state's ability to exploit the exercise of rights by the accused against him/her since that could be interpreted as punishment for exercising those rights.

CHAPTER 10

Identification Procedures: A Special Class of Search and Seizure

Similar to the electronic surveillance area, there is little constitutional law and protections for the accused when it comes to identification procedures. Identification procedures include such items as blood and DNA analysis, chemical analyses (such as drugs), fingerprints, ballistics, and lineups.

BLOOD SAMPLES

In an early ruling (*Breithaupt v. Abram*, 352 U.S. 432, 1957), the Supreme Court set the trend for this area by holding that a blood sample taken by a skilled technician from an unconscious man was admissible in court. Underlying the police activity in this case was the need for a quick analysis of the defendant's blood so as to ascertain its alcohol content and to prove a DUI offense. Even still, Chief Justice Warren was joined in dissent by Justices Black and Douglas in arguing that the action was "repulsive" and constituted a due process violation, as claimed by the defendant.

The lead case in this area, however, is *Schmerber v. California* (384 U.S. 757, 1966). Here, a blood sample was taken by a physician from a conscious person who objected to the procedure. Schmerber raised Fourth (search and seizure), Fifth (self-incrimination), and Fourteenth

Amendment (due process) claims. In a 5–4 ruling, the Court rejected all of Schmerber's claims. The Court dispensed with the Fifth Amendment issue by pointing out that the blood sample did not constitute compelled testimony (or any communication), which would deserve the Amendment's protection; only Justice Black saw the blood extraction and admission as proof of a DUI as a Fifth Amendment violation. The exigency of having to quickly submit the blood sample for analysis before it would degrade convinced the Court to permit this warrantless seizure of evidence; the absence of a warrant was also justified here since the search was incident to arrest. Accordingly, the Fourth Amendment claim was rejected. Although the majority failed to see a due process violation in this case, Chief Justice Warren and Justice Fortas (both in dissent) thought there was one. Justice Fortas went so far as to identify this as an act of violence. Justice Douglas also dissented, believing that taking blood samples in this manner violated a right to privacy. Although all of these positions are interesting, perhaps the most remarkable aspect of the decision is that Justice Brennan, eventually considered one of the most liberal justices to ever have served on the Supreme Court, wrote the opinion upholding the forcible taking of the blood sample.

The Court took the Fifth Amendment aspect of *Schmerber* one step further in *South Dakota v. Neville* (459 U.S. 553, 1983). In this case the Court ruled that a prosecutor can use a defendant's refusal to submit to a blood test as evidence of guilt and admit this evidence at trial without committing a Fifth Amendment violation.

The Supreme Court has modified somewhat its position toward blood samples in this century. In *Missouri v. McNeely* (569 U.S. 141, 2013), the Court held that if police can get a warrant in a DUI case without jeopardizing the evidence, they must do so. McNeely was stopped for a possible DUI, failed a field sobriety test, refused a breathalyzer test, and, after being transported to a hospital, refused to submit to ta blood test. The arresting officer, without pursuing a warrant, directed a lab technician to take the suspect's blood. The Supreme Court upheld what the trial court and the Missouri Supreme

Court had determined. In the absence of a verifiable exigency, a warrant is necessary to forcibly take a blood sample from a suspect. The U.S. Supreme Court explained it will utilize a TOC test to evaluate the need for a warrant in these cases. The Court also commented that the availability of telephonic warrants, which the officer can pursue while transporting the suspect to a hospital, should remove much of the exigency in these cases.

Very recently, the Court reaffirmed *McNeely* by holding that an exigent circumstance is necessary to dispense with the warrant requirement in taking blood samples from suspected DUI drivers, even when it would be incident to arrest (*Birchfield v. North Dakota*, 579 U.S. ___, 136 S.Ct. 2160, 2016).

FIELD SOBRIETY TESTS

Similar to its rulings in blood sample cases, in *Pennsylvania v. Muniz* (496 U.S. 582, 1990), the Court held that police can put a suspect through physical tests (or a field sobriety test) without Fifth Amendment implications. The interaction may be videotaped and the officer can ask several questions, such as: name, address, height, weight, eye color, date of birth, and current age. Nevertheless, police cannot ask certain questions such as the date of the suspect's sixth birthday because that answer would trigger what the Court considers a testimonial response, requiring that the suspect has been *Mirandized*.

DNA SAMPLES

To date the Court has issued one ruling in collecting DNA samples. Maryland law provided that suspects arrested for violent crimes or burglary could be swabbed for his/her DNA, after a judge had verified the existence of PC at an arraignment. In *Maryland v. King* (569 U.S. ___, 133 S.Ct. 1958, 2013), a suspect was arrested for an assault. Police took a DNA swab from King's cheek, which was a routine booking step in the previously mentioned serious cases. The DNA matched an open rape case from six years earlier. The Supreme

Court ruled that taking the sample was a search, but it was a reasonable one since the Maryland statute was narrow. The statute limited the crimes for which DNA swabs could be collected, the judge had to find PC for the current crime, and the sample was destroyed if there was no PC or an acquittal or eventual permanent reversal or pardon. Another interesting aspect of the case is that the typically liberal Justice Breyer was in the majority, while the typically conservative Justice Scalia was among the dissenters.

OTHER EXAMPLES OF CONSTITUTIONAL IRRELEVANCE

Other methods of identification also lack constitutional protections due to either a lack of REP (for Fourth Amendment search and seizure considerations), a lack of a testimonial nature in the evidence (for Fifth Amendment self-incrimination purposes), a lack of confrontation (for Sixth Amendment right to counsel purposes), or a lack of shocking the conscience or suggestiveness (for Fourteenth Amendment Due Process purposes). Consequently, the Supreme Court has rejected claims of these constitutional violations as applied to fingerprinting or photographing as well as to more controversial items, such as providing voice samples or talking at a lineup (e.g., uttering the words the robber used) (*U.S. v. Wade*, 388 U.S. 218, 1967; *U.S. v. Dionisio*, 410 U.S. 1, 1973) or providing writing exemplars (*U.S. v. Mara*, 410 U.S. 19, 1973). Collecting items for scientific analysis (as well as the analysis itself) can also be accomplished without the interference of constitutional rights, such as a right to counsel.

LINEUPS AND THE RIGHT TO COUNSEL

The one aspect of the identification process that is surrounded with constitutional protection is the lineup, depending upon when it occurs. In 1967, the Court issued two rulings that established a right to counsel at a lineup once a suspect has been charged/indicted. In *U.S. v. Wade* (388 U.S. 218, 1967), the Court explained that a right to counsel applies at this stage because it is a critical one. A *critical stage* exists when there is a physical confrontation between the defendant and the state, which cannot be duplicated in a scientific or systematic way by the defense at trial, and, may result in prejudice to the accused (e.g., lineups, interrogation, court proceedings).

Counsel is needed at a lineup so as to promote a defendant's Sixth Amendment right to confrontation and to protect against any improper influence at a lineup. In a companion case (*Gilbert v. California*, 388 U.S. 263, 1967), the Court reaffirmed the previous decision, provided the suspect has been charged with a crime. These cases have always been considered inseparable (since they apply the same ruling to both federal and state policing agents) and are known as the Wade-Gilbert Rule.

The more conservative Supreme Court of the 1970s assured that Wade-Gilbert would not be expanded by re-emphasizing that this right to counsel is limited and specifically is not applicable to:

- Pre-charge showups/lineups (*Kirby v. Illinois*, 406 U.S. 682, 1972); and,

- Photo Identifications both pre- and post-charging because the defendant has no right to appear (and will not likely appear) so there is no "trial-like adversary confrontation" (*U.S. v. Ash*, 413 U.S. 300, 1973).

LINEUPS AND SHOWUPS AND THE FOURTEENTH AMENDMENT DUE PROCESS CLAUSE

There was a third case associated with Wade-Gilbert that provided a final constitutional protection to the identification process, especially in the showup and lineup contexts. A showup is a one-to-one identification encounter between a suspect and a witness. In *Stovall v. Denno* (388 U.S. 293, 1967), the Court determined that there is a due process right to exclude eyewitness identification that has been arrived at by excessively suggestive procedures. The showup is arguably unavoidably suggestive, the lineup can be constituted so as to be the same. The Court explained it will use a TOC test to determine suggestiveness. *Stovall* involved a one-person showup at the hospital bed of a victim who could have died. The urgency here prompted the court to find no due process problem with the identification.

A couple of years later, in *Foster v. California* (394 U.S. 440, 1969) the Court definitively held that a suggestive lineup violates due process. Foster was in a lineup in which he was considerably taller than the other two suspects. Following the lineup, Foster was then brought alone into a room with the witness because the latter had asked to speak with him. On both of these occasions the witness could not identify the suspect. Sometime later there was a second lineup that included Foster and four different people. The witness finally identified Foster, and repeated this identification at trial. The Court invalidated the identification and characterized it as compellingly unfair.

The TOC test the Court mentioned in *Stovall* was given substance years later in *Neil v. Biggers* (409 U.S. 188, 1972). This case involved a rape after which the victim identified the alleged assailant via a showup at the police station. The Court upheld the identification achieved in the case after applying the following factors from the TOC test:

- The opportunity of the witness to view the criminal at the time of the crime;

- The witness' degree of attention;

- The accuracy of the witness' prior description of the criminal;

- The level of certainty demonstrated by the witness at the time of the confrontation; and,

- The length of time between the crime and the confrontation (*Id.*, at 199–200).

The use of a TOC test whenever there is an unnecessarily suggestive confrontation procedure was itself tested in *Manson v. Brathwaite* (432 U.S. 98, 1977). The case involved an undercover agent

(Glover) who purchased drugs from Brathwaite. Glover described the seller to his partner (D'Onofrio) who thought it could be Brathwaite. D'Onofrio showed a picture of Brathwaite to Glover who stated he thought it was the guy. Brathwaite was convicted of the drug sale. His conviction was reversed on appeal, however, by the Second Circuit of Appeals that adopted a *per se* approach. This approach would require the exclusion of any out-of-court identification whenever it was obtained through unnecessarily suggestive confrontation procedures, even if it was reliable. Exacerbating the situation in this case was that the identification wasn't secured as the result of an emergency. Nevertheless, the Supreme Court insisted on employing its TOC test here. As a result of this test, the Court concluded that it would permit the admission of Glover's identification, despite its suggestiveness, since the identification "possesses certain features of reliability." The Supreme Court thought the *per se* rule went too far. The dissent, on the other hand, wanted the *per se* approach so as to act as a deterrent for the police and due to the inherent unreliability of witness identifications.

The Supreme Court recently required that in order to challenge the admissibility of an identification, the police must be at fault for any impermissible suggestiveness that occurs in an identification. In *Perry v. New Hampshire* (565 U.S. 228, 2012), the police were talking to the potential offender in public and were observed by the eyewitness (who had glanced out a window and saw the interaction). The witness identified the accused after this observation. The Court refused to apply the TOC test of suggestiveness when the police did not cause the problem. The 8–1 ruling had only Justice Sotomayer dissenting due to her belief that it's the suggestiveness that is the problem, rather than the fault of the police. She argued that an erroneous conviction can stem from any suggestive identification process, regardless of wrongdoing by the police.

CHAPTER 11

Grand Jury Investigations

There are two types of grand juries. The one that is probably better known is the one that ratifies or rejects the prosecutor's request for an indictment against the accused. This is called the *charging grand jury*. It has arguably become what most would consider an irrelevant operation. The saying goes, that a prosecutor can indict a ham sandwich. The charging grand jury is beyond the scope of this text.

The second type of grand jury is the *investigative grand jury*. It is probably best known for investigating and deciding whether to bring charges against prominent, often government-related officials (think of the Watergate, Whitewater/Clinton, Trump/Russia Grand Juries). The most likely knock on this grand jury is not irrelevancy, but rather a possible abuse of power. The reason behind this possible characterization is that the constitution does not control the behavior of this grand jury (or the charging one for that matter). The reason constitutional limitations do not apply is that this body is comprised of private citizens and not government agents to whom the Constitution most certainly does apply.

The investigative grand jury can require people to appear before it and to testify (assuming there is no Fifth Amendment implications), as well as to bring documents and papers to submit to the grand jury. There is a threat of contempt for those who refuse to comply. If the individual is being called upon to testify, there will be a *subpoena ad testificandum* issued, while if papers/documents are the target, a *subpoena duces tecum* will be issued.

Nearly a century ago the Court described the grand jury operation as follows:

> It is a grand inquest, a body with powers of investigation and inquisition, the scope of whose inquiries is not to be limited narrowly by questions or propriety or forecasts of the probable results of the investigation, or by the doubts whether any particular individual will be found properly subject to an accused action of crime (*Blair v. U.S.*, 250 U.S. 273, 282, 1919).

The lack of control over the grand jury is believed to be justified by the grand jury's need for full information (a complete inquiry), and an unlikely abuse of power. Grand jurors are regular citizens who are supposed to operate without bias. The Court said in *Costello v. U.S.* (350 U.S. 359, 1956) that the grand jury is "a body of laymen, free from technical rules, acting in secret, pledged to indict no one because of prejudice and to free no one because of special favor (*Id.*, at 362)."

The grand jury's subpoena power was fully recognized in *U.S. v. Dionisio* (410 U.S. 1, 1973). In this case the grand jury wanted to collect voice exemplars from Dionisio so as to compare them with recorded conversations being used as evidence against him. Dionisio refused to comply and claimed to do so would violate his Fourth and Fifth Amendment rights. He lost at the district court level but prevailed at the Seventh Circuit Court of Appeals, which agreed with the Fourth Amendment claim. The basis for this claim was that the Fourth Amendment did apply to the grand jury and that there should be a showing of reasonableness for any subpoena the grand jury issues. The Circuit Court determined that there was a lack of probable cause to arrest Dionisio and that the grand jury here was simply trying to accomplish what the police could not; thus, the seizure was unreasonable.

The Supreme Court explained, however, that a Fourth Amendment claim requires a REP (which we addressed in Chapter 3) that does not extend to one's voice. The Fourth Amendment does not cover what one knowingly exposes to the public as in a voice. Physical characteristics do not have a REP, according to the Court. Moreover, the Court noted that a subpoena is not a Fourth Amendment seizure since it involves having to appear and give evidence and thus it is not equal to an arrest or stop. The Court also commented that the only way the Fourth Amendment applies is if the subpoena is too sweeping and unreasonable, if it were to operate as an instrument of oppression. The Court concluded that the grand jury is subject to judicial control and subpoenas can be quashed.

As to the Fifth Amendment claim the Court observed that witnesses cannot be compelled to testify in violation of their right to not self-incriminate, but the Amendment does not apply to voice samples. The sample of voice does not serve as testimony, as required for Fifth Amendment relevance.

In a companion case, *U.S. v. Mara* (410 U.S. 19, 1973), the Court applied the same reasoning to handwriting and printing exemplars. Justice Marshall wrote a spirited dissent in which he saw a Fourth Amendment connection. The Justice envisioned grand juries as effecting "official investigatory seizures which interfere with personal liberty *(Id.*, at 40)." As the Justice saw it: "The Fourth Amendment was placed in our Bill of Rights to protect the individual citizen from . . . potentially disruptive governmental intrusion into his private life unless conducted reasonably and with sufficient cause *(Id.*, at 44)."

Essentially, the Supreme Court has declared that the grand jury must be let alone.

Witnesses can be compelled to testify before the grand jury (as in the trial, too), even if the testimony is incriminating, provided they are granted immunity. *Transactional immunity* is complete in that it protects against *any prosecution* for *any crime* associated with the testimony. For obvious reasons, defendants prefer this type of immunity. *Use immunity*, on the other hand, protects against using *only the testimony given by the witness*. In *Kastigar v. U.S.* (406 U.S. 441, 1972) the Supreme Court ruled that use immunity is constitutionally compatible and that witnesses can be forced to testify if given that immunity; transactional immunity went beyond the requirements of the self-incrimination protection, according to the majority.

Otherwise the Supreme Court has ruled:

- A witness appearing before a grand jury does not need to be warned that he/she is a potential defendant in danger of indictment, although some states do require a warning (*U.S. v. Washington*, 431 U.S. 181, 1977); and,

- There is no Sixth Amendment right to counsel being present during grand jury testimony, but some states allow it (*U.S. v. Mandujano*, 425 U.S. 564, 1976).

Index